THE HEART OF BUSINESS
Ethics, Power and Philosophy

THE HEART OF BUSINESS
Ethics, Power and Philosophy

by

Peter Koestenbaum

Saybrook Publishing Company

San Francisco • Dallas • New York

THE HEART OF BUSINESS, by Peter Koestenbaum

Recognition for permission to quote from copyrighted material is found in the "Acknowledgments" section at the end of this book.

Second Printing

Library of Congress Cataloging-in-Publication Data

Koestenbaum, Peter, 1928–
    The heart of business.

    1. Business.   2. Philosophy.   3. Intellect.
4. Interpersonal communication.   5. Leadership.
6. Business ethics.   I. Title.
HF5351.K584   1987   658.4'09   87–13665
ISBN   0-933071-15-9

Saybrook Publishing Co., Inc.
4223 Cole Avenue, Suite Four, Dallas TX 75205

Printed in the United States of America

Distributed by W. W. Norton & Company
500 Fifth Avenue, New York, NY 10110

This book would not have come to life but for the inspired and devoted help of many kind-hearted friends. My debt to them is vast and no less is my gratitude. Each one of them knows, privately, the unique depth of their contribution, and I need them to feel fully acknowledged: Peter Block, Rollo May, Jean T. Settlemyre, Nancy Badore, Jean-Louis Servan-Schreiber, Frank D. Anthony, George Friedman, Robert P. Mueller, Mark X. Feck, John Lyman.

My publisher, Pat Howell, deserves a mountain of kudos for his enthusiastic commitment and his client-centered imagination.

Regrettably, many friends are omitted. I hope they will generously forgive me and know I profoundly appreciate and esteem them.

Peter Koestenbaum
Farmington Hills, Michigan
May, 1987

THE HEART OF BUSINESS
Contents

TO BE OR NOT TO BE IN BUSINESS

The Heart of Business has one primary theme: the leadership mind. It examines this topic from the perspective of how philosophy—and its related fields in the study of human existence—can contribute to leadership thinking and enrich it. Although theory is needed to give meaning to applications, the emphasis is on the practical uses of philosophy in business.

The leadership theme is analyzed through three major ideas: Mental expansion through the Theory of Multiple Intelligences, character development through Deep Structure Theory, and the courage to reach genius and power levels of authentic leadership and ethical action.

This guide to philosophy in business is for executives and decision-makers. It is expected that persons who become familiar with this material will improve in their capacity to think, to be creative, to be of strong character, to be courageous, and to relate well to persons and to teams who depend on them. But the necessity for leadership is not limited to business. It concerns as much political figures, school administrators, and professionals, including those in medicine and in the law, and all those who aspire to take charge of their lives and of their fates.

My purpose in writing this book is simple: to inspire and motivate the leadership mind. For without inspiration and motivation, the way America does business cannot be changed. Required first of all is a new perception of the multiple intelligences that can broaden the mind and expand it. Required, second, is a new vision of human existence, a new depth, a new character, and a new courage that comes with the study of the deep structures. And then, the leadership mind is ready for transformation to genius level performance and to the power level of ethical action. This is the power of authenticity. In this way dignity can be restored to business as a profession and a calling.

A book of inspiration for the business community? Yes, unequivocally. For the past several years it has been my privilege to work with executives from the world's largest international corporations. My workshop/seminars on creativity and the development of leadership intelligence have convinced me that the problems facing top business leaders today are not only profits, productivity, and personnel, but issues of personal integrity, meaning, and value. Today's crisis in the business world is not simply fiscal or cultural, it is personal, internal and—in a word—*spiritual*. My contact and work with these leaders has led me to think of what I do as a genuine "ministry."

To speak of ministry and inspiration within the context of business leadership is not to suggest that it has been my job to console disgruntled CEOs or dry the eyes of frustrated junior executives! What philosophy contributes to business is not comfort, but challenge, *provocation*. Participants in my seminars will tell you that the tasks of expanding intelligence and deepening character are difficult, often painful, ones. Change is required—and the change involves facing and discarding old prejudices, inviting new vision, and a willingness to take off in directions that have never been tried before. Like the poet, who prods and stirs language, provoking it to take shape in new meanings, my job as a philosopher "ministering" among business leaders has been to provoke and inspire—with a view to transformation at that level of being and action which philosophers have traditionally called "ethics."

For ethics in action is ultimately what this book is about—and what it hopes to demonstrate is an authentic possibility for today's leaders. Ethics means profits. We must acknowledge that attention to the emotional and ethical needs of employees also means attention to productivity and profits. There does not need to be any opposition between effective profit-and-production orientation and orientation toward the humanizing (i.e., nonproduction) goals of business. Roger Harrison, a consultant and author, says it well:

> The business leaders who articulated and practiced philosophies of benevolence toward their employees were moved by deep caring and a sense of personal responsibility. *They did not take care of their employees primarily because they thought it was good business to do so: rather, it became good business because they did it with heart.*

I have entitled my book *The Heart of Business* with precisely this point of view in mind. Good business is what results when leaders struggle to achieve that personal transformation which results in responsible, genuine caring for others *from the heart*. This book will, I hope, serve as an introduction and an invitation to begin that transformative process.

Developing the leadership mind means transforming it. By expanding its creativity and deepening its character it can go through a metamorphosis to authenticity. Authenticity means a new integrity, a new level of power and influence, a new height of vision, and more ethical courage.

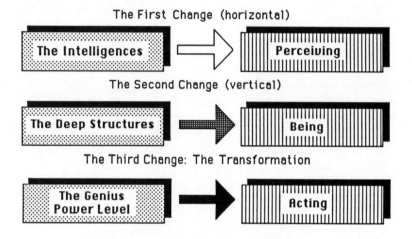

The First Change (horizontal)

The Intelligences ⟹ Perceiving

The Second Change (vertical)

The Deep Structures ⟹ Being

The Third Change: The Transformation

The Genius Power Level ⟹ Acting

The transformation of the leadership mind

We will briefly examine the eight different kinds of intelligences that everyone has and then help you construct a personal intelligence profile unique to you.

PART ONE

THE FIRST PERSONAL CHANGE:
MENTAL EXPANSION

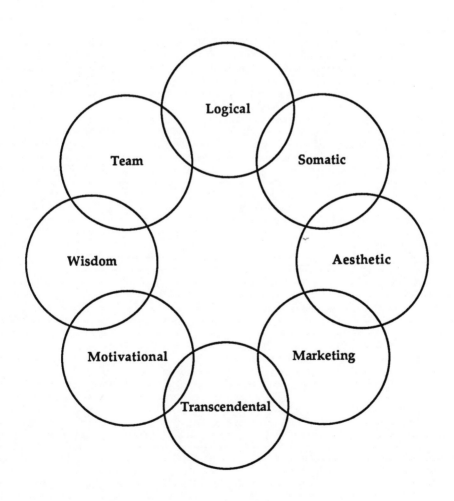

CHAPTER 1

Developing Multiple Intelligences

Today, the most alive force in the world is business. The way business goes the world goes. *The Heart of Business* is for leaders of that new world. To prepare for leadership is to enlarge the intelligence.

Intelligence is a multiple phenomenon. We have for too long restricted our conception of intelligence. To truly expand our minds, we need to evolve, especially in our own lives. We can do that only by understanding that there are many more ways to be intelligent than those usually measured.

And expanding our intelligences is surprisingly easy. It is also pleasurable, healthful, and gives life new hope and meaning. Also, intelligence is profitable, just as ethics is profitable. These are affirmations of faith, not empirical facts, but leaders can make them into facts.

To be ethical because it is profitable is not ethical, but to be ethical *is* profitable.

Jonas Salk distinguishes between the dollar value of the human and the human value of the dollar. Most organizations are concerned with the dollar value of the human. Human beings are a cost, and their employment and development are measured in terms of dollars for the company. The reverse is to consider the human value of the dollar. The dollar has an important human dimension—expanded intelligences working through deep structures. Developing the human aspect of the dollar is the secret success formula for increasing the dollar value of the corporation.

To see it all in context, we must talk about the significance of multiple intelligences, that is, of different ways of being smart, of different styles of adapting to the world. We must make room for multiple lifestyles.

Socrates was perhaps the first man with the courage to think for himself, within his own alienated and politicized state. He was murdered, and became the 2500-year-old model for leadership through integrity and wisdom.

To be intelligent means first of all to be unique and unusual, and to be so in a desirable way. It means that the intelligent person has something that makes him or her superior to other persons or to his or her earlier condition. Intelligence is valued, even envied, but never degraded, for even those who think they do not "have" intelligence value it. It need not be a "thing" that one "possesses." It is a way of being, a manner of doing things.

Perhaps most important, intelligence allows free movement within reality. Intelligence means highly developed adaptation and therefore success and facility in operating within the many chambers of reality. The intelligences are, in Aldous Huxley's famous phrase, the "doors of perception."

The truly intelligent person operates with what the Italians of the Renaissance called *sprezzatura*, a facility, an elegance, a sureness, a sagacity born of talent, training, and experience. We see it in great artists, such as the dancer Rudolph Nureyev. He richly displays "somatic intelligence." To be intelligent is to be at home everywhere; it means success in dealing with any situation. Intelligence is the expanded mind, the stretched consciousness.

Intelligence is the extent to which one has command over a domain, be it that of the market, of abstract thought, of the emotions, of the body, of one's consciousness, or of one's pure free will.

An intelligence is a way of approaching the world, of valuing things. It is the way the mind organizes experience so that the world is intelligible and has meaning.

The world is not what it is objectively. It becomes what it is by the way in which consciousness acts on it. These acts, sometimes called projections, are like directives or programs, which the mind or consciousness imposes on the world. A computer program cannot be seen. But its effects on the monitor can be seen. Consciousness cannot be seen, but its effects on the world can be seen. Control over the powers of the mind, over the organizing function of consciousness, is also control over our intelligence.

Intelligence acts according to its powers and to its understanding of these powers. This means that consciousness constructs a life in keeping with its principal mode of perception. But in so doing, consciousness defines itself, that is, it constructs the self, and also, in a manner of speaking, creates reality and ethical values. These definitions of the self and of the world are changeable if we desire it and if we invest the requisite energy. Definitions of self are chosen. They are rooted in our deepest freedom. In the end, this freedom means control over the way we are intelligent and over the ethical meaning of our lives—true freedom and the true happiness. We need a theory of multiple intelligences because there are many rooms in the mansion of reality.

The eight intelligences can be summarized as follows:

LOGICAL
Abstract Reasoning
Visualization
Analysis
SOMATIC
The Language of Sensuality
Muscular (dexterity and strength)
Kinetic Orientation
Health (physical and nutritional)
AESTHETIC
Verbal
Musical
Pictorial
TRANSCENDENTAL
Consciousness (consciousness as fact)
Non-Attachment
Exploration of Inner Space-Time
MARKETING
Survival
Systems
Wonder (flexibility, adaptability)
MOTIVATIONAL
The Preeminence of Action
Self-Energization (will)
Greatness
WISDOM
Experience
Communication Skills
Philosophy of Life
TEAM
Identity Through Community
Service
Working Through and With Others

Intelligence can be increased. There seems to be little doubt that we can improve what we do and how we do it, that we can be inspired by charismatic figures, and that we can follow example and enhance our performance. The entire educational enterprise, formal and informal, is based on the premise that we can and should enhance the ways we are intelligent in the world.

But the pragmatic consideration is the most important of all. Why live at all if we cannot go through life convinced that our potential is greater than our realization of it, that we can vastly improve our capacities and our meanings? To have the faith that intelligence can be increased is one of a class of convictions, beginning with Pascal's notion of belief as a wager and developed in William James's famous essay "The Will to Believe," that faith is a rational part of life. Faith can make things happen, and provides therefore its own confirmation. Saint Anselm's well known *credo ut intelligam,* "I believe so that I may understand," is still a major truth. And faith need not only be religious. Faith is the conviction that something can be done; and it is then the strength of that conviction that makes it real. There is no intelligence without it.

If you expand your mind through the study and the practice of multiple intelligences, what will happen? How can this philosophy be of service to business? It can effect change in the corporate mind. Philosophy can affect the profitability of a company by accomplishing a change in the executive consciousness. The changed corporate intelligence will change the organization. In what directions, specifically, can the corporate intelligence be expected to grow?

- Creativity. Leaders will become more innovative, that is, they will encourage the free-ranging mind to think of new ways of doing things.

    They will develop the habit of spontaneity. Spontaneity is the opposite of will power. New ideas spring spontaneously from the mind that has worked its way through all of the eight intelligences. Spontaneity is a sign of the freedom of the will. And the more freedom we have the more human we are, and the more effective we shall be.

    Leaders who explore the eight intelligences will develop their intuition—by trusting it and by knowing that it is their access to the unconscious. And the unconscious is the source of some of the best and most mysterious creativity. Intuition means that we have kept open the channels to the unconscious. It means that we allow ourselves to benefit from experience. We understand that important decisions cannot be calculated into being but require maturation to be made and carried out.

- Energy. Decision makers will work from enthusiasm, joy, hope, and meaning. Their energy level will increase sharply. They will become more awake and alert, more enthusiastic, happier, and healthier.

- Communication. Executives will develop the ability to inspire, to evoke loyalty, they will achieve contact, encounter, and engagement, and will know how to delegate.

- Clarity. Leaders will increase concentration, focus; develop a panoramic access to inner data; improve the power for eliminating distractions; tighten control over their minds. These skills lead to lucidity, to sharpness, to intuitive and intellectual penetration, to brilliance. The mind then operates like a premium camera.

  Memory is enhanced, for memory seems to be connected with expanding the field of consciousness and sharpening our vision of it.

  To increase concentration is the ability to clear the mind of clutter, to pursue a single vision. Clarity is one of the most obvious signs of intelligence. What was difficult yesterday becomes self-evident today. What was opaque before is now transparent. Intelligence is vision, both inner and outer.

- Ethics. Leaders endeavor to increase their understanding and their commitment to the higher purposes of human existence, for they know that there can be no meaningful leadership without unassailable integrity and a highly matured sense of fairness. Integrity is not negotiable. It is the foundation for human dignity. With ethics, compassion and empathy increase. One understands what it feels like to see the world from inside another consciousness. And one gains the skill to make another person feel it.

Abstract Reasoning

Visualization

Analysis

Logical Intelligence

When we stop to think that our universities give admission tests in logical intelligence, and that it is very difficult for a student performing poorly on such tests either to get into a good university or, if he or she does get in, to do well in that institution, then we realize the profound effect such a selection process has on the entire population. Just imagine some alternatives: somatic, or marketing, or aesthetic, or even transcendental intelligence might become the test for admission to a university! The curriculum, the definition of success, and certainly the mindset of the graduates—and with them, the future of society—would be unimaginably altered!

Logical intelligence consists of the capacity for abstraction (or seeing relations or abstract relations), for visualization, and for analysis (as opposed to synthesis or seeing wholes). This is the intelligence that is usually measured.

It is calculating; it is deductive, inferential, relational, mathematical, geometric, abstract. It can be spatial and visual. It is highly developed in what one might call a technological, scientific, or engineering mind.

Abstract thinking is first and foremost non-visual thinking. It is what is most valued in traditional intelligence tests. Its best illustration perhaps is in analogies: "Color is to house as (a) white is to green; (b) soft is to hard; (c) outside is to inside; (d) property is to thing; and (e) worker is to boss." (The answer is (d).) Or, "Water is to grass as (a) brother is to sister; (b) green is to blue; (c) cause is to effect; (d) effect is to cause; (e) science is to nature." (The answer is (c).)

Logical intelligence means speed and competence in managing abstract relations. It means to be comfortable and quick in such matters as the syllogism: "All men are mortal; Socrates is a man; therefore Socrates is mortal." It means to be quick in thinking up analogies and metaphors: "To take arms against a sea of troubles." "Great oaks from little acorns grow" "The trainee's sales talk was as hesitant as one's first bite of squid."

Logical intelligence also means to enjoy and to have facility with mathematics; to be a natural at calculations and computations. It means to be at ease with proofs, of which there are plenty in logic and in geometry. It is to excel at debating. It is to be familiar with arguments—both formal and informal, both relations and connections. Logical intelligence as abstraction and relations means the capacity to use the mind without visualization. It is to abstract and to find relations, without visualization.

But logical intelligence also means having a clear spatial, that is, visual, orientation: competence in managing spatial relations, being good at mechanical reasoning, excellent at visualization. A person with a high capacity for visualization has a mind like a map. Abstract relations is to think without visualization. Visualization is to think intuitively, to have the gift of achieving the encompassing inner vision. They are not opposite traits of logical intelligence, just complementaries. For example,

> Three brothers, A, B, and C, stand in a row, so that C sees the heads of both A and B, B sees only A's head, and A sees no one's head. Among them they own five hats: three black ones and two white ones. While the brothers close their eyes, a stranger places a hat on each head. When they open their eyes and look ahead, they are asked these questions:
>
> "Mr. C, please tell me what color is your hat?" Mr. C replies, "I don't know."
>
> "Mr. B, please tell me what color is your hat?" Mr. B answers likewise, "I don't know."
>
> The question of the riddle is, what color hat does A wear?

Examine what is required, intellectually, emotionally, motivationally, and from the point of view of the will and self-discipline, to deal successfully with this problem.

Answer: C says he does not know the color of his hat only because the two hats that he sees are not *both* white. For if the latter were the case, then his must be black—since they own only two white hats. The alternatives derived from his answer are that either both of the hats that he sees are black, or only one of them is white.

Armed with that information, B would know the color of his hat if A's hat were white. Since he does not know, we must infer that A's hat is black.

And that is the answer.

Let us look at another example.

An army scout starts Monday morning at sunrise from his base camp at the foot of a tall mountain. He walks up a steep mountain road and reaches the outlook at the top by sunset. He camps overnight and at next day's sunrise, which is Tuesday, he returns to his base camp. His return trip was twice as fast as his upward journey. Is there one specific spot on the road where the scout was at the exact same time Monday and Tuesday?

That there is such a spot can be discovered through visual intelligence. For all that is necessary is to imagine two scouts going in opposite directions on the *same* day. They must meet, and where they do is of course one and the same specific spot. And therefore such a spot exists. However, to discover precisely *where* that spot is requires relatively complex calculations and therefore both analytic and abstract-relations intelligence.

In going over these puzzles, we must keep in mind that we are studying one intelligence. We do not do the exercises and the examples exclusively for amusement—although they are enjoyable—but to study how the logical mind works. And then we must use that understanding to amplify, intensify, and enhance precisely that kind of thinking.

One must learn and generalize from working this and other examples. One must examine how life would be different if one were always like that. One must ask, What acts of consciousness are required in order to think logically? What moods accompany that mindset? Could they be boredom, frustration, anger, embarrassment? Do we experience fun and pleasure, hope, accomplishment, success, competition, intensity, or something else?

Logical intelligence is also strong on analysis. We should take a difficult paragraph or problem as an object of analysis—perhaps a chronicle from history, a case study from a business or a law school, a current political or economic controversy. We must be competent in being able to divide the problem into as many significant components as possible and then try to resolve or design action plans for each of its elements.

In other words, logical intelligence in its analytical mode signifies meticulous attention to the most minute detail. Many of the other intelligences tend to rely more on intuition and to be more global than analytical thought in their mode of apprehending reality. People with logical intelligence make good administrators—they are cool and rational and, like good bureaucrats, are often impervious to personal and emotional appeals.

In sum, logical intelligence means abstract reasoning, internal visualization, and analysis.

Much of mathematics—pure, that is, by itself and when used with applied science, like physics, chemistry, etc.—is abstract reasoning and thinking in abstract relations. People who try to visualize or work out in any non-abstract or pictorial fashion problems in abstract reasoning will always end up thinking of themselves as inadequate. For the logical mind is fast, and to work things out by intuition is slow. Every high school algebra student knows that to solve an algebraic problem mathematically, that is, through the manipulation of abstract symbols, may be a matter of a few seconds; but to work it out in words or pictures may take hours—or may be outright impossible.

Visualization is the ability to work with pictures in the mind, especially three-dimensional ones, without the use of physical models, i.e., visual aids. Good examples of this kind of intelligence, also very much valued in the sciences and in the academic world generally, are exercises in which two- or three-dimensional geometric figures are turned around and the subject is asked which one of several likely candidates is the actual inversion of the original figure. Some people have real difficulties, to the point of vertigo, with such problems. Others can solve them instantaneously. But here, as elsewhere, practice makes perfect. We can tell people's skill in this intelligence when they are called upon to assemble objects, such as toys and furniture, and must follow the diagrams in the instructions.

Analysis, the converse of holistic and systemic thinking, is the ability to take a problem apart into its mutlifarious and detailed parts and then handle or manage or solve each singly. This is a most highly prized virtue in business and industry. And it is very difficult to succeed in business with only one of these two important skills. Required are both analysis and synthesis. One is not likely to ever find a list of traits, competencies, or criteria for management positions that does not include the ability to analyze a problem into its component parts.

We can train ourselves to improve in the skill of analysis by simply making the effort. It is very much like speed reading, swimming, or rhyming: practice does make perfect. Think for example how your personal life and your professional enterprises would be different if you were better at this intelligence.

No doubt we each have our own proclivities and areas of comfort in living these intelligences. But we also have a choice. We can motivate ourselves and we can instruct our minds to desire this particular intelligence, to value it, to constitute themselves to *be* that intelligence—to practice thinking in, for example, logical terms, as would a student preparing for the SAT or GRE or LSAT—and to apply it, use it, and experience its potential for survival.

If you are frustrated at not being accomplished in logical intelligence, you can always be reassured by the fact that there are seven more intelligences to go!

The Language of
Sensuality

Muscular

Kinetic Orientation

Health

CHAPTER 3

Somatic
Intelligence

Mens sana in corpore sano was a motto of the Romans, borrowed from the Greeks—a healthy mind in a healthy body. In this way, our society has extolled athletics in conjunction with the mathematical sciences. These are the two skills that matter. But somatic intelligence is more than just athletics.

Somatic intelligence can also be called "manual intelligence." It consists first of the capacity for being sensual, which includes our general physical health and the good feelings that go with it. Sensuality is the language of the body. Second, it consists of dexterity and of strength. And, third, it is the intelligence for orienting oneself in space (and also time), that is, for having a good sense of place and of direction. Finally, somatic intelligence consists of physical health, which means also nutrition, for they are the ways to tune the instrument. The first uses the whole body, whereas the second uses the small and large muscles.

Somatic intelligence is the kinetic sense, the use of a conscious, living body. It activates body awareness as the primary mode of being in the world, and it exhibits the skills of large and small muscles: its practitioners include mechanics, technicians, surgeons, musicians, athletes, farmers, carpenters, craftsmen and women, magicians, and body therapists. It has blue collar as well as athletic connotations. It means thinking with the body, existing with the hands, and coping somatically or manually with the demands of reality. The do-it-yourself mythos in America responds to this kind of intelligence. It makes physiology the root metaphor for all existence: in psychology this is known as energetics or bioenergetics.

Somatic intelligence includes everything that has to do with health and holistic medicine. It covers nutrition and exercise, diet, and all our knowledge about what a healthy body needs to feel well, to be joyous, and to live long.

Sensuality is a part of the life of the body. Animals are sensuous, and so are human beings. The more we live in conscious and deliberate contact with these primitive aspects of who we are, the healthier we are likely to be, and the happier. For then we are more closely in tune with what we are and who we are. Idealism, mysticism, and spirituality must not consist of the denial of the body, but rather integrate the spiritual with what is and what was the body.

In order to understand somatic intelligence we must distinguish the objective or social body and the felt, lived, or experienced body. Subjectively speaking, my body is an unknown area in one sense, and an intimate one in another. My body is both subject and object—a fact that is not true of any other body or thing in the world, at least not in my world. What does that mean? It means that I can use my body as sense organ—the eye, the touch of any part of the body—and at the same time as object, for I can see it and I can touch it.

The subjective part of my body is exclusively my own. I am not in touch with the subjectivity of any other person. We approximate that contact when we love others—our children, our parents, our spouses.

For example, I can use my finger to feel my cheek—that makes the finger the subject and the cheek the object. Conversely, I can also feel my finger with my cheek—externally there is no difference. In that case, my cheek becomes the subject and my finger the object. My body is like the house of being. I dwell in it.

Only I feel my physical pain, my physical anxiety, and my physical vulnerability. I empathize with the pain of others, but I do not feel it directly. I do not see with your eyes, only with mine, although I understand the language you use to describe what your eyes see. The objective body we can see in a photograph and in a mirror. But the subjective body can be fully disclosed and explored only by a poet, a philosopher, an artist, a psychoanalyst, or a mystic. And the subjective body cannot be reflected. An approximation is in love, for one soul can mirror another. The sensuous intelligence is the subjective body—the body as sense organ, the body as self.

Constant awareness of the ubiquitousness of our body, and of its mystery, of its dominance and of its wisdom, is crucial to the life of a fulfilled somatic intelligence. We must trust our body. We must listen to our body.

Listening is the key. Is that difficult? Can we not take time out and allow the feelings in our body and the sensations on its surface to speak to us? Can we not encourage fantasies to accompany these body sensations? Cannot ancient myths, religions, and beliefs, anthropomorphic ideations and what have you, feed the imagination with ideas and hypotheses—like dreams—about what our body wants and says? Healing, mental and physical, economic and academic, political and social, and good living in general, are closely tied to this unprejudiced sensitivity to the body and to its language. The body's voices are like the stars on a smoggy evening—we know they are there even though we may not see them clearly.

But we can learn. And learn we must. For true leadership can spring only from the wisdom of our ancient bodies. We are one with nature, one with our history, one with evolution. Let us feel that, live it, enjoy it, participate in it, and be fulfilled by it.

Large-muscle control is the world of athletics. It is the somatic intelligence of strength. That world is vast; it is popular. In fact, the sports pages of the nation's newspapers are by far the most widely read. And it is easily accessible. It includes the world of the joggers and the sports fans, of the weightlifters, the tennis players, and the swimmers. It includes the world of nutrition—of attention to vitamins, fiber, diets, low cholesterol.

The somatic intelligence of strength has enormously important psychological implications. Many executives religiously practice their exercises. It is important in high executive office to be trim—not only for the sake of appearances, but, more importantly, for the sake of physical health. But most significant of all, the somatic intelligence of strength means not merely brute physical force, but spiritual power. One of the best ways to acquire courage and self-confidence, which are part of spiritual strength, is through empowering the body. This is a technology now understood by many people. A physically fit person is a far more effective leader than one who shows no respect for his or her body.

Brute strength, it is sometimes thought, may reflect a crude materialism. But there is no necessary connection between the cultivation of the body and the values one entertains. As a matter of fact, the body is a temple, and the worship of the body also contains within it, as the Greek artists of the age of Pericles so ably demonstrated, respect for holiness. We can feel that veneration for the holy in the living in classical sculptures, especially in the delicate suppleness of arrested motion. If there is a connection, it is perhaps between strength and idealism made visible.

The somatic intelligence of dexterity requires its practitioners to take up crafts and skills demanding minute muscle control—from actors and mimics, to clowns, to weavers and carvers, cabinetmakers, blacksmiths. Dexterity is a wonderful intelligence. It absorbs the soul, purifies the spirit, pacifies the psyche, and beautifies the world.

But dexterity also includes surgeons and artists, especially in the crafts. A life that takes pleasure in the value of fast chromatic scales on the piano, painting miniatures, or in delicate sculpting—as is done in the Orient with elephant tusks—is in tune with its dexterity.

A full presentation of the sensuality aspect alone of somatic intelligence would require a full course and practicum in one of the body therapies, such as energetic therapy, dance therapy, and even what was once popular, primal scream therapy. The names do not matter. Their content does.

The word "therapy" may sound ominous to the business mind. It evokes the specter of illness, or worse, of craziness. That should not be. Therapy is part of education. Therapy teaches us through personal experience about who we are and how we became that way. Therapy teaches us how personal responsibility plays a role in who we are. Therapy teaches us how we relate to others and how important other people are in the conduct of our lives. And therapy helps us claim our freedom and take charge of our lives. These are all elements of growing up and of getting a complete education.

Body centered therapy is the lifestyle conversion, the concerted effort, to simply live our biological truth. We were not created yesterday. Today's yuppies do not have in their hands the authentic way of life. Even such a dominant religion as the Judeo-Christian tradition can hardly be unequivocally accepted as the final word on human nature, for it represents but a minuscule percentage of biological life on earth. If Christianity is 2000 years old, and Judaism over 5000, and if life on earth has existed for two billion years (or four billion years, if we consider that earth and life are continuous phenomena), then simple arithmetic tells us that Christianity arose at the last .0001% of biological time and Judaism at the last .00025% of the time of life on earth. If all of the history of life were compressed on a 24-hour day (86,400 seconds), then Christianity arose 9 one-hundredth (0.0864) of one second before the end—less than one-tenth of a second before the end of the 24-hour day, which is then all there is to today's historical period.

And these calculations assume that our bodies started with life. Why not go further back? What, after all, is the difference between life and inert matter? Is it not purely definitional? If life arose from inert matter, then why not say that inert matter is alive too? Why is the whirring electron not as much alive as the whirring humming-bird?

It makes sense, therefore, that most of our lives are governed by biological forces and inheritances. Technically we say that it "is in the genes." We distinguish ourselves from our evolutionary background, but that is a cultural bias and not a natural hypothesis.

Our critical functions as human beings occur automatically. Our biological mechanism takes care of us. The homeostasis of our physiology is exquisitely delicate. Consider some examples from the body: temperature control, heartbeats, breathing, digestion, the vast spectrum of healing—from sunburns to cuts and bruises, from major surgery and accidents to viral and bacterial infections. All these are miracles. And we can do little ourselves to control them. Other functions, such as procreating, loving, being ambitious, wishing to survive, jealousy, competition, anger, moods, reflexes, and so forth, also have their origins in our biological heritage. So does our adaptation to old age and our desire to die.

Let us be proud of our bodies. Those who are somatically intelligent are intelligent in an ancient way, a way that is healthful and must be respected. Somatic intelligence creates the scaffolding and the base for the artistic creation of leadership.

CHAPTER 4

Verbal

Musical

Pictorial

Aesthetic Intelligence

Aesthetic intelligence is really the intelligence of language—but here language is used not for abstract reasoning but to winnow images from our life-world and transform them for use in expressing the emotional truths of our existence.

Aesthetic intelligence can help to develop or produce, express, and communicate emotions, feelings, the unconscious, the primitive, ethics and morality, the ethnic, tradition, and other personal, social, and anthropological phenomena.

This intelligence consists of three subsidiary intelligences: verbal, musical, and pictorial.

Aesthetic intelligence has elements of primitive and concrete thought. It expresses our total being-in-the-world wrapped in one fresh, clearly delineated, surprising, and powerful image or symbol. That is art.

The arts have solved problems that neither science nor politics, neither psychology nor medicine, seem to be able to touch. The Cold War stopped in a tearful embrace of the two superpowers when the American citizen and native Russian, Vladimir Horowitz, returned for the first time in sixty years to his motherland to give a piano concert. Polyphonic music proves that differences and contradictions are beautiful and harmonious and far richer than a single statement. And it demonstrates that conflict is required for harmony. No one will tell Johann Sebastian Bach to make up his mind which melody in a fugue is the right one or which theme in a concerto shall prevail!

Understanding the arts helps the business leader in communication. That is obvious: any student of advertising knows how much creative art goes into its production.

But an even more important consequence of understanding the arts is what might be called self-expression. Self-expression is much more than it at first appears to be. It has to do with the important philosophic and psychological concepts of grounding. Persons are not real or complete until they are perceived, and perceive themselves, as an integral part of nature. The voice that speaks must feel itself come out of the viscera. The mind that imagines must see itself at one with the nature that it describes.

Our quest for beauty makes possible such unity with all existence. The arts are thus essential for integrating us into the world—the world of space and geography and the world of time and history.

And not only do the arts integrate us with the external world, they connect us with our inwardness. In fact, the arts help create that inner world. The arts bring up our deepest emotions, emotions we would otherwise not know we had. The arts create the life of the emotions. These emotions bring insights; they come to us as truths; they are given to us as revelations, as knowledge. The poet, said Novalis, is the true scientist. The artist of genius, said Schopenhauer, has direct access to ultimate reality, as opposed to the rest of us, who are in touch with only appearances.

The arts are our new languages. Any business mind that needs to think along new paths, that requires innovative and penetrating analyses into the lived human reality, that must find more persuasive ways to say what needs to be said, that needs to communicate it better, and that needs to stir up enthusiasm, loyalty, and commitment among employees and customers, must embrace the arts, saturate itself with the arts, immerse itself in them.

In order to sharpen aesthetic intelligence and understand that the arts are a language, let us take a look, by way of example, at music.

Music must be both conceptualized and perceived as a language.

What is the alphabet of music? What are its letters and its words, its molecular and its atomic constituents?

In listening to sounds made by any event, musical or otherwise, we concentrate our consciousness on several possible tasks:

- To distinguish the aesthetic from the practical. An automobile horn and a red traffic light each have unique and intrinsic qualities on which we can focus. They can be vibrant or dull, sharp or obtuse, penetrating or shallow, dominant or inconspicuous. We can heighten our senses, and perceive what to us earlier was obtuse. That is the aesthetic attitude.

  The practical attitude is when we but marginally perceive the sound or the light, and when the sound or the light are signs for action. The horn means Watch out! and the red light means Stop!—and no more.

- To concentrate on the intrinsic quality of the sound, the timbre. How does a train sound as it approaches a crossing? What is the sound of a jet engine? Of a baby crying? What are the acoustical details of a bird's call? What is the sound of silence? How can these sounds be recreated? Re-evoked?

  The same attention must be given to listening to musical instruments. We must always ask, what is the sound of the instrument? Do we hear all of its richness? How is it being played? What might be different? Of what does it remind us? In other words, what are our associations?

- To attend to the associations we make with sounds. These associations could be feelings or memories, images of nature or of civilization, ideas or facts, hopes or tragedies, vigor or depression, the birth of God or the death of God.

  What associations do you have with these instruments?

    Horn?
    Trumpet?
    Organ?
    Flute?
    Drums?
    The human voice, the premier instrument?

  These sounds and their associations give us the raw material for making music.

  A trained ear attends perceptually, emotionally, and with associations to all these sounds and their nuances.

Similar things can be said about the other arts. For painting, color and lines, contrasts and figures become the raw material. In poetry, the raw material is words, but more than that, the images that the words evoke. It is also the sounds of the language and the rhythms of the lines that express and convey meanings.

But let us return to music.

Listen to music, preferably live music. Then, play around with it yourself. Make it easy and make it fun. There are innumerable ways to be a musician. Some are very difficult and others are simple enough for infants.

Do the same with other arts, such as painting. Just play around with them. Insist always on inspiration—technique can be taught later. Write some poetry or short stories. Savor the language. Play with your imagination; in fact, acknowledge your imagination as your spark of divinity.

The principles of composition apply not only to music but also to painting, sculpture (i. e. , the visual arts,) and literature. Composition in paintings has to do with the abstract form of the total painting and what that form does, what it says, and how it relates itself to the viewer. Of particular importance is how the viewer is invited into the picture through the composition, how the viewer is made to feel once inside the picture, and where the process comes to a halt. The specific content, story, or depiction—a still life, a landscape— becomes then only one of the elements of the artwork.

Language communicates and expresses. Language is one kind of voice.

What is voice? Voice does not mean necessarily sound made by a human being. "The voice of the turtle" is not human. Nor must voice be a sound. Voice refers to any and all forms of communication and expression by humans and by any and all other beings. Voice is the general expression of a living thing on this earth and it is an expression about the earth, something that comes from the earth, and something that is of the earth, or returns to the earth. There are many forms of expression, what we call language is only one of them.

But above all, language organizes experience. Language creates a world of meaning for us. It makes sense out of our world. Being resides within language, not the other way around. Different languages create different perceptions, interpret the world differently, construct different universes. Not only do French and German, Sanskrit and Hopi create different worlds, but so does body language, painting and sculpting language, and so forth.

The arts are language, and through them four things happen, all of prime importance: expression, communication, organization, and revelation—the penetration into a deeper realm of reality.

The arts as language can reveal a separate reality (which implies a theory of multiple realities). As we discover the arts, we discover new realms of values, ideals, and organizations of being. As we discover new realities, we can dedicate our lives to new beliefs and convictions, give life a new direction.

Executives often do not feel the power of these different realities until their children start to espouse them. They then discover the differences between idealism and materialism, mysticism and science, between a Sakharov and a Steve Ross, a St. Francis of Assisi and a Ross Perot, and a Martin Luther King and a Douglas Mac Arthur.

These separate realities are intimately connected with motivation and enthusiasm, with the ability to think for ourselves, with the power to create our own world, with energy, and with joy. The arts help us to understand how to initiate action and make room for paradigm shifts. To be open to a separate reality is to own the richness of our possibilities and also to claim the fullness of our freedom. Aesthetic intelligence can give us a glimpse of how profoundly different our world could be.

A genuine business leader is not just a logical and abstract thinker. Nor does a leader merely know how to work with people—or act with initiative and self-discipline. A leader is a grounded, rooted, emotionally richly endowed human being. A leader is a person who participates fully in life—the life of the body, of the inner soul, and of the outside world. A leader shares completely in the world of society and in the world of nature, the world of the atom and the world of cosmology. The decision maker who loves the arts can, through them, reach a high level of energy and of enthusiasm, of mental health and happiness.

The artist, as Rollo May has said so very frequently, is entrusted with the sacred task of creating the myths and the symbols for tomorrow.

The artist is emotional. And the artist wants to be emotional, for the emotions are the bridge—better call them roots—to reality. The emotions suck sap from the earth as the roots of a tree extract their nourishment from the soil. The eagle flies home into the wind towards the mist blanketing the mountain top, for the bird is one with nature. So is it with us—we must sense, savor, fulfill our appetite and satiate our hunger for the richness of the living world of which we are a part and with which we are one. Also we fly high into being. The world is fulfilled by our filling it as we are fulfilled by the world filling us.

The arts should open up a new reality, a new set of values, a new vision, a new spirit, a new life. The arts can make you see the world with the heart. The arts can change your life. And the arts are the most powerful agent of exhortation, persuasion, and communication.

Leadership in all fields can be truly creative and genuinely human only when enriched by the arts. Enriched by the arts, lawyers, accountants, and engineers all deserve to be promoted to leadership positions. So do marketing geniuses. Plato argued that philosophers ought to be kings or kings philosophers. We must argue here, as an additional truth, that artists must be leaders and leaders must be artists.

Consciousness as Fact

Non-Attachment

Exploration of Inner Space-Time

Transcendental Intelligence

Transcendental intelligence understands the nature of consciousness as a fundamental aspect of the world and ingredient of reality. It means we understand the power of non-attachment as a fundamental mode of being in the world. The person with transcendental intelligence has a clear vision of inner space-time and recognizes it as a major zone for exploration. We know that this exploration has been carried out, primarily through the history of ideas and through religious mysticism. It has yielded subjectively testable and introspectively repeatable results, and we can personally, through our own intuition, verify the conclusions of these researches into the realm of inner space and inner time. Through our study of ideas and our experience of mysticism we know this exploration occurred.

It seems strange to insert this intelligence into the business context. Yet precisely because this intelligence is alien to many business decision makers, the benefits of exploring this realm may be exceptional.

Transcendental intelligence is the exploration of inner space and inner time, the ability to withdraw from the world and reflect dispassionately on reality, rather than to be enmeshed in it. Transcendental intelligence is to practice the art of non-attachment.

It has to do with clarity of inner vision, with openness to non-ordinary modes of thought, with meditation, which is the practice of dwelling in this realm of infinite inner space and inner time. This inner vision can be explored through non-attachment. To choose to cultivate the region of our pure inner consciousness is to make a deliberate effort to develop one's mind.

Clarity of inner vision means that we illuminate and magnify the inner mind. During this process of deep introspection, the mind must feel at rest, for emotional agitation is like muddying a pond by stirring it.

Transcendental intelligence involves accepting the independent reality of pure consciousness and recognizing that we are this consciousness.

There is little interest in this form of intelligence in the West, especially in the hard circles of the business world. True, many executives do meditate, and they have found that such expeditions into inwardness indeed have healthful effects on their business: meditation helps them keep calm, maintain their perspective, keep their values, remain honest. They become imperturbable, and they gain security and strength from the religious side of meditation. Nevertheless, the transcendental is seldom valued or even understood among American executives. In the Orient, on the other hand, it is probably the most highly prized form of intelligence. If we simply were to put the matter to a vote, transcendental intelligence would prevail by the sheer numbers of its adherents.

Transcendental intelligence is valuable to business because it can dramatically enhance most of the other forms of intelligence. This intelligence clears the mind of distractions and debris; it diminishes the magnetism of irrelevancies. It reestablishes control over the mind and simplifies self-discipline.

Transcendental intelligence is usually at the bottom of any profile or ranking of the eight intelligences in the business community. In one seminar, a VP, in profiling the company's performance and prospects, placed transcendental intelligence at the bottom, as expected. His chart was posted on the wall: marketing and motivational intelligence were at the top.

After some discussion, it became evident that if transcendental intelligence could be mobilized for use in the high-technology and administrative problems this company was having, it should rank at the very top. We were not talking about stress reduction through meditation or an escapist form of mysticism. Nothing of the kind. We were talking of expanding the mind and clarifying consciousness in the finest and purest sense possible. We were talking about enhancing concentration and increasing memory, about cultivating the most pristine workings of the mind and of reason.

After the break, the group noticed that the VP had inverted his chart on the wall so that transcendental intelligence appeared on top!

This is the most difficult of the intelligences to analyze. It may also be the most fruitful. Some people have no understanding of even the basics, that is, that consciousness is real. We must bring consciousness back into our everyday vocabulary. Moreover, the analyses of consciousness are quasi-scientific explorations. Contrary to what most people seem to think, one can describe consciousness in much the same way as a plant, a comet, or a dream. They are all objects to the subjective ego. The study of consciousness is one of the most constructive and helpful activities in which we can engage. And reference here is to more than meditation, more than mysticism in religion. It is to cool and dispassionate philosophical examinations and explorations of consciousness. It is discussed at length under Consciousness and Transcendental intelligence.

Transcendental intelligence contrasts sharply with its opposite, the marketing mind.

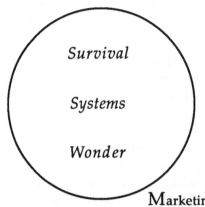

Survival

Systems

Wonder

Chapter 6

Marketing Intelligence

Marketing intelligence possesses the characteristics of survival, systems thinking, and that proverbial beginning of all philosophy, wonder. It can also be called pragmatic or prudential intelligence—a term of special meaning in the philosophic community.

Marketing intelligence is the intuitive survival intelligence. The marketing intelligence has made a non-negotiable commitment to stay alive. It is pragmatic, prudential, the art of the possible. It is results-oriented and eminently practical. Marketing intelligence characterizes the effective executive, especially the leader, perhaps more than any other of the intelligences. It is the global vision, the ability to see and to respond, to conceptualize and then to act, over ever-larger time frames, spaces, and territories, and especially systems.

The decision-maker who has marketing intelligence is governed by wonder, thirsting for learning and knowledge, always looking, always fascinated by the novelty of it all, the leader whose skin to the outside world is always porous. Abraham Maslow calls it freshness of appreciation.

With this kind of intelligence the world falls naturally into simple ideas. Complex issues—or issues that appear complex to non-marketing minds—fall naturally into patterns of the most obvious simplicity: Solve unemployment and absenteeism with one stroke by splitting jobs into equal and cooperating halves. Recontact all your clients with a new product or a renewed old product. Send them a newsletter. Give them a new idea.

The marketing intelligence always and instantaneously adapts. It has but one thought, to survive; and it always finds a way.

It may even be that the study of animals with high survival strengths, such as eagles and cats, can assist us in the anthropological and ethological study of this kind of intelligence. The key seems to be utmost alertness, quickness of adaptation, and independence.

Insects survive not as individuals but only as colonies and as species, because they reproduce astronomically. Their actions are stupidly repetitive and mechanical. But foxes and panthers, eagles and cats, survive as individuals. And it is because of the sharpness, the responsiveness, and the wide range of their perceptions, and of the speed of their reactions that they survive so well in the jungle. That is also the posture marketing intelligence takes towards its world of products and finance.

Survival orientation means uncompromising single-mindedness. "Those who say it can't be done must get out of the way of those who are doing it!" is the appropriate motto.

The marketing intelligence adapts instantly to the most variable of circumstances and, even beyond that, it makes chaos simple. It has the capacity for innovation. The flexible mind is tempered only by the constraints of common sense, ethics, and the laws.

One interesting aspect of the survival mode of marketing intelligence is its concrete thinking. It thinks in terms of concrete objects. The marketing intelligence thinks principally through examples, pictures, stories, images, and visions.

This intelligence can be fostered, encouraged, developed, by mimicking the external appearances of what it does. We can train ourselves to think concretely, to learn our metaphors, to look for stories, and to find interest in myths. In so doing, we reshape the way in which we view the world. And since our social world, or life-world, is in great measure what our projections make it, concrete thinking will enhance the survival element within our marketing intelligence.

Marketing intelligence is also political intelligence. It is the willingness to be political. The marketing intelligence thinks in political terms and, since politics is the art of the possible, it makes the continuous adaptation to reality and to the need of managing and manipulating it the primary mode of thought. Strategic thinking is the manipulative arm of marketing intelligence. It is the objective analysis of a situation (an industry, a constituency) and a plan of attack in every sense like a military operation. Marketing intelligence focuses on effectiveness and outcomes.

Marketing intelligence is the ability to grasp in one simple mental act ever larger systems. This act is one, unitary, and it is simple; it is obvious and commonsensical.

Systems thinking is the ability to take large gobs of information and see them as simple wholes. Marketing intelligence is able to make everything simple. And it is a simplicity that works. Systems thinking is not simplistic but smart and effective. Without marketing intelligence, business would be unmanageably complex.

Integration and wholeness work because a person can do only one thing in one lifetime. It must feel subjectively like one thing although objectively it may look like many. Integration does not mean 100 ten-minute appointments sputtering like the cylinders in an internal combustion engine, one after the other, but instead may mean leisurely, intensive, and exploratory sessions.

Business executives have large numbers of conflicting obligations: dozens of incompatible business interests, family, eternal questions, leisure commitments. Balance or compromise does not work for long; it does not give lasting satisfaction. Fragmentation is contrary to human nature, which is one and whole, as Plato says of the soul in the *Phaedo*. Fragmentation is anathema to quality. Quality grows with wholeness and with integration. The analytic mind fragments for purposes of practical action. Fragmentation is an important ingredient in scientific leadership. But it is not marketing.

The systems element of marketing intelligence consists in turn of three forms: space, time, and logical wholes. Spatial systems are a form of geography; they involve the ability to see internationally, or to see large territories with one glance, however literally or metaphorically we may care to define the terms "geography" and "territory." That is a skill, and it can be practiced—even while you drive, you must learn to get the big picture.

Systems thinking, as thinking in logical wholes, is another and different way to survive. Marketing intelligence means harmony with the environment. Difficulties are signs that we are out of tune with our environment. Roger Harrison, in "Strategies for a New Age," says:

> When goals become very difficult to achieve, and it begins to seem as though the environment is hostile and unsupportive, it is typical of our culture to engage in problem solving—to identify the barriers to success and to work and plan to overcome them. We can, however, take the point of view that our organization has an appropriate place in the larger system, and that our task as managers and leaders is to attune our

organization to the environment in order to discover what our part is and play it. The difficulties we experience are inter- preted as signs and signals from the environment that we are somehow out of resonance with our true role. We read events as messages, rather than as judgments.

But the most important aspect of the form of marketing intelli- gence called systems thinking is what happens with regard to time. True, a human being is his or her "whole space." But above and be- yond that, a human being is his or her time, the time of his or her life. The leader is a person who thinks not in units of hours or days, not of weeks and months, not even years. The wider the time span the more effective the leader. Elliott Jaques suggests that the chairman of an international conglomerate needs to think of time in units of twenty years. The president or prime minister of a major power must think of time in units of 35 to 50 years, at minimum.

Increasing these time-span units can be practiced and cultivated. You just do it, and continue to do it, as with speed reading. And the world responds.

Here are some questions to help increase the time frame:

1. What is a realistic prediction of what I shall be doing next year at this time?
2. What is an idealized projection of what I would like to be doing next year at this time?
3. What are the obstacles that prevent me from achieving that ideal?
4. What am I meant to learn from these obstacles?
5. What must I do now to increase the chances that I might achieve my ideal at a later time?

The next time you are on your way to work, think of yourself—and of your company—as 5 or 10 years older. Just as in driving or walking you look ahead and around you, so as you live your life now you must see as far ahead as you can (or wish). As you go through the day, remember that it is always later—you are older, your colleagues are older, and your company is older. Think especially of how you will look different at that time. Train yourself to think ahead.

A good example of an increased time frame exercise is to prepare a rectangular chart, with 84 smaller rectangles, forming 7 vertical and

12 horizontal divisions and representing the life expectancy of one born today (it can be actuarially adjusted for older people). Each small rectangular box represents one year of your life. And that year is represented by a small but complete 365-day calendar. Now cross off, one by one, the years past. As you do that, reflect on each year. Attach stickers to major choice points or turning events in your life. Now reflect on the meaning of what is left! Make some decisions as a result of that reflection.

Increasing your space frame is also a part of systems thinking. It can be achieved by having maps, photographs, and articles on your wall to remind you of other nations and other lands. You should carry in your mind a map of your city. Try to always be conscious of where you are in relation to the city as a whole (or the countryside, if that is where you reside).

Make a deliberate effort not to be influenced by your surroundings but think of the places where you have been and the people you have known and imagine being there and being with them.

Compare marketing intelligence to speed reading. It means we intuit and absorb ever larger wholes. As we feel comfortable with one whole, we are ready for the next and larger whole. We see the unity of things. The key word is "simplicity."

For practice take a look at any complex phenomenon: a landscape, a painting, a meeting, a conversation, a business transaction, a class, a novel. Then think of the words "wholes," "unity," and "simplicity" and ask yourself what insights about the phenomenon develop, what patterns emerge, what shapes are implicit, what new idea emerges. This is how an artist plans a painting.

Marketing intelligence in its systems mode is the genius for simplification. Simplicity to the degree of ludicrousness is often not a mistake when it leads to seeing things from a marketing perspective: "At Ford Quality Is Job One" puts the company's entire philosophy into simple workman's language.

Management by objectives, goal directedness, and task orientation are further synonyms for the ideals of the marketing intelligence. The survival aspect of marketing intelligence is solution oriented. The interest lies in the outcome. It matters little how we get there—as long as our means are moral. But the most common obstacle to outcomes are pride and self-pity. We blame others—which we must do if it is true and good for our souls. But in practice it does little more than to "cut your nose to spite your face." Marketing intelligence, in its survival mode, indulges little our personal sensitivities, for its concern is with outcomes. This intelligence is tough, it is hard.

Survival in marketing intelligence is what in psychology is called reality testing. The survivor survives because he or she tests reality continuously and responds accordingly with appropriate action.

Marketing Intelligence as survival we see in the alertness of a condor.

It helps to remember that business is not commerce—an abstraction in economics—but a determined survival and a "can-do" attitude. Business is a lifestyle where effectiveness and accountability are the principal orientations to the world. Effectiveness is of course a key hallmark of leadership. All the other intelligences must then be harnessed in the service of "making outcomes happen."

Survival is more a matter of instinct than of calculation, of experience than of reasoning.

It is always helpful to study, beyond what we want, what prevents us from achieving it. If one finds systems thinking and survival thinking, as they are here described, difficult, one should ask, "What in my childhood gave me the sense of false security, that I did not have to struggle for my safety in this world? I got a good education, so that I did not need to rise through the ranks. We had money when I was a child, so that I did not need to fight for food, attention, shelter, and education. We always lived in safe neighborhoods, so that I did not need to protect myself. I have never been in a revolution or in a war, so that I always sleep peacefully at night."

What is the motivation for enhancing marketing intelligence? Money is not a sufficient answer. The marketing desire must grow from the needs of the soul. It must spring from the spiritual requirements of the character, not from the material consensus of the culture. And here resides the true difficulty. "Marketing minds are born, not made" is a good rule of thumb. From this it follows that if you wish to grow in this intelligence, and enhance it, you must be born again. What is required is a deep conversion, not a shallow technique. A marketing intelligence is a superb politician. It is an intelligence that demands motivation more than skill.

The marketing intelligence can be trained through survival-oriented sports such as sky diving, hang gliding, rock climbing, rafting, sailing, survival training. In each, life depends on the level of alertness that one can summon.

Finally, marketing intelligence can be defined as wonder, thirst for learning, freshness of appreciation, excitement about life, desire for novelty.

The marketing mind is attuned to the mystery and the miracle of being. It is flexible. It makes no assumptions. Its openness to reality is virginal. It is not bound by tradition. Wonder means responsiveness, listening, learning, and eagerness. Walt Whitman wrote, "A mouse is miracle enough to stagger sextillions of infidels." Everyone knows Tennyson's "Flower on the Crannied Wall":

> Flower in the crannied wall,
> I pluck you out of the crannies,
> I hold you here, root and all, in my hand,
> Little flower—but *if* I could understand
> What you are, root and all, and all in all,
> I should know what God and man is.

There are always resistances to expanding the mind: they are as understandable as they are lethal. We must neutralize immediately and directly this pathology of "psychosclerosis"—Ashley Montagu's term for the hardening of the mind.

The fundamental assumption behind the theory of multiple intelligences is also the final message of the principles of developing leadership intelligence, namely, that thinking about thinking stretches thinking.

Although the ability to integrate and use these things simply and whole is part of marketing intelligence, its value far transcends the marketing function in business. The real whole is not the business but one's total life.

The aesthetic intelligence, for example, provides a good adjunct to a successful marketing intelligence. Analysis is not as effective as "impressionism." The kind of categories that apply to marketing come closer to impressionistic descriptions of the general "feel" of things than the meticulous analyses of behavioral scientists and statisticians. Listening to effective and entrepreneurial marketing minds talk to one another is closer to hearing poets, painters, and psychotherapists describe the realities of their art than it is to hearing scientists and engineers discuss their latest proofs and calculations.

But what about the will?

CHAPTER 7

The Preeminence
of Action

Self-Energization
(will)

Greatness

Motivational
Intelligence

Motivational intelligence is the courage for greatness, the discovery of destiny, and the commitment to meaning.

Motivational intelligence is first of all a philosophy of action. Action is the interface between idea and reality, mind and matter, soul and body. Action is neither mental nor the material, neither subjective or objective. It is instead the living contact between the two. It is the view that God is not only an essence (a blueprint or a plan or a program) and not a mere existence (an object), but is that extraordinary Being in whom existence and essence merge. God's essence is His existence.

Furthermore, motivational intelligence is self-creation, self-energization, will power, or, as it is commonly known, motivation. It comes from within; and its true source is never known. It is the strong sense of self, the autonomous ego, the ownership of one's acts and of their consequences. It means responsibility. Self-energization is the antidote to depression. To be self-energized is to claim your freedom and your power. Self-energization is will, will power, self-discipline, positive thinking, and enthusiasm. It is the starter engine. Tennyson reminds us of "So many worlds, so much to do,/ So little done, such things to be."

If we admire a family of cranes that arrives at a local New England pond, survives the hot summer months, keeps a secret nest for the evenings, and flies south to escape the bitter winters, what in fact happens is that we envy them for their marvelous adaptation. We could not survive all year, naked and without amenities, in the wilderness. In our own way, we must be home again like the cranes—one with nature, integrated with ancient, evolutionary, botanical, geographic, and biological realities. This connectedness gives us a sense that can best be expressed through the arts. This type of groundedness is one of the key ingredients of leadership.

All the discussions of the will in the history of ideas, beginning with the ancient Hindus, the yogis, and the Greek Stoics, illustrate one element of self-energization: the power of the will. Motivational intelligence is tethered to the will. G. Gordon Liddy is a radical example. Asked, "At home, does your family fear you?", he answers,

I respond to people as they respond to me. I am absolutely no danger whatsoever to anybody who means me no harm. When I was in the FBI, for example, I was so thoroughly trained, and I practiced so well, got so good at the use of firearms, that when I walked down the mean streets in some of the worst cities in the United States, I knew I was the most dangerous person walking down the street, but only to someone who meant me harm.

USA Today.

The core of motivational intelligence is the pinpoint of freedom that exists at the center of the "sphere" that is a human being. One can go no deeper than the center of the earth, for as one apparently moves deeper, one is instead moving closer to the surface on the other side. That center point is the source of one's freedom. It is a key concept in existential psychotherapy. Viktor Frankl and Rollo May have said it movingly and well:

There is nothing conceivable that would so condition a man as to leave him without the slightest freedom. Therefore, a residue of freedom, however limited it may be, is left to man in neurotic and even psychotic cases. Indeed, the innermost core of the patient's personality is not even touched by a psychosis . . . . An incurably psychotic individual may lose his usefulness but yet retain the dignity of a human being. This is my psychiatric credo. Without it I could not think it worthwhile to be a psychiatrist.

Viktor Frankl, Man's Search for Meaning.

There is agreement among many psychotherapists that the enlarging of the individual's responsible freedom is one of the goals, if not the central goal of therapy.

Rollo May, Psychology and the Human Dilemma.

Spontaneity, the opposite of will power, leads to intuition and innovation. It is letting be. It is to witness the inner magic that wants to voice its song.

This kind of intelligence understands the meanings of the pursuit of *greatness*, the need for courage. Motivational intelligence has a sense of the heroic. There can be no true greatness, no true heroic ego, without a firm commitment to morality, to ethics, to a moral goal, to the conviction that the moral consciousness is the defining characteristic of the human species. No analysis of morality is more profound, more trenchant, than that of Immanuel Kant, the eighteenth-century German philosopher. People are moral, he said, not because they seek rewards or fear punishment, but because they make an independent and spontaneous choice to be moral human beings. The capacity to make that choice is exclusively human. And that is how, through the personal support of a human soul, we literally create the morality and the justice of the world.

Motivational intelligence is the point where ideas and spirit connect with the world and become action. Here thoughts take root. Action is never another idea but is what gives flesh, blood, and life to ideas. It is where the soul touches the ground. Motivation is connected with moods, which are mostly genetic or chemical. If not, their origins reach far into early childhood, or even into anthropological ancestry. Motivational intelligence means not to be depressed, but to take responsibility for one's high spirits.

Motivational intelligence is to be enthusiastic about life. It is to be self-created. Motivational intelligence is the ability to energize oneself. We can call it "self-energizing," self-starting. It is autonomy. It is the ownership of the soul. It is to understand the secret of responsibility, to claim one's freedom and power.

The heart of the free human being lies in the concept of self-energization. God himself is the realization, the essence, or the symbol of self-energization, for God created the world out of nothing. Self-energization is the explanation and the implementation of autonomy. The body grows up physiologically, but the soul evolves by increasing its effectiveness in self-energization.

Motivational intelligence is also the search for independence, individuality, and identity. It is to say, with God, "I AM WHO I AM." Motivation is a form of intelligence different from all others. It is the willingness to risk, the capacity for choice. When no evidence is relevant anymore to sway a decision, the truth emerges: decisions are acts. They are not thoughts nor insights, not truths nor knowledge. In action, the black and white score becomes another dimension—the glorious sound of music.

In general, motivational intelligence is the intelligence of enthusiasm. It is excitement, the decision to think big. It is the faith in positive thinking. It is to move fast and never stop, to be a fast-paced person and a fast-track organization. It is the ability to move forward and not look back, not to show concern for small failures or bureaucratic details, but to forge ahead at all costs and make the final goal more important than the details along the way. Warren Bennis says, "Managers do things right; leaders do the right thing." That is wisdom.

CHAPTER 8

Experience

*Communication
Skills*

Philosophy of Life

The Intelligence
of Wisdom

This intelligence, among the most desirable, consists of experience, which is mostly a function of age and of having lived a full and variegated existence, of communication skills, and of a philosophy of life. Wisdom refers to therapeutic skills. To be wise is to be experienced; to be mellow. It is to know about death and about compassion. It is to have the desire and the skill to see the world through the eyes of another. To be wise is to be humble.

Thus, the intelligence of wisdom consists of a serviceable world view, based on broad experience, that comes only through the maturity and mellowness of age. It consists of communication skills, including intimacy and confrontation; and it is acquaintance with the eternal questions of human existence, such as death, freedom, love, guilt, beauty, anxiety, and self-respect.

Communication skills are based on seeing the world through the eyes of another. Moreover, the soul is bombarded with conflicting messages, from both without and within, which it then attempts to organize into peace, harmony, tranquility, minimal chaos, and reduced conflict. That is a condition of homeostasis.

Attendant to this "homeostatophilia" (love of balance) is the feeling of rightness, of fit. We call it truth. Some call it convictions or belief systems. Others call it attitudes, values, world views. Some will die for it, others even kill for it. Most marry for it, have children for it, and style their lives for it.

To have someone else's homeostatic world view enter one's own is frightening. One responds in panic and with rage. For an alien homeostasis, like a viral infection, can only be fought primitively, with a direct assault. This explains severe political differences, ethnic controversies, differences in raising children, conflicting views on the meaning of money, and the enormous variation in career goals.

And the defenses to maintain this system in being can be outright staggering. Their rigidity can be monstrous and the energy invested in holding up their structure outrageous and wasteful. But what makes these defenses even more effective is their cunning deceitfulness and their gentle seduction.

The wise person, the authentic leader, goes beyond the restrictions of his or her own limited homeostasis. Such a person reaches a higher state of perspective, a wiser synthesis, and finds meaning and joy in experiencing the homeostasis of another. The pain of the conflict is also the euphoria of personal growth. From the vantage point of that higher perspective there is greater freedom. Intelligent decisions, leading to team solutions, can follow from such a quantum leap of growth in the soul. Effectiveness in communication is thus to harmonize world views or to understand without fear world views radically different from our own.

But we also need an immortality project, a philosophy of life. The sense of destiny haunts us early in life, while we have the energy and the ambition of youth—which is but the life force spurting effusively from the soul—and also in the middle of life—when the guilt of paltry accomplishments burdens the conscience. We need to make a decision for something greater than ourselves—and company missions and business philosophies are meant to do precisely that, to elevate employees above the mundane and the pedestrian. For an immortality project can relieve us forever from the panic of death. Our mortality is a daily truth. And death means more than the last stage of growth: it is to say good-bye to all there is.

Business problems naturally lead to personal questions. Here is where psychology and philosophy have significant roles. There is more than comfort in knowing that daily aggravations and pressures in business are really expressions of deep and universal human issues. There are answers here, solutions. It is at the deeper levels of personality structures that these problems can be dealt with. Correlatively, if we avoid the depth we cannot solve them. And this is a helpful insight for all who struggle daily with their business.

The surest path to wisdom is the constructive use of anxiety. This position is neither a gimmick nor mere technique, but instead the application to business of the philosophy of Kierkegaard.

Anxiety is normal and is a sign of health. It is also the most severe pain known to humans. Fortunately, our confrontation with, and integration of, anxiety reveal deep truths—about the self and its world, and about emotions and meanings.

Anxiety must be experienced and lived through. The journey through anxiety is an existential crisis, whose secret is transforming anxiety into security. There is no happiness without the wisdom that pain has meaning. We all need to learn the value of dialoguing with our anxiety.

The world is my projection. That may not be altogether accurate; and thinking it may lead to unnecessary guilt. But these caveats aside, here lies an answer for people who ask, what can I do to apply philosophy? It is useful to view the social reality in which we find ourselves as our unconscious made visible. It is helpful to interpret our life-world as something we have set up. The cliché that people play games is part of this same advice. Look upon what you do not as real but as pretense—as a game, a sport. Get into the habit of not taking yourself too seriously. Begin to realize that there are alternative perceptions of what you do and of who you are. When we accept the world as our projection, we can ferret out our hidden motives, our unconscious needs. In this way we can become masters of our fate and with that new power help ourselves to a better life.

There is the problem of evil, with the reality of evil. We must learn how to dialogue with evil, for evil can be the source of potency. A student said, "I find strength in 'eating the void!'"

The theory of polarity tells us that life is paradoxical and inherently ambiguous. Linear thinking denies ambiguity, it is a deception that will hinder us from succeeding in life and in business. For the analytic approach to human issues has shown itself to be no longer viable. Polarity or ambiguity in the world is the projection onto reality of the mystery of free will, which is the deepest inner secret of the mind.

The importance of experience in wisdom is obvious. But a tangential thought about the importance of experience might be useful. Experience includes knowledge. Researches in artificial intelligence, especially those done by Feigenbaum, have discovered that AI programs work only to the degree that the "knowledge base" is differentiated from reasoning or from what AI specialists euphemistically call the "inference engine." In ordinary life, knowledge comes with maturity and results from a lifelong history of curiosity and education. It is the key to making intelligent choices.

But no leader can be successful alone.

Identity Through
Community

Service

Working Through
and With Others

CHAPTER 9

Team
Intelligence

All of the previous intelligences potentially are expressions of individualism. But whenever we deal with organizations we become keenly aware of the centrality of team effort. In fact, team effort may often overshadow all else, even within a highly individualistic culture such as our larger society. The abilities to function in a team and also to lead it—are sui generis. Team intelligence, like most of the others, has three elements.

The social is the ultimate reality. Identity through community or social consciousness is the first characteristic of team intelligence. For this person the sense of identity is achieved through the social. The team intelligent person understands the primacy of social reality. This person has social consciousness. All perception for this person is first filtered through the social consciousness.

The team-intelligent person is engaged; he or she knows the meaning and the importance of engagement. The engaged person has his or her teeth sunk into reality. Engaged, i.e. centered, people make good lovers, good parents, good teachers, and good executives—in short, good leaders. They love to function in teams—authentically, genuinely, not as escape or substitution, or as Machiavellian manipulation.

When Tom Peters and Robert Waterman talk about "management by walking around" and about being customer-driven, and when Terry Deal and Allan Kennedy talk about the war stories of a culture, they refer to that part of engagement which is made *visible*. To be visible is to be extroverted, other-directed, to mingle, to shake hands, to be a politician, to want to get elected, to love contact with the public. That is the engagement factor in team intelligence.

Many executives enjoy problem solving. They see a difficult situation, and they work on it, struggle with it, and then hope to see results. This is another characteristic of team intelligence. What underlies this feeling? The word is *engagement*. The close encounter, the struggle, the wrestling, the dialoguing with reality is a sign of fierce interpenetration with reality. The willingness to express this carnal, primitive, and concrete part of our human potential manifests the engagement element in marketing intelligence. It is a sign of general health and aliveness.

The team-intelligent executive has exceptional organization skills and is adept at designing programs, teams, and task forces. This person understands how teams work and that work must be done by getting teams to do the work. This person's interest and focus are always on the organization. This person stimulates others to behave like a team aligned to a common vision and purpose, and knows the secret that you get work done by finding and stimulating others to do it. You do not know how to do it yourself and you do not want to know. A person exhibiting this intelligence has organizational design skills, developed by thinking ceaselessly in these other-directed modes.

Good managers are team intelligent in that they work well through people. But they also work well with people. They understand the ethics of cooperation. They also know that good will often is not enough and that what is needed is to install systems and processes that help people work well together.

The team empowers the individual. It can make each member feel more effective, more powerful, more valuable, more worthy, and more fulfilled than working alone, than struggling independently. This feeling of fulfillment results from satisfying instinctual needs. And teamwork, like gregariousness, is an instinct, which, if fulfilled, leads to a deep sense of satisfaction. Teamwork has ample support in the history of the evolution of the species. And relying on a team can be learned for example at sea, where passengers may be restricted to a small ship and everyone's welfare is conspicuously connected.

There is of course a paradox between needs for personal freedom and independence on the one hand and for security on the other, being protected and taken care of by a large organization. But this paradox is healthy because it is normal. It is built into the structure of reality. Coping with it elevates us to a higher state of being. To cope is to feel the conflict and allow it to reveal to us its deeper truth, to yield its message of a higher and healthier perspective. Choosing one pole only of the polarity remains always unfulfilling. Transcendence and

integration are the important words, more than choice and resignation.

The effect of conceptualizing oneself and groups in these terms is
that it helps us recognize the importance of groups. It shows the
value of belonging to a group and how group processes define one's
identity. Feelings of warmth and hope, of common solutions and
companionship are central to team intelligence. The team intelligence of patriotism—as well as that of ethnic, religious, and family
loyalties—is a further example of how a person can find his or her
identity through the group.

Team intelligence means a real spirit of cooperation. It means joy
in togetherness. It means that it is fruitless to think individualisti-
cally, that everything done or imagined, needed or performed must
be with other people. A team-intelligent person may be soft, just as a
motivational intelligence may be hard.

The point to emphasize is the predominantly relational aspect of
the human enterprise. In philosophy, this emphasis is associated
with the work of Martin Buber and the life of dialogue. In the
lifestyle of team intelligence everything is conceptualized and experienced as existing in relationship. The science of cultural anthropology and the philosophic movement known as structuralism, as set
forth by Claude Lévi-Strauss, make care and caring the fundamental
nature of the social relations. In their terms, the concept of the self
results directly from social structure. When we concentrate this kind
of structural and systems thinking exclusively on the economic life of
a society, then of course we get welfare societies.

Only in dealing with the behavior of systems do we have the
opportunity to change the organization. This team-intelligence
management of a problem appears to be among the most successful
methods of transformation.

CHAPTER 10

Your Personal Intelligence Profile

Diagnosis

We must commit ourselves to the creation of a self, of an identity. We are nothing—a "nothingness," in the words of Sartre. We need to become something—"being," again in Sartre's words. That something is a concrete, visible object. I recognize it and so does the world. It is what gives us an identity. That identity is a symbol, the hard object with which you show yourself to the world. Your unique combination of the eight intelligences can be expressed as your personal intelligence profile—your symbol. I must see myself in that symbol, and the world must recognize and respect me in that same symbol. It must satisfy the need for being, for identity—at the gut level.

Constructing a personal intelligence profile in the following practice will help. This is a diagnostic exercise, associated with the theory of multiple intelligences, that starts with the premise that each intelligence is not only the way the mind works but implies a whole style of living. With each intelligence there comes a lifestyle. For example, the logical intelligence, or the primarily logically intelligent individual operating alone, could imply a lifestyle of withdrawal, into the abstractions of mathematics, let us say. That person we perhaps imagine as an isolated individual, because the extraversion of the team intelligence is of little relevance to him or her. On the other hand, preeminence of the aesthetic intelligence implies the life of an artistic genius, perhaps dissipated like the logical genius but also rife with feelings and passions, with *Weltschmerz*, and with the impractical nature that typify what we believe to be the artistic genius. The somatically intelligent person is not intellectual, is perhaps brawny, possibly a blue-collar worker or an athletic coach. We have stereotypes for all: scrawny logician with a book under his arm filled with mysterious and dehumanized symbols—a permanent student at some prestigious university; the aesthetician, disheveled hair, full of melodies and metaphors, or colors and shapes, images and sounds, who spends most of his creative time in a state of passionate euphoria. And the mechanic, using his big muscles, and some small muscles, who loves to tinker on cars, does not mind getting dirty, and is supremely effective with steel and cast iron. And so on. These examples are far from accurate. But the point is that each intelligence represents a lifestyle, a character structure, a set of values, a personality, a way of experiencing reality, and a manner of being in this world.

Raising Intelligence

1. Apply each intelligence to a real setting. Intelligence training is autodiagnostic and autodidactic. In other words, you can do it yourself.
2. Focus on two or three realistic issues, important to you and in need of genius-level creativity. One issue may be philosophic, such as how to deal with the matter of death and immortality. Another may be personal, such as how to gain more energy, how to lose weight, or how to improve your marriage. And a third should be a business issue, such as how to develop a marketing plan.
3. Describe each intelligence yourself. Learn to apply introspection, self-appraisal, detachment, perspective in order to achieve a "meta-view." These efforts will force you to pay keen attention to the subject matter, and that is the key to learning—to understanding as well as remembering.
4. Evaluate therapeutically your resistance to each intelligence, that is, disclose the resistances you have to it. The obstacles to intelligence are the most important part of the analysis.

   There are always resistances; they are a matter of degree only. To resist an intelligence means that you can improve and enhance it, but you will not do it—unless you go beyond the resistance. We make the useful assumption that each person has virtually unlimited capacities for every one of the eight intelligences, but it is not easy to develop them all fully.
5. Examine how your strength and weakness regarding each one of the intelligences affects your organization and your personal life. Give examples.

6. Speculate or fantasize how life would be different if you were better at each one of the intelligences. Consider both your professional and your personal life.

7. Develop a personalized *intelligence education plan*. Design it for yourself or for your organization. Select one or more intelligences and prepare an imaginative and multimedia training program—one which involves traditional liberal arts education as well as exercises and experiences, to enhance one intelligence focus or a full intelligence profile.

   The program must be results oriented and be rationally and maturely integrated with the business purposes of the organization.

8. Develop an action plan. Present decisions that include people, dates, and places.

9. Construct a series of utopian societies, each with one of the eight intelligences as its highest value. Compare how a society based on aesthetic intelligence, for example, might differ from one based on logical intelligence.

   Ask yourself whether societies actually exist based on, for instance, somatic or transcendental intelligence. And then examine how they can be distinguished from one another.

10. Specifically, how might the following concerns be affected, how might they be transformed, if we took seriously variations among the eight intelligences:

    - Recruitment? Incentives? Promotions? Benefits?
    - Sales, marketing, advertising?
    - Accounting, bookkeeping, records?
    - Leadership and management?
    - Investments?
    - Education?
    - Medicine?
    - Psychology?
    - Architecture?
    - Government?
    - Law enforcement?
    - Taxation?
    - City planning?
    - Foreign policy?

Action Plans for the study and integration of the eight intelligences:

1. The leadership learning curve or feedback system. We can also call this "the Socratic self-correcting feedback system."

   The elements of this system are homeostasis (which defines it as a living system), feedback (the so-called negative feedback loop leads to balance through self-correction), and the danger of the suppressed (especially the resistance to the fullness of life, which we can call the "*Becker*" factor—after Ernest Becker, who wrote *The Denial of Death*).

2. Learning to learn is the key to implementation and improvement.

   —We learn from our own successes and failures.

   —We learn through the stimulation of others and from new experiences.

   —We learn by uncovering what we do not know, for the great danger lies in continuing to make mistakes that we do not know we are making.

   And the most common mistakes are to be found in ignorance about human nature, in lack of understanding of what it means to be a human being.

3. We must assess our competence in each of the key personal leadership elements.

   —All assessments can be discussed in groups.

   There are three classes of evaluations for each intelligence:

   —"I am like that . . . ."

   —"I am perceived like that by others [who might be specified, such as subordinates, peers, or superiors] . . . ."

   and

   —"I perceive ___(name a significant person)___ like that . . . ."

   Use this scale:

   0. Never
   1. Rarely
   2. Occasionally
   3. Frequently
   4. Most of the time
   5. Always

Worksheet

1. The personal focus.

Do you understand the intelligence in general and each one of its elements? Define and describe in your own words each intelligence and component.

Where have you seen it used, applied, exemplified, or modeled? Lacking, abused, or ignored?

How much interest and motivation do you have and show for each one of the intelligences? How much ability and skill?

2. The business focus.

Assess impartially and mercilessly how your intelligence strengths and weaknesses impact your organization. Be specific.

What are the effects on your organization of your personal leadership assets? Cite cases. Discuss the perception you think others have of you.

What are the effects on your organization of your intelligence deficits? Cite cases. Discuss the perception of others.

What are the obstacles to your self-improvement? To your peak performance? What were you meant to learn from these obstacles?

(It is more productive to explore the obstacles to doing what you know you must do than to simply ask what it is that you must do. Most people know what they must do, but do not know why they do not do it.)

3. Develop an action plan.

Make at least one new and clear decision, indicating dates, people, and places, to the degree that they are appropriate.

Case Study

Ned R. is a high-level executive, just below a vice-president, in one of the world's largest and most prosperous international high-technology firms. He has just been promoted and put in charge of the entire quality-control program for all the divisions of the company. Considering the severity of the worldwide competition, this program was critical to the future of his organization.

Ned is brilliant. He is an engineer by training, with extensive managerial experience. He has a potent intuitive mind. He grasps solutions "out of nowhere," it appears. He is impatient with detail, although he can understand it. He thinks, reflects, grins, and suddenly an inspired and simple solution crosses his mind.

He has been entrusted with the basic task, partially self-chosen—for it is too complex for many of his superiors to understand—to devise subsystems within one large system to reorganize how the company works and thinks about its work.

He must develop that system quickly, imaginatively, with originality. It is groundbreaking, for indeed it has no precedent. He must then pass it on, first to his superiors, who must be sold on this life-saving idea, and then to all their subordinates. In short, he must find ways to change the culture. Wall Street analysts agree that only in this way can the organization survive—regardless of how well it may be doing now.

Objectively speaking, Ned has answers. The company will do especially well if they give Ned freedom, support, and resources. But that can happen only if Ned is ahead of his time—no, ahead of his superiors, who are behind the times. He must solve not only the systems problem but also the ignorance problem. And the meaning of his life, not to speak of the future of the company, is at stake.

Ned wants to make an imprint on the organization he has known all his life. He wants his contribution to make a difference, to be of genuine benefit. He wants his design to live after he retires. He knows that all he needs is a chance. And he knows that the company needs him. But with the intense competition for solutions, which seems more a sport played for the sake of winning than a commitment to help the organization's future, he fears for his life when it comes to seeing the program through.

Ned is very conscious of the politics of his organization. People mean well, at least most of them, but turf is a primary issue. Competition for virtually everything is intense, and yet whoever appears in the slightest not to be a team player is, in the company's jargon, "dead."

There is envy and politesse, kindness and backbiting. The effect of all this conflict is paralysis. The consequences for the company are disastrous, for nothing produces more waste than employees willing to sacrifice the interests of the company for their own narrowly perceived needs.

The company needs a genius and a diplomat, an engineer and a psychiatrist, a hard and a soft man, a person who is committed but will feel secure in his heart if he fails. Is Ned the man? Will the company recognize him as such? Will the management committee give him a chance, for the sake of the stockholders and the employees?

Look at Ned's profile. His high points clearly equip him intellectually for the task. He is high in Logical Intelligence (9), not quite as high in motivational (7), perhaps he gets discouraged more readily than he should, and fairly high in team (8), which he has learned as a survival technique at the company. His marketing (4) should be higher. But that is not difficult to improve with some training.

Somatic (3) (low in the area of sensuality) and Transcendental (1) he felt were irrelevant to his task, which are possibly significant errors on his part. His aesthetic (3) and wisdom (3) scores indicate he could do more to inspire those he seeks to influence and more to have a sturdy ground and center on which to fall back during periods of rejection. This requires education and a committed teacher.

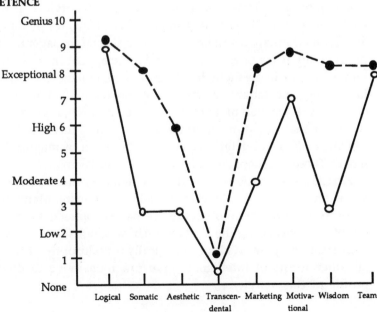

Personal Intelligence Profile
Level of achievement: where I am ————————
Level of interest: where I want to be— — — —

Name: *Ned*

COMPETENCE

INTELLIGENCE

An inventive and consistent bottom-line-oriented program designed to enhance the intelligences in which he is low should go a long way to give him the tools and the power to push ahead with his life's ambition and opportunity. Such a program must have integrity, that is, be deep and sophisticated, and it must be fully integrated with the business goals of the company.

Such a program should enhance his creativity, that is, his access to his unconscious, and give him greater clarity of mind and purpose, greater brilliance and transparency of mind, coupled with a sharper memory. It should greatly enhance his skills of effective communication, elevate his energy level substantially, and protect him against the constant threat of depression. Finally, it should double the credibility of his already well-developed but still too fragile character.

With each of the intelligences we must ask at least two distinct diagnostic questions: What is your level of interest in this intelligence? and What is your level of achievement in this intelligence? The answers could be given on a scale from a low (L) of 1 to a high (H) of 5.

Then we ask some pragmatic questions:

How would an increase in your self-evaluation or self-rating under either interest or achievement affect your productivity? It helps to spell out specifically how that might work. Thus, for instance, how would an information systems director or general manager improve in productivity if his or her interest and achievement in transcendental intelligence or in aesthetic intelligence were enhanced? Perhaps an interesting speculation! Or, conversely, how would an orchestra conductor or a teacher of poetry increase his or her productivity—whatever that might mean under these circumstances—if his or her somatic or logical intelligence became the target of intense development? These questions should lead to new horizons.

Another exercise is to rank the intelligences, first by interest and value, and second by achievement and development. Many people—and this is a peripheral observation—have expressed as their greatest interest increasing the intelligence of wisdom. Quite a few executives seem to value wisdom, specifically a philosophy of life, above all other forms of intelligence. We can then move to develop a profile of this activity.

When you have created a profile of the present or real you by virtue of the first set of answers, you are now ready to develop a profile of the ideal you. See the previous case study and then fill out your own scale.

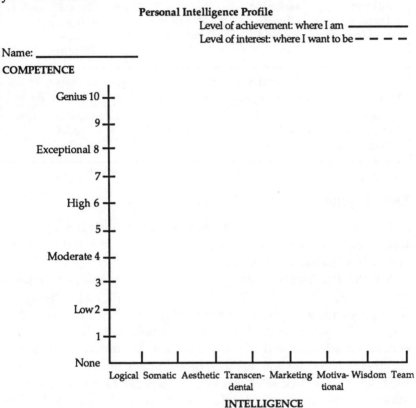

Personal Intelligence Profile

Level of achievement: where I am ──────

Level of interest: where I want to be ─ ─ ─ ─

Name: _____

COMPETENCE

Genius 10

9

Exceptional 8

7

High 6

5

Moderate 4

3

Low 2

1

None

Logical Somatic Aesthetic Transcen- Marketing Motiva- Wisdom Team
dental tional

INTELLIGENCE

The following table may help clarify the concept and the uses of the theory of multiple intelligences:

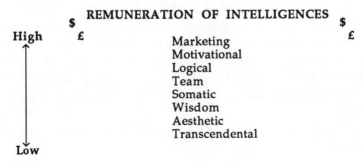

REMUNERATION OF INTELLIGENCES

$ £ $ £

High

Marketing
Motivational
Logical
Team
Somatic
Wisdom
Aesthetic
Transcendental

Low

SAMPLE INTELLIGENCES PROFILE

Carpenter	Effective Executive	Attorney	Scholar
Somatic	Motivational	Logical	Logical
Aesthetic	Marketing	Team	Transcendental/Aesthetic
Team	Team	Marketing	Motivational
Marketing	Logical	Wisdom	Team
			Wisdom

Accountant	Scientist Technologist	Mechanic	Priest, Minister, Monk Nun, Religious Person
Logical	Logical	Somatic	Transcendental/Wisdom
Marketing	Team/Motivational	Team	Team
Team		Marketing	Aesthetic

Development

Each intelligence can be cultivated in its own unique way. To do this is exciting, for intelligence has the hope of youth and the attraction of success. A few examples:

Somatic intelligence: Somatic intelligence is developed in well-known ways. Sensuality is cultivated through body therapies, through dance and poetry, through styles of life, through understanding body languages. Strength characterizes the lifestyle which centers on athletics and physical prowess. Dexterity, like the rest, requires practice. It takes as much time and devotion to live through the full body (sensual intelligence) as it does to tone the body to high athletic achievement (the intelligence of strength) and to develop small muscle expertise, as would a pianist (the intelligence of dexterity). Kinetic orientation can be practiced through mountain climbing, sailing, map reading, and just plain determination.

Aesthetic intelligence: Aesthetic intelligence can be cultivated by emphasizing heavily the unconscious. We can deliberately attend to our intuitions and especially to our dreams. In so doing we modify our entire life, because the sharp and alert person, who gets up bright and early for calisthenics and works and plays hard all day, will barely have the tranquility to slide gently into the trance of sleep and dreaming.

But this is true of all the intelligences; each requires a unique style of living.

The aesthetic intelligence is romantic. It presumes that there is another reality, a separate reality, that Nature speaks to us through appearances, and that there is a God behind what we sense who has a mission for us: to report His Word. The arts then become a language. That language is the only way to reveal the hidden reality behind appearances. And the motto that best describes it is "Truth through passion." If the passion is intense enough the vision is also clear enough. Let the metaphors invite themselves, but we shall strain to use them. The heroic ego is a romantic ideal. Its destiny is to report the deeper reality which it has seen. And that reality is noble, elevated, ethereal, redeeming, and provides salvation.

Aesthetic intelligence can also be passive, in which case it relies on the unconscious, invites expression, and acts more like a priestess through whom the god speaks or a prophet whose voice is really that of God rather than that of an autonomous human being. Such a state can produce great art, is unpredictable, and *uses* the artists—in the sense that the artist is spent, sucked dry, and prevented from living a normal life—to the latter's detriment.

But aesthetic intelligence can also be active, in which case the artist is a social or political force, as in the cases of the Spaniards Pablo Picasso and Pablo Casals.

Both aesthetic intelligences take the Bohemian risk. What matters is beauty, harmony, depth, and truth. The practical issues are neglected, even obstructed. The aesthetic intelligence finds it difficult to be disciplined.

How is aesthetic intelligence connected to leadership? Through aesthetics you move people, touch their hearts, thunder into their souls, flood their spirits with tears of joy. Leadership means to reach people, to inspire them, not in their five percent of logical intelligence nor their ten percent of ignorance, greed, and fear, but in their eighty-five percent of feelings and emotions, of unreason and of heart. The world respects the artist because the artist's life, poor as it may be, speaks integrity. And integrity leads; it also leads to trust, is never envied, uplifts, creates meaning, and builds loyalty. In some ways, aesthetic intelligence is the diametric opposite of marketing intelligence. The latter does not compromise on survival, the former could not care less. The former adapts, like a chameleon; the latter does not even know the word.

Aesthetic intelligence is a form of language. And linguistic facility in general is a learned skill, one which reveals our earliest relation to the world. Our language habits and language forms (expressions used and avoided, facility or trepidation, joy or horror) relate to how we were accepted, how we were loved, how much attention was lavished on us, how guilty we were made to feel, or how guilty our inner impulses made us. All of that should become transparent when we hear ourselves use language—any language, including that of the body.

Each intelligence can be encouraged in its own way.

Reviewing the eight intelligences, we become increasingly clear that each is profoundly associated with a specific style of life. To practice the intelligence is to change your life: to be an athlete, a pianist, a priest, an inventor of new mathematical proofs, a Green Beret, an ascetic who is perfect in renunciation by the firm stoic harnessing of the will. For a person fantasizing in detail, intensively, and with all the senses—in the spirit of the imaging therapies popular in business today—each of the intelligences can have an invigorating effect on achieving goals or changing habits.

Developing intelligence is to develop the self.

Any of the eight intelligences can be enhanced by practicing certain exercises:

- Name examples of where each intelligence can be useful.
- Describe a problem and indicate what each of the intelligences can do in the analysis and the solution of that specific problem.
- Think of someone—known personally to you, through the news media, or in history—who excels in each one of the eight intelligences. What can you learn from that person and that lifestyle?
- Ask yourself how your work and your behavior would be different if you had increased or improved in any one particular intelligence. Create a vision, a fantasy, of the goal—and sustain it in view and fill it with psychic energy.
- Practice developing successive personal intelligences profiles. Keep them before you, like a mirror, and keep a log in which you record daily your reflections and actions to increase your intelligences.

- Involve others in your practice. Develop a profile for them. Discuss your profiles with each other. Create quality circles among yourselves with the goal of developing your intelligences. Whatever you do will make a difference. Any time and thought spent on this will improve your thinking.
- Report your efforts to expand your intelligence. And discuss with others how you have applied these attempts to enhance your Intelligences and what the effects have been. To what extent have you succeeded? Failed? Explain why.
- Develop your own daily lesson plan or programmed study guide.
- Construct a profile or a collage of the eight intelligences in terms of how you wish to organize your life. Thus, for example, you may feel that writing poetry is your goal—as more than one CEO has emphatically stated. Then, based on your own example, create a picture—perhaps a tree, a landscape, a flower, a bird or animal, a person, or an abstraction—on which you graft the proper relationship among the intelligences in your life. Some intelligences may be centrally relevant; others of no interest at all. Play around with this profile: is it serviceable? How would it be for you to invert it? What do others think?

Enhancement

You must assume personal responsibility for designing a program of intelligence development or intelligence enhancement. A separate module for each intelligence can be created.

We can enhance an intelligence by naming it. We can enhance logical intelligence by doing logical exercises, such as puzzles. Examining Zeno's paradox of the turtle and the hare is one example. (How can the hare ever overcome a turtle in a race in which the latter has a head start? Consider that whenever the hare catches up with the turtle, the latter will have advanced, even slightly. And this logic is infinite. Zeno used this paradox to argue that motion is an illusion.)

We can enhance aesthetic intelligence by listening to a series of musical selections and then determining which we like best, and trying to explain why that might be.

We can enhance somatic intelligence by moving physically closer to a person than is comfortable and by then articulating the feelings thus aroused.

We can also enhance intelligence by acting directly on our awareness itself, rather than renaming the objects it observes. That is a bit more difficult—because it may be less interesting. But it is of course more direct, and pure consciousness is certainly always available to us. We try to have direct control over the functioning of the mind.

If you wish to enhance the intelligence of wisdom, and you are thinking of therapeutic or communications skills, then make the deliberate effort to throw your mind, like a ventriloquist, into that of another person and see the world from that new point of view. Above all, see yourself through those other eyes.

Make a deliberate decision to be a kind of intelligence or to enhance a kind of intelligence. If the issue is team intelligence, then you must make the concerted effort to get things done through other people. Catch yourself at doing things yourself you could be delegating. If the issue is greatness (motivational intelligence), then quickly look for an image of greatness, either self-created or gleaned from memory, and be resolute about imitating that image. Have pictures of great leaders on display—Gandhi and Einstein, Churchill and John F. Kennedy, Mother Teresa and Picasso, and so forth.

Visualize the intelligence. If you are concerned to enhance transcendental intelligence, then clear your mind of rust and cobwebs, turn on the inner floodlights, expand the inner size of your cranium, and vigorously start looking around and leaping about freely in that refreshing spaciousness.

Look for living examples. The world is full of intelligent people. Seek them out. Imitate them. Experience what that feels like. These are all inner acts you can undertake. They are self-perpetuating and self-enhancing. They snowball, for once you start learning by imitation with every attempt the rewards increase your success.

How can we accelerate our personal evolution? Understanding multiple intelligences can do it. We need only analyze resistances, for they exist in our customers as well as in ourselves. We can achieve results by studying the obstacles which prevent us reaching them.

Cultivate your multiple intelligences daily. The resulting increased intelligence will also enhance the effectiveness of the intelligence-training itself. This becomes a self-accelerating system, and your intelligence can be expected to increase at a growing pace.

You must be aware of all the multiple intelligences before you can select the one intelligence that will help you develop and apply the others. This is accelerated evolution. The effect is spiraling progress.

Accelerated effectiveness will become accelerated evolution, and it will show itself in terms of measurements you yourself have chosen—be they profits, promotions, recognition, self-satisfaction, knowledge, and meaning.

The same point can be made through a feedback loop diagram:

Develop a workbook, capitalizing on the feedback loop that builds momentum and that will enable you to:

- identify a problem;
- select relevant Intelligences;
- enhance them;
- try solutions, that is, apply the intelligences to the problem;
- deepen your identification and clarification of the problem;

this may, in turn, change your choice of relevant intelligence and improve your enhancement of the intelligence and your creativity in meeting the problem. You can continue this upward spiral habitually and indefinitely. That is accelerated evolution in multiple intelligences.

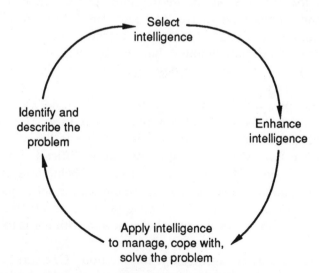

Let us now consider the example more specifically.

Develop a representative problem. Identify what you guess are relevant and serviceable intelligences.

Clarify the intelligences. Read the descriptions. Improve on them and add your own. Do exercises, prescribed or invented. Place your mind into the frame of the chosen intelligence. Be aware that in each instance you are placing your mind into a different world, with a different focus, creating a different picture, and developing a new image. Your lifestyle itself will be affected by this projection into different intelligences.

Fantasize the full lifestyle of each intelligence. Apply it to whatever you are doing right now—driving, flying, banking your money, having a coffee break, working on an assembly line, skiing, attending a meeting, planning, making a sales presentation. How would a person accomplished in one of the intelligences that you have chosen handle the particular situation in which you find yourself right now?

Also, fantasize how you, committed to a certain intelligence, would now be doing something different. Examples might be painting instead of calculating, managing instead of working with your hands, planning instead of executing, seeking love instead of success, and so forth.

Living the Intelligences

Look, for example, at marketing intelligence. View the issue systemically. Look for patterns, and therefore for depth. What are the real issues? The issue of evil, for example, cannot be settled by going around it, circumventing it, but only by integrating evil within yourself: identify with the otherness of evil and experience your own resulting potency.

For example, your mother is dying of cancer, she wants to live with you her last months, and you invite her to do so. The situation is painful because all the childhood deficiencies in the relationship come back in intensified form: your mother is difficult and critical; she condemns you at the very time that you are being most devoted. She blames you for her failures. She is unpleasant, crabby, uncooperative. Her residing with you is affecting your career adversely. And yet the guilt of abandoning her or being severe with her is too much for you to bear.

What is the problem and what is the solution? One version of the problem is that the situation is enmeshed with evil: she is evil to you and your response threatens to be evil as well with her And the total situation is an evil one to begin with. You are in pain and you are paralyzed, your two issues, because your mother's hostility touches the evil potential in you. And that evil potential generates so much energy and conflict in you—it rivets you so much that you are forced against your will to spend 80 percent of your energy dealing with your mother—that you must deal with the personal evil in you before you can rationally handle your mother's oncoming death. But facing your own evil, owning it rather than denying it, is the secret to strength, objectivity, control, discipline, rationality, good judgment, centeredness, peace of mind, and all those character structures which enable you to deal with ease and authenticity with the most pernicious problems life thrusts upon us.

Then try motivational intelligence. Consider the importance of self-energization and of the powers of the will. Recognize that the source of high spirits and of enthusiasm is you. Lift your spirits, all by yourself, so that you can manage your problem with renewed hope and rekindled enthusiasm. Anatol Shcharansky, imprisoned in Russia for nine years, much of it in solitary confinement (the "punishment cell"), energized himself with a sense of humor. Asked if he would do it again, he made allusion to what Warren Bennis calls the "Wallenda factor"—a certain foolhardiness and impulsiveness, necessary for courageous actions.

The act of self-energization can lead to boundless confidence. But sobering reality must always be seen against the background and the horizon. In is no accident that Freud considered reality testing the hallmark of mental health. And reality-testing, being the key to survival, is an aspect of marketing intelligence. How well that is stated in this passage from Ecclesiastes:

> I returned, and saw under the sun, that the race is not to the swift, nor the battle to the strong, neither yet bread to the wise, nor yet riches to men of understanding, nor yet favor to men of skill; but time and chance happeneth to them all.

Then try team intelligence—organizational skills, working through others. It seems fairly obvious that others will not only help implement solutions to one's problems, but more than that, they will think of what these solutions might be in the first place. You must find people for dialogue, quality circles, therapy, especially in groups, brainstorming, team building. You must find people to do the work which heretofore you thought was yours alone to do.

You may need imagination, creativity, lateral thinking, and more, to achieve new solutions for the practical and financial elements of the primary problem described above. And that gets one to:

Transcendental intelligence: Transcendental intelligence is cultivated through understanding its truth and importance as the foundation of knowledge. For all understanding is rooted in consciousness. Transcendental intelligence is therefore the key to many of the other intelligences, especially logical intelligence.

For to move the mind to higher levels of intelligence one must engage in what philosophers call the "reduction," (literally, "stepping back") which is the conscious act of non-attachment, of stepping out of the stream of life, and into the vast void, the realm of inner space and inner time. In fact, the latter are in essence is not much different from its cognates of external space and external time. It is the successive lifting of the center of attention out of its usual place and dimension that is the secret of the true imagination. For to exist on a point is to have no understanding of a point, much less of a line. It is only by moving out of the dimension of the point—the "zero" dimension of existence—that the point as reality even appears. But it is only from the perspective of a line that a point can be conceived to exist.

To know that a point is on a line requires the transcendence of the line; and the line is overcome by stepping out of it, by looking at it, by practicing non-attachment to the line. And that conscious act is the step that moves us—the ego, the source, the center of awareness—into a plane, which we call then the second dimension. And when we "look at" a plane— rather than existing on it—which can be done only by minds exercised in the art of non-attachment, then reality is transformed into the third dimension, for we are now spatial.

Each step into a higher dimension is produced by detaching consciousness from its object. When you look at a point, you must be on a line. And in order to look at a line, you must be on a plane. And in order to look at plane, you must be detached from the plane, which places you in a volume or third dimension.

To understand these secrets of the operations of consciousness is the key to clear thinking, to transformative thinking, and is the origin of authentic innovation. And here practice makes perfect. Such mental transformations, such internal suggestions, such meditative mindsets create the conscious environment for meaningful breakthroughs.

We now move to the utilization of the intelligence of wisdom. For that we must remember these homilies:

Anxiety is beautiful.

We must develop the art of dialogue and therapeutic or communication skills.

We need a sense of greatness, we need to look for charisma, and we need not be embarrassed to deliver enthusiasm-arousing pep talks.

We should feel free to use guided fantasies in order to create the ambience either of one intelligence (e.g., logical) or one element within wisdom (e.g., a philosophy of life).

Be ready for action. Get self-energized, self-started, daily. Develop the discipline (which is a matter of the will, which in turn is the phenomenon of self-energization) of persistence, perseverance. Monitor how you operate and discover the tricks that work for you. On the basis of that create a daily startup schedule: organizing your office, writing in your journal, sharing dreams, reading inspirational literature, scheduling physical exercise, playing or listening to music. Find a system that works for you and stick to it.

Never forget your need for organizational skills, performing work through others.

Become a product advocate, and in conjunction with that develop an impeccable priority system. The product is you and what you can accomplish. For that is the marketing intelligence's way to survival.

Resistances

Here are some resistances to creativity and the innovations which come with broadening the intelligences.

Traditionally, the obstacles are on this list, sometimes referred to as killer phrases (A few of the items are found in Roger von Oech's, *A Whack on the Side of the Head*, published by Warner Books, New York):

"Killer Phrases" or Resistances

Silence.
Hostility.
It can't be done.
The right answer.
It's not logical.

Follow the rules.
Be practical.
Avoid ambiguity.
To err is wrong.
Play is frivolous.
It's not my area.
Don't be foolish.
I'm not creative.
It's not in the budget.
We're not ready for it.
Everybody does it this way.
Too hard to administer.
Too theoretical.
Production won't accept it.
Personnel isn't ready for this.
Not timely.
The old people won't use it.
The new people won't understand it.
Takes too much time (work).
Don't move too fast.
Has anyone else ever tried it?
Let's make a market test first.
Let's form a committee.
Won't work in our territory.
Too big (or too small) for us.
We don't have the manpower.
We tried that before.
Too academic.
It's a gimmick.
You'll never sell that to management.
Stretches the imagination too much.
Let's wait and see.
Too much trouble to get started.
It's never been done before?
The union will scream.
Let's put it in writing.
We are doing it already.
It makes me feel uncomfortable.
We do not have enough time.

The culture does not tolerate mistakes.
Heroes get shot down.
People and their accomplishments are not
  acknowledged.
Take a deeper dive.
We let that guy go.
We identify the entrepreneurs so that we
  can fire them.

But we go beyond these classic ploys of resistance.

In any practical discussion of creativity and innovation, resistances naturally seem to arise.

They are of several kinds. There is the anxiety caused by opening up the mind full throttle. That leads to the fear of non-conformity on the one hand, for creativity entails boundless imagination, and the fear of death on the other, for to live fully is also to arouse the consciousness of life's end. Ernest Becker said it well,

The deepest need is to be free of the anxiety of death and
annihilation;
but it is life itself which awakens it,
and so we must shrink from being fully alive.
[This is true literally and symbolically.]

It is painful to stretch the mind. The matter is no different from stretching unused muscles.

Sometimes we look at an optical illusion or an ambiguous and vague picture. Maybe a figure in the dark that we cannot make out. To strain the mind to think what it might be, like solving a difficult puzzle, or trying to remember an important but long-lost memory, leads to vertigo, dizziness, nausea. That is like the pain of creativity. Accept it, want it, plunge into it. That is the price we pay for an expanded mind, for a consciousness that has been stretched.

There is also the danger of getting into the wrong type of innovation. For creativity can be shallow, as in a game of chess, or profound, as in the commitment to a new life. True creativity is not just to have a new insight, as potent and beautiful as that may be. Authentic creativity is also the commitment to make that idea live; it is the knowledge that the idea is important, that the vision is monumental, that the image is rooted in what is real. We must therefore not talk merely of creativity and innovation, but of mature creativity and mature innovation.

In other words, creativity cannot be used merely to invent a new product. It requires also the commitment of becoming a product advocate.

Imagine how a person of broadened intelligence would function in our circumstances. And the image must be held before us as vividly as possible: in the mode of all our senses, through stories, with symbols, rituals, social support, and with pristine clarity.

And it must be believable. That is best accomplished with a living, or at least a real, example. If all else fails, one can be a model to oneself and to others.

What are the obstacles to your success? What are the limits you impose upon yourself? You have three operating images in your unconscious: perfect, current reality, and inadequate. Which one dominates? How did it get there? What are your resistances to change? Which image would you like to dominate? How do you propose to achieve that?

Resistances are real and they are powerful. We resist not only access to our true feelings but also to our possibilities, to our enormous potential. And there are reasons for resistances. Some are psychological and neurotic, perhaps with origins in childhood, and others are existential or simply part of the human condition. Resistances must be respected.

Conclusion

Perhaps, in conclusion, the following story can help us understand the roots of the intelligences. The story can help us understand what it really means to give a gift to someone we love—the ultimate gift.

THE ULTIMATE GIFT FROM THE HEART

Donna Ashlock was a freckle-faced 14 year-old who liked bicycles and basketball. Felipe Garza was an energetic 15-year-old with a passion for break-dancing. They were both high-school freshmen in Patterson, Calif., a small farming town 75 miles southeast of San Francisco. After school Felipe would often drop by The Tigers Den, a hamburger stand where Donna worked part time, to play video games and make wisecracks to gain her attention. Felipe had a crush on Donna, but she chose someone else to be her boyfriend.

One day last month, Donna suddenly began gasping for breath while working at the hamburger stand. Doctors said she had cardiomyopathy, a weakening of the heart muscle that would kill her in six to eight weeks unless she had a transplant. When Felipe learned of Donna's condition, he calmly told his mother: "I'm going to die so I can give my heart to my girlfriend."

Since their son appeared to be in perfect health, Felipe's parents paid little heed to the grim premonition—they didn't know, as his friends later reported, that he had been experiencing blackouts and headaches. A week ago a blood vessel burst in Felipe's head; he was brain dead before he reached the hospital. Hours later his family carried out Felipe's wish by donating their son's heart to the girl he loved. "If it weren't for Felipe, my daughter would also be dead," said Donna's father, Raymond Ashlock, after the transplant operation at a San Francisco hospital. "He's a hero."

Later, Ashlock—who had not known Felipe or his family before the boy's death—told his daughter what had happened. "I explained that he had donated his kidneys and eyes," he said. "And I have his heart?" asked Donna. "Yes," Ashlock said. Donna's expression "changed just a little" at the news.

After the funeral Felipe's father, Felipe Garza Sr., said he did not think his son had willed his own death. "Maybe he had a feeling; I don't know," he said. "I'm proud of what he did and the way he went—to give his heart to this girl-friend." Added Felipe's half-brother John Sanchez: "it's making us think that every time she's around, something of him will be around."

Newsweek, January 20, 1986.

Now we shall explore the deep structures. The heart is their symbol. The heart means that feelings reveal deeper truths; the heart means that love, commitment, and care are life's highest values. And, finally, heart, *coeur* in French, means courage, the courage to enter the deep structures of our being.

PART TWO

THE SECOND PERSONAL CHANGE:
CHARACTER DEPTH

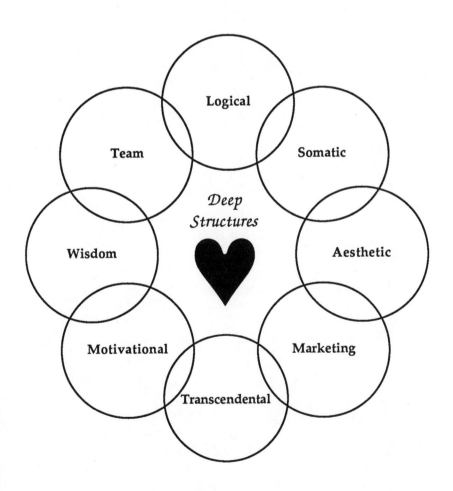

CHAPTER 11

Existential
Ultimate Concerns

The first section concerned itself with broadening the mind through understanding and applying the eight intelligences. Mind expansion enhances innovation.

This section deals with the deepening rather than the broadening of mind. Its key concept is ethics.

This latter part of the analysis of the philosophy and business intersection is perhaps the most important of all. What makes ethics a distinctive ally of business is not so much that it helps expand the mind but that it challenges it to deepen. Business needs courage and roots even more than it needs innovation.

Deep structure theory talks about ultimate concerns, feelings, and actions as the three principal categories of explanation of the human being.

The roots of our being begin with ultimate concerns. They enter the realm of the real only to the degree that they become emotional, part of the feeling domain. Hence, they exist in the realm of feeling. And they burst forth into the realm of action, the connection of feelings with the real world.

Deep structure theory is the foundation of a philosophical contribution to the realm of the practical, an attempt to encapsulate the current philosophic wisdom about what a human being is into a few practical propositions. No depth needs to be sacrificed in the attempt to make philosophy truly useful.

The reader must be reminded that in order for philosophy to be effective each person must be a philosopher, an expert in the philosophic understanding of the human condition. This is different from the sciences, where an outside expert will do. The message for leaders is, "Do it yourself!"

The following table lists the ideas, the concepts, and the theories about what we need to survive as persons with dignity. These are the thoughts that concern us ultimately—that is why they are called our ultimate concerns, an expression originally coined by the philosopher and theologian Paul Tillich.

The undergirding question is religious. Do we see the world with secular eyes? or with mystical eyes? We therefore speak of two kinds of ultimate concerns. On the one hand there are the existential ultimate concerns, which are fundamentally non-religious, or at least do not require religion to give them meaning, nor need their focus be on religious views of human existence. On the other hand, there are the religious concerns, which are here called the transpersonal ultimate concerns. These are the fundamentally religious, mostly mystical, forms of approaching human existence and of perceiving the world in which we transact our history.

Let us look first at the secular world-view. It gives us twelve existential or personal ultimate concerns:

- Death and finitude
- Freedom and responsibility
- Aloneness and isolation
- Meaning and work
- Being-a-body and being-in-the-world
- Independent individual identity
- Reality and the Other
- Ground and home
- Love and intimacy
- Growth, creativity, and spontaneous play
- Beauty and the aesthetic
- Ethics and morality

The existential ultimate concerns, when fully understood and integrated into our lives, give us our sense of potency, energy, engagement, roots, centeredness, aliveness, joy, liberation, and hope. They provide us with a confident and exhilarating sense of moving into the future. They are what is needed to "get our act together." They are the key ingredient in an autonomous character structure and form the basis for maturity and effectiveness in one's personality.

Successful integration of an applied understanding of the existential ultimate concerns into one's total life leads to the felt conviction that life is truly good, that it is far better than one had, in realistic moments, thought possible. The existential ultimate concerns are the key ingredients in one's decision for greatness. They lead to strength, to courage, to autonomy. They explain what it means to take life seriously.

Following is a brief description of each one of the existential ultimate concerns. As you read, pause and ponder how these relate to you personally and to your business problems and decisions. Ask yourself how much or how little you have thought about them, and how much or how little you have allowed these thoughts to influence your daily life. Consider how your life and your company might be different if these themes were constantly before you, if you felt and understood their importance at all times, and if you have any significant answers to the questions they imply.

Death and finitude. Our ultimate limit is the certainty of our death. Death calls everything into question; its inescapability can lead either to despair or to strength. We respond authentically to the fear of death when we create immortality projects. We feel alive and we also perceive the pressure of time only because we anticipate that we will die.

Freedom and responsibility. We always choose. The quality of free will in me, says Descartes, is exactly as perfect and as total as it is in God himself. Freedom is sui generis, that is to say, it is of its own kind and cannot be reduced to or equated with anything objective, visible, or material. Freedom is the powerful but also dangerous capacity to make totally arbitrary decisions—from donating a kidney to a brother to detonating a terrorist bomb on an airplane. The general rule is that I am responsible for my social world as much as for my personality, for the former likewise reflects the consequences of my freely chosen actions.

Aloneness and isolation. Life's crises—losses, criticisms, and difficult choices—underscore the painful truth of one's inevitable isolation. To be comfortable in this pit of aloneness is the secret of leadership and of ego autonomy.

Meaning and work. Every human being needs to feel worthy, useful, and important. We can do that by discovering a destiny or a task more significant and durable than we are. Excellence in one's work also improves the quality of the experience of one's soul.

Being-a-body and being-in-the-world. We are first and foremost members of the biological and of the geological orders. Our primitive instincts, the needs of our bodies, dominate a major portion of our existence. Our reality is the physical and the social world in which we live. From it we derive our support and into it we project our hopes. We are of course more than our bodies, but human existence as we know it depends also upon being a body and upon living in an environment that is compatible with that body.

Independent individual identity. Each of us is unique and special. We must be recognizable as such by having a distinct identity. We cherish our independence and our rights as individuals above all else. We must be acknowledged and valued for ourselves and for our accomplishments. The soul has a natural tendency and desire to evolve towards autonomy.

The primary sources for an individual's identity are his or her job, career, or profession, and his or her family. Moreover, independence is not only a personal but also a national and even an international commitment of our society and of our nation. We can be helped towards achieving our independent individual identity if we explore the obstacles and resistances to achieving it. These obstacles can be both internal, that is, self-imposed and self-generated, and external, that is, economic, social, and political.

Reality and the Other. In order to cope with life successfully we require a highly developed sense of what is real. We do not have the luxury to deny what is a fact, nor can we with impunity subscribe to an illusion. Both the world of people and the world of things differ in kind from the world of my own personal and inward ego. That is why the external world must always be referred to as "the Other."

Ground and home. We need a source of security and a place to call home. These supports, the zones where we are accepted unconditionally, come to our rescue in times of distress. To say that I am grounded is to say also that I am entitled, that I have rights, that I belong, that I love myself, and that I take care of myself, in the sense that I look after my own needs and interests.

Love and intimacy. Love means devotion, commitment, and caring; it means contact, communication, and engagement. Intimacy is the mirroring of souls; it is mutual reflecting and a spiritual union. Both mean deep validation by an open and accepting world. And that welcoming world is usually the emotional bosom and the free and unconditional commitment of another human inwardness, of another personal freedom. Love is encounter, contact, meeting. Without it the child does not develop nor can the adult survive with integrity.

Growth, creativity, and spontaneous play. Life and consciousness are joyous as long as they expand continuously into a world ready to receive them and into a future that welcomes them. The wonder and excitement of continual learning is the essence of life. Laughter, innocence, and self-expression bring hope and freshness to everything they touch.

Beauty and the aesthetic. Art is the language of depth. It hears the eternal voices of nature—the messages from the stars and the flowers, the messages from the hills and the glaciers. The beauty of our environment reflects the beauty of our souls. It is through our aesthetic sense that we penetrate the essence of Being itself.

Beauty is a natural resource and an environmental necessity.

Ethics and morality. Little else is as distinctively human as our ethical conscience and our moral sense. To be ethical means to live by the stern demands of reason and not to be governed or swayed by the seduction of the emotions. To be ethical is to be just, consistent, and predictable. It is preeminently our capacity to act ethically and our possession of a moral sense, which set us aside from the animals.

Deep Structure Exercises

The existential ultimate concerns can be used to stimulate discussions and promote brainstorming. The following questions ask you to draw on your understanding, your experience, and your opinion regarding each one of the above twelve existential ultimate concerns, covering these points:

What does each individual theme mean to you? In other words, how would you define it? For example, when it comes to death, one might write, "Death is my greatest fear, I do not know how a human being can face death. Belief in God, which I do not have, seems nevertheless a necessity. I believe my lack of inner strength is tied to the fact that I have not dealt with my own death." Someone else might say, "I rarely think about death. I believe it is a distraction from work and from fun. I only hope that I will die painlessly and in my sleep."

Give a specific example of how this issue affects your life, or how it might affect it. An illustrative answer is, "My mother has cancer and I am worried over her health. We have always been very close and I do not know how I will respond when her death comes. I am frightened by this situation." Or one could say, "I am reassured by the fact that we have professionals who can deal with death—physicians and nurses on the one side and morticians and ministers on the other. In this way our emotional burdens can be minimal."

What message does each particular Existential Ultimate Concern hold for the greatness of your company? Some answers might be, "My job security is like protection against death. The uncertainties of the price of our product and concern over mounting competition lead me constantly to fear the death of this company. I must handle its death as I must manage my own, for the threat of unemployment is to me very much like the threat of death. Both must be managed in a similar way. In fact, strange as it may seem, it appears that I cannot manage my anxiety about unemployment until I have managed my anxiety about death." Or, "Our products (for instance, pharmaceuticals) are a symbolic answer to death for many of our customers. It is that symbolism which makes my job worthwhile." Or, "Our company philosophy as well as our marketing policy should emphasize that the goal of this firm is to protect as far as is possible both patients and consumers in general from premature death."

After you have developed a feeling for each of the existential ultimate concerns, rank them according to the intensity with which they function in your own life and in the life of your organization. From one to three ultimate concerns should be listed as primary—aloneness, freedom, and love, for example—and then many of the others can be interpreted in terms of these.

For example, a woman might say that an analysis of her existential situation discloses that she must make the free decision, within her aloneness, to love. Those are for her then the primary values. Subsidiary to them are the insights that this must be accomplished before death; that this will bring meaning to her life; that her decision must be carried out in an ethical manner and with a refined sense of beauty. Such a lifestyle will transform her into an effective individual and assure at the same time her independence and protect her unique identity. In order to succeed she must clearly face reality, which includes attention to the needs of her body. And so forth. Profiles can then be prepared and compared.

Profiles for companies and for organizations can also be prepared, after the proper examination of the existential situation of the firm in question.

The group then distributes each of the answers to everyone and they work their way jointly to the following goal: what specific and precise steps—visible and behavioral—can we take in this organization to integrate and activate the results of our brainstorming and discussion session?

One characteristic but oversimplified answer is "This company must stand for greatness in its relations to employees, customers, stockholders, and the public. Its products must have meaning and authentic value. We must therefore redesign our promotion campaigns and redefine our marketing practices. And here are specific examples . . . ." Or, "Employees must feel that they can make meaningful choices in this company. This means a revision of the organization chart. Here are our recommendations . . . ." Or, "This company's high-sounding words about its mission, values, philosophy, and guiding principles must be also felt in the heart of its employees. It is always difficult to separate personal immaturity and paranoia on the part of the employees from systematic corporate indifference and callous selfishness on the part of the organization and of its top management. Here are specific grievances. Let us examine them and offer solutions . . . ."

CHAPTER 12

Transpersonal
Ultimate Concerns

The big decision in life is how to view religion. It is the question of whether or not God exists, and whether or not there can be salvation and resurrection—love, justice, and eternal life. Carl Gustav Jung said, "I have treated many hundreds of patients. Among those over thirty-five, there has not been one whose problem in the last resort was not that of finding a religious outlook on life."

The essentials of a religious perspective are best referred to by the less doctrinaire expression, "the transpersonal world-view." The transpersonal world-view gives us the following list of ten Transpersonal (or religious) Ultimate Concerns:

- The world is a continuous field.
- There is an inner and an outer world.
- There is an inner and an outer self.
- Everything is paradox and conflict.
- Consciousness can be expanded.
- Consciousness is the God inside.
- God is the miracle of being.
- Everything is seen from a subjective perspective.
- Reality is ambiguous.
- We have the power to assign meanings to existence.

Of special interest to leaders is that the transpersonal ultimate concerns seem to hold the secret for effective brainstorming and for the improvement of the creative and innovative uses of the imagination. They also seem to be intimately tied to improving logical intelligence. (This point was discussed earlier in the analysis of Transcendental Intelligence.)

The Transpersonal Ultimate Concerns are life's religious or metaphysical issues. When life is good we do not wish to give it up. We therefore begin to take seriously the religious or metaphysical hypothesis about eternal life and about the role and purpose of human existence within the scheme of the cosmos. And when life is bad we also hope for a better existence, a reward for suffering, a fulfillment of our frustrated needs, in the hereafter.

The transpersonal ultimate concerns, when activated and fully developed, can lead to peace and tranquility, to a sense of resolution, to answers, to hope, and even to a sense of having attained salvation, deep reconciliation, right here on earth.

Let us now examine each transpersonal ultimate concern in turn.

The world is a continuous field. Reality and life are seen as a spatial, a temporal, and a logical (which means a systemic) field. But they are also viewed as a process. The reality of these various levels of continuity leads to a sense of unity and wholeness, and of holistic, integrative, contextual thinking. All existence, which of course centrally includes human beings, is one—it is one event in space, one process in time, and one system in logic. God is one. The universe is one. God and the universe are one. And I as well am one with being.

Neither you nor your company live in isolation. The interdependency between you and the world is real. A company operated as a family business, even if it has been so operated over several generations, may have a different commitment to certain values than one run by a hired CEO. Nevertheless, the theme of continuity between the past, present, and future is always there. If nothing else, that interconnectedness will surface in the boardroom.

There is an inner and an outer world. There exist an inner world and an outer world, and they are mirror images of each other. Often we project our inner conflicts out into the world and this affects our working environment. Or perhaps the reverse is true. Business problems become nightmares as we try to solve them in our dreams or with our hallucinations. The recognition of these two worlds also represents the meeting of East and West, where the East is perceived (in an oversimplified fashion) as living in the inner world and the West is perceived (also in an oversimplified fashion) as living in the outer world.

There is an inner and an outer self. Inside, every person is innately a pure consciousness, sometimes called a spirit or a soul, surrounded with an acquired psychological ego. The latter consists of a character and a personality, of a physical body, of many social roles, and so forth. The body is like a pearl to the soul, which, like a grain of sand, has activated its creation and is then surrounded by the jewel. This distinction between the two selves, inner and outer, is useful in counseling for the reconstitution or the reconstruction of a client's personality and of his or her world. This knowledge is useful also when one is under stress—the inner self, as the Stoic philosophers and martyrs of all ages so well knew, is our final refuge. This belief structure is not an escape from either contact or commitment, but provides a safe place where one can feel comfortable and at home even under the most adverse conditions.

Everything is paradox and conflict. This category of our being-in-the-world refers to the pervasiveness of polarity, to the reality of contradictions, to ambiguity and uncertainty, to the conviction that there are two sides to most human issues, both of which, while incompatible, may nevertheless be true at the same time. Opposites coexist; contradictions are real.

Opposition, alienation, dialogue, and dialectic are the laws of the universe, from physics to politics, from astronomy to psychology, from the symmetry of living things to the monogamous relationships in love. Polarity makes conflict, tragedy, and stress the fundamental principles of all living beings and of all inert existence.

Conflicting feelings result from trying to do two or more incompatible things at the same time, such as remembering and forgetting a dream, wanting and not wanting to marry someone, wishing to work and wishing to sleep, and so forth. Furthermore, we believe in incompatible opposites at one and the same time: we think that a person is essentially good and decent, but is also essentially destructive and evil. All life is conflict, paradox, and contradiction. Only the written word and the abstract thought, which are dead, can be logical and consistent. Life, however, pulsates with excitation, vibrates with conflict, and, in general, thrives on the fertilization of opposition. The dialectic is the essence of maturity and of team work, as it is of democracy.

Consciousness can be expanded. This characteristic of awareness is expressed by such ideas as mind expansion and consciousness raising, altered states of consciousness, and new modes of being. We assume that we are only partially conscious and that all persons, with help, can experience altered, improved, and expanded states of consciousness. This is the core of creativity, the heart of innovation, and the source of the imagination. It is also the foundation, in the words of

Spinoza, of "the improvement of the understanding." On this principle rests the theory of multiple intelligences.

Consciousness is the God inside. This transpersonal ultimate concern represents the ideal of sainthood, asceticism, monasticism. It means silence, reflection, meditation, inner search. It stands for humility, self-abnegation, and self-sacrificing love. It is the experience of the reality of the inner spirit or self, and the belief in God as an immanent (as opposed to a transcendent) being.

In philosophy, this deep structure stands for the concept of pure consciousness: there is a consciousness within us which is as mysterious as it is important. It is transparent, yet also substantial, real. And that consciousness is no other than ourselves. I am in fact that consciousness—no more and no less. This dimension of thought provides also one of the fundamental sources of personal and of emotional security. It is mysticism's solution to the problem of existence.

God is the miracle of being. This deep structure describes God as the *ground of Being.* It complements the previous category. Whether or not one thinks of oneself as religious, one can have nevertheless a sense for the miracle of being, which is the miracle that exists behind the world and which supports the world in its being. That miracle is terrifying, overwhelming. But it also lends support, yields bliss. It is a separate reality, as well as the ultimate support of the universe. This dimension of thought is a second source of security. It is traditional religion's (rather than mysticism's) answer to the problem of existence. It is the theory of a transcendent God—God as the external confronter, the law, the judge, and the giver of grace.

Everything is seen from a subjective perspective. This deep structure refers to the fact that every time the self (the subject) interacts with the word (the object), it cannot avoid a subjective perspective, no matter how hard it tries to be "objective." This is sometimes called the egocentric predicament. It alludes to the preeminence of subject-object interdependency, of dialectic and dialogic. Subjectivity is also the source of the justified feeling of being special. We must always ask, before we can accurately describe any event, from whose subjective perspective it is to be analyzed.

Reality is ambiguous. This category refers to the flexible, fluid, and indefinite character of perception and of reality. Reality is inherently flowing. Fixed points are essentially illusions, and structures are arbitrary and changeable superimpositions on the flux of experience. Ambiguity is an inescapable characteristic of the objective world. This fact makes possible the next structure.

We have the power to assign meanings to existence. This theme is the power we possess to invent world-views: we are free to choose the meaning that this world shall have. World-views are basically chosen rather than discovered. This fact helps to explain the significance of the study of cultures, religions, and mythologies.

This so-called "transcendental freedom" is our godlike capacity to develop systems of reality—different cultures have developed diverging and often opposing systems—on which we then base our lives, our decisions, our institutions, our politics, and even our wars. There is power in this idea. And this power is both the glory and the terror of human history.

A paradigm shift—which we need urgently to insure world peace—is a decision made at this deep level about the meaning of the world, of ourselves, and of our neighbors. It is an ultra choice made about being right, and about considering that those who we "know" are wrong may after all be partially right. It entertains the possibility that we, sure to be right, could in fact actually be wrong. Only to the degree that such redefinitions take place are we entitled to hope for a civilized future.

Deep structure theory examines the boundaries of the human conditions. And they are existential as well as transpersonal, that is, secular as well as religious. We must distinguish sharply between a belief system based on the reality of our being-in-the-world, our incarnation, our situation, on the one hand, and a mystical otherworldy view, in which reality is found in the exploration of our pure, universal, and eternal consciousness. A comprehensive view of human existence must explore sympathetically both of these disparate poles of the spectrum of our experience.

CHAPTER 13

Feelings

Ultimate concerns are about human beings in the world. Now we take a look at the second set of philosophic deep structures of human existence. These are the feelings, or moods and emotions, mobilized when we struggle with the above ultimate concerns:

- Anxiety: abandonment, assault, ridicule, insanity
- Tragedy: loss without redemption
- Anger: self-against-self, self-against-other, and other-against-self
- Guilt, nausea
- Loss of self-respect, inferiority complex
- Disorientation, vertigo, amnesia, confusion
- Physical pain
- Disability
- Depression, boredom, withdrawal, giving up

Feelings are the emotions we all suffer as we confront or deny, fail or succeed to cope with, the existential and the transpersonal ultimate concerns. These feelings are often called symptoms, because they are typical of the complaints patients bring to physicians and psychotherapists. They are the roots of the moods and emotions that trouble people, and in our culture are given intensive and expensive medical care and psychological attention. These feelings can be positive or negative, depending on our attitude towards them. But prima facie they are all negative. The close to a half-trillion-dollar health bill of this nation can be attributed mostly to our mismanagement of these feelings about our ultimate concerns.

Thus, *anxiety*, the first feeling or symptom, can be a diseased condition or it can be the sense of excitement preceding any important act or major decision. Anxiety is normal and healthy; it is the denial of anxiety that leads to illness. You deal with anxiety by "going with it!"

There are four distinct sources of anxiety: abandonment, assault, ridicule, and fear of insanity. The latter includes also the fear of doubt, uncertainty, and error: we must act decisively even though we fear that we may be fundamentally wrong. We can add to that list the anxiety about death, the anxiety produced by our freedom in making difficult decisions, the anxiety of change, and the anxiety brought about by the guilt that we might be evil.

Much of life's energy is squandered in avoiding these feelings, and much effort is wasted in elaborate strategies to deny them. Compulsive behavior is but one example of how we try to protect ourselves from anxiety.

In a healthy person, a strong ego functions as a defense against anxiety. The ego is the manager of anxiety. Extreme anxiety, however, can become unmanageable panic and hysteria. In clinical philosophy, we would call that an intolerable overdose of the truth. In this connection, phobias—perhaps the most pervasive form of anxiety in the United States—can be managed by acknowledging that they are, as is true of many other forms of mental illness, a last-resort cry for authenticity.

Tragedy is the feeling (or the objective truth) that there can be no redemption. Certain losses—a death, an unrequited love, defeat in war, betrayals, years wasted languishing in prison—are unacceptable. To be forced nevertheless to accept the unacceptable is tragic. Moreover, certain values about which we cannot compromise— eternal life, eternal love, true justice, authentic respect for human dignity—may never be realized. That is tragic, for we can do nothing. We call such experiences the tragic sense of life.

Anger is different from hate. Hate is evil, but anger can be frustrated communication. Sometimes anger tries desperately to break through the walls that separate us from other persons. Anger is panic; it is a desperate demand for contact, an ultimate response to the frustration of obstacles and obstructions. Anger is also the last possibility for self-affirmation. When perceived in this way, much anger—whether directed at us or coming from us—can still feel good and healthy rather than just plain bad and sick.

Guilt is neurotic when it is taught in childhood. In other words, guilt through which we are controlled, which ties us down and limits our freedom, is neurotic guilt. To act on it is to destroy our integrity. But guilt which stems from the depths of our natures is authentic and existential.

That genuine guilt—which does not lead to symptoms but can be a source of energy—comes in four forms. Most people are embarrassed to admit that they are too weak to solve their own problems. That is one of the shapes of guilt. Another form is guilt over not fulfilling one's potential. A third source is one's lack of autonomy, a lack for which one feels fully responsible, for we must remember that the natural direction of the soul's growth is towards autonomy. Finally, guilt is the sense of self-betrayal, the feeling that we have not been true to ourselves, that we have missed out on life. Even the promises of immortality and of reincarnation offer little solace, for having missed living once, we will be punished for this omission by even more diminished existences hereafter.

The feeling of guilt leads to nausea, because one must expel what one has illicitly admitted into one's emotional digestive system. Evil, like an inert gas or a toxin, cannot be assimilated.

Loss of self-respect is the feeling of inadequacy and inferiority. It leads to a sense of emptiness. It is the nihilism, the sense of abject worthlessness of being no one and belonging nowhere that lurks deep inside the human breast. Pride and dignity are human necessities like air and bread. Honor, dignity, and pride are the words we use to deal with our fears of inadequacy.

Disorientation, which is like vertigo, is the feeling that the whole world is dissolving; it is confusion about what is real and what is right. When structures crumble the mind can go mad. On the other hand, disorientation shows us the flexibility of the mind. It opens up new ways of perceiving and of understanding the world. It displays before us the zone of our possibilities.

Physical pain and disability can be chronic conditions. They can therefore become opportunities and challenges to demonstrate one's unique mode of coping with the toughness of life's ultimate concerns. As medicine becomes increasingly sophisticated, people who in earlier days would have died remain alive. But they are often crippled or disabled, and many of them suffer acute and chronic pain. Pain and disability, however, can also develop character, allowing the sufferer to set an example, to display the nobility of the human spirit. By increasing religious depth, pain and suffering can help the consciousness pierce the barriers to wisdom.

Depression is to give up on life. It comes out as boredom. It may be the least authentic of these feelings and the most difficult to treat,

CHAPTER 14

Actions

We have at our disposal a vast armamentarium of coping devices, management tools, strategies, and helping techniques that can assist us to understand and resolve the issues underlying our daily personal and business problems. Here are a few:

- Full presence, awareness, self-consciousness
- Contact, commitment, engagement
- Listening, hearing
- Exploration and description; confrontation and challenge
- Identification of defenses—denial, projection, displacement, sublimation
- Rational reflection, spirituality
- Courage, the existential crisis, and claiming one's power
- Integration of evil through dialogue
- Acceptance of ambiguity and integration of polarities

Full presence, awareness, and self-consciousness means to be fully aware of all feelings, thoughts, emotions, fears, hopes, dreams, anticipations, anxieties, cares, concerns that are "present to oneself" at this particular time and in this particular place. It means to be fully and totally conscious and alive now and here.

Presence also means to have uncovered the underlying, unconscious depth of *me* at this space-time point. The depth goes beyond the childhood-caused psychological conflicts to the more profound problems of ethnic identification that often touch people's most devastating emotions—and right on to the even deeper underlying philosophical and ontological issues that make up the human condition, the fate of men and women, the destiny of being human.

The psychologist J.F.T. Bugental describes therapy as follows: "At the beginning of therapy I instruct the client that therapy is the demand to be fully present to oneself. Therapy is concluded when the client is in fact fully present to him- or herself." Presence is achieved through contact.

Contact, commitment, and engagement are the supreme goals of the human enterprise. Most people understand contact to mean praise, judgment, criticism, meeting role criteria, fulfilling functions, and so on. In truth, however, contact is non-judgmental, interested, caring, compassionate. The key word for contact is witness: a fully aware appreciation and acknowledgment of who another person is and what another human being feels. To meet another person in depth is to see the world through his or her eyes and to understand what the real messages are which language and actions can transmit only feebly.

Contact is also called encounter. It is a very special sense of having touched the reality point in another person—and having the corresponding point touched in oneself. The effect of contact is the glowing feeling of security and the warm sensation of finally being understood. If there are miracles, then they occur in the human touch.

Listening, hearing. People do not need answers nor do they need advice as much as they need to know that they are being listened to, that they are being heard. To be heard validates one's subjective consciousness, it clarifies one's feelings, and it is often all that people ask. To be listened to validates one's identity, and feels healthy and makes one strong. And yet in actual fact, people use talk to not listen.

Listening is a skill, but so is learning how to talk to a good listener. This means not to make unreasonable demands on the listener to take action to solve one's own problem. There is a glow in the soul that shines each time one is heard by another self.

Exploration and description; confrontation and challenge. Healing occurs through searching for answers, and not by being given answers. It is the search that heals, not the answers. Advice stops growth. The benefit of swimming derives not from understanding how to swim but from actually swimming. Growth is stimulated by intelligent confrontations and loving challenges, not by crudeness, insensitivity, or indifference. People need active listening, not advice. A simple point, but it is amazing how many times it is missed altogether.

Identification of defenses—denial, projection, displacement, sublimation. When we are stuck in the agonizing process of trying to make an important decision, then a useful question is "What part of yourself must you give up before you can make your decision? The dreamer part? The practical part?" The deep wish or profound character structure that you must abandon in every major growth step is also your dominant *resistance* to authenticity. Sometimes it is to give up the security of your childhood. Or it may be that independence requires giving up the love of your mother or your father. Or it may be that you have not yet made the decision to grow up, to be an independent identity, to have courage, or to be willing to go through the feelings of intense anxiety.

Typical defense mechanism are outright denial, projection of subjective feeling on to objective reality, displacing emotions from, let us say, anger at the boss to kicking the dog, and sublimation—where we might follow rigid ethical rules or write a poem to express some forbidden primitive feeling.

Rational reflection, spirituality. This can also be called distancing and non-attachment. Stoics and many Oriental philosophers have discovered the security of the inner self, detached from the stresses of the world. The extreme form that this coping device takes is the asceticism of the monastic life. The monk or nun gives up the world, gives up desire, secular attachment, and dependency. The mind thus non-attached is spared the agony of loss and deprivation, the pain of competition and the frustration of unrequited love. The executive, when faced with ugly realities and unpleasant choices, can also adopt this posture of retreating to the silent and solitary center and find therein the refuge, the security, and the strength to act resolutely against the tide. The earlier discussions of transcendental intelligence and of the Transpersonal Ultimate Concerns have addressed themselves to this time-honored solution to the travails and the exigencies of life.

Courage, the existential crisis, and claiming one's power. Life cannot be lived without courage. To be an adult is to have experienced the success of this truth. The world responds to courageous leaders. Nature is designed for independent adults, not dependent children. To have courage is to act in spite of anxiety and guilt. Courage means to be energized by failure and buoyed up by rejection. It is the willingness to be alone and like it.

Integration of evil through dialogue. This is the integration of the demonic, the shadow. Human beings are bothered by dark fears and sometimes by dark desires. The fears do not go away. Irrational behavior and self-destructive and sabotaging relationships reveal how we can be prisoners and slaves of these unconscious regions inside the psyche. A crisis, sometimes of major proportions, is often needed in order for us to cross this barrier to health and to growth.

It can be achieved by befriending rather than fighting the problem, the demonic. We feed the fantasy monster. The beauty kisses the beast. The union of the two opposite poles—the sacred and the profane, good and evil—is also their integration. By thus wrestling with our demons, we achieve the wholeness and the power to confront life's gravest difficulties. Allowing ourselves to go through a crisis rather than to defeat it and permitting ourselves to experience our shadows rather than to repress them will finally set us free. We can thus realize the proverb of Christopher Morley, "The only true success . . . is to be able to live your life in your own way."

Acceptance of ambiguity and integration of polarities. Dogmatism is an attitude of the inexperienced. Life has two sides to every issue. Niels Bohr said "A great idea is an idea whose opposite is also a great idea." It is unreasonable to demand that one either breathe in or out, but not both. To make courageous choices comfortably in an ambience of confusion and in the absence of precision is the mark of a developed person.

Life is difficult. It is difficult for everyone, not just for tragic figures. And it is not until one has opened the pores of one's consciousness to the tragic sense of life that one can claim even a modest degree of maturity. Each person has his or her own difficulties: a difficult parent, a difficult marriage, a difficult child, a difficult education, financial difficulties, a difficult boss, a difficult neighborhood, not to speak of a death in the family, famine, serious illness, war, oppression, injustice, crime, prison, and other horrors. That is when the need to face the eternal questions becomes paramount.

CHAPTER 15

The Master Table

Philosophy in business, especially in its aspect of ethics in action, develops and elaborates the "deep structures." They are the underlying issues, themes, and concerns in small and in large, in minor and in major human problems. They are the categories we must investigate and the themes we must address if we wish in-depth solutions to the enduring human problems.

Everyone has the capacity to understand the deep structures. Most people can learn to apply these insights to their own lives and to their businesses. The sole requirement is practice. And there should be little of importance about human beings and their needs that is not covered in one way or another by deep structure theory. To understand the deep structures is, to mix a metaphor, "To get a handle on what makes people tick."

The *master table* is based on the three categories of deep structures: ultimate concerns, feelings, and actions. In a complete life, thoughts, feelings, and actions go together in the harmonious flow of one's personal history. Only by avoiding the fragmentation, the splitting, and the compartmentalization of thoughts, feelings, and actions can we acquire an integrated, whole, authentic, and self-actualizing personal history.

For example, to be cerebral, or to be excessively emotional, or to "act out" by virtue of insufficient impulse control, is to suffer a fragmented soul, to be plagued with an aberrant and deviant personality. Only a balanced interweaving of thoughts, feelings, and actions—of head, heart, and body—can lead to a well-functioning personal life and satisfactory career advancement.

Whereas the categories of thoughts, feelings, and actions apply to all human beings, your personal history is exclusively yours. It will always be unique, for you are first and foremost an individual. To feel to be you is unique: it is to know that you have never been before and that you will never be again; it is to feel that you are a singular event in the vast history of the cosmos.

There is a significant qualitative difference between understanding oneself through theory and experiencing oneself as the unique I. Fully understanding and integrating wisdom about one's being cannot help but affect the way one feels about oneself and about those one meets in the marketplace.

Following is an mnemonic outline of the master table.

Can the master table be illustrated with a diagram? The Master Table can be summarized and remembered through the diagram of a triangle within a circle. Ultimate Concerns are at the peak of the equilateral triangle, and feelings and actions are at the base of its two legs. The circle, representing your personal history, encloses the triangle. Your personal life contains and envelopes all of the theoretical ideas of the master table. And all of it rests on a foundation of systematic philosophy—which means metaphysics and epistemology, a theory of reality and a theory of knowledge respectively.

The foundation of the master table lies in the contemporary philosophical movements known as existentialism and phenomenology, both the religious and the non-religious varieties. The master table also includes information from the behavioral sciences, which includes various forms of psychotherapy. The great metaphysical visions, which have reached a high stage of development intellectually in the West and experientially in the East, are also an important ingredient of the master table. Many of these have found expressions in theology and in mythology, and also in literature and the arts.

The master table consists of *new maps* of the *"bodymindworld."* The master table is a map that gives you a workable geographic overview of the deep issues required to understand people and communicate effectively with them. It is new because it purports to be a contemporary account of insights into human nature, and at the same time attempts to incorporate the wisdom of the past and of other lands and other civilizations in its personality theory.

It is a bodymindworld because it is alert to the intimate interdependency among body, mind, and the surrounding world. An action in one area produces a reaction elsewhere. This insight regarding the pervasiveness of systems and of interactions, of structure and of context, becomes a fundamental principle in personal transformation to the genius level of performance and the power level of ethical action in business organizations and in their markets.

The master table is therefore a response to the question, "What is a human being?" or "What is a person?" or "Who am I?" Since mind, body, and world are one integrated system, questions about the nature of persons—including questions like, "What is *my* world?" and "What is *the* nature of the world?"—become questions about the total *nature of being*.

The master table can also be seen as an intimate analysis of the structure of the I-am experience or of the I-process. The life force, when it appears in us, becomes the I-am experience. That is the meaning of God saying to Moses in *Exodus*, "I AM THAT I AM."

Evil is any obstruction that confronts the I-am experience. Evil can destroy the I-am experience, in which case it more than bends the spirit—it cracks it. Aging, since it is the experience of slow death, may be the most pernicious obstacle of all to the I-am experience. Death gives rise to the pressures of time. We must guard against depression in such cases. It follows then that the role of philosophy-in-business is to act as the guardian of the integrity of this I-am experience.

The master table is for people who are interested in becoming self-disclosed and transparent, not for those who are fighting against understanding their own nature. It is for those who can and want to see. It is not for those who have chosen to be blind. The total effect of the study and of the application of the master table should be to facilitate and help you to experience the reality of your own existence so that you do not reflect on life but live it.

What is the value of dividing the master table into ultimate concerns, feelings, and actions? These categories are diagnostic. Some people are preeminently thinkers. They become the scholars and the scientists of our society. Some people are primarily feeling or emotional individuals; these then may become the artists and the lovers among us. And then there are people who are primarily action-oriented, such as politicians and business executives.

In addition, these three categories can be therapeutic. Therapy is the effort to translate one's dominant category into another, or to explore the others, which may have been hidden. Thus, for example, for a thought-oriented person to be in therapy is to encompass and embrace the corresponding feelings and actions as well. Symptoms in the lives of thought people—such as unsatisfactory personal relationships and frequent bouts with depression—may be traced to the denial of their feeling and action dimensions. Conversely, a primarily action-oriented person may be limited and needs to learn more about the possibilities of human experience and the rich feelings waiting to be felt.

Ultimate concerns give meaning to feelings. An action gives credibility to or validates both ultimate concerns and feelings. And thoughts and feelings are both empty unless translated into actions.

An example of these interconnections would be a difficult personal decision, such as giving up something to which one is addicted, like alcohol, excessive food, or cigarettes. To stop smoking may be only a thought. But we are unlikely to actually stop smoking unless we are also appropriately angry, which is a feeling. And combining the two, thought with feeling, gives us also a chance for meaningful and effective action.

Coping with these negative feelings is the necessary precondition for solid joy rather than brittle happiness. Positive feelings, such as hope, joy, pleasure, and fulfillment, are a function of negative feelings. We can, through an existential crisis, transform our negative feelings into positive states. We also support our positive feelings with the knowledge that we can manage comfortably any negative feelings which might threaten them—as a singer is supported by an orchestra. In emphasizing the negative, we give both credibility and foundation to the positive. If you can handle anxiety, guilt, anger, depression, and the like, then you need never fear that your joy is in danger.

The biological curve of life first rises and then promptly falls again. It is like a bell-shaped curve, because of its evolutionary and involutionary phases. The soul, however, unlike the body, always grows. And here is where philosophy and biology part ways. For the philosophic curve, on the other hand, is the unfolding of the deep structures, the journey to authenticity. It rises steadily and need not come to an end before death.

Technical training and professional experience are helpful in applying the insights from the master table to actual problems in the business environment.

Case Study: Sandra

In one of the seminars we saw in Sandra a simple example of the master table at work in a business setting. Sandra was disgruntled. She could not stand her immediate supervisor. He was contemptuous of women, patronizing, selfish, insensitive, narrow, unpredictable. Sandra had several options. She could adopt a stoic and withdrawn posture, lead a life of protected inwardness, perform as best she could, and continue in this armored fashion until the day that she retired. American corporations are peppered with such embittered employees. Or she could muster her courage and leave the organization, become perhaps a self-sufficient entrepreneur—realizing fully the discipline required and the anxiety such a high-risk choice would release.

Or, Sandra might choose to confront her adversary intelligently by understanding that to dialogue with her evil can be the most effective path to self-fulfillment. Such dialogue requires discrimination between our culture's contribution to her despair and her own personal contribution to that same alienation. She must invite others to discuss with her the undiscussable. She must teach others how to be truthful with her, about even the most sensitive matters. Only in this way can there be emotional progress with people who experience themselves as trapped and are desperate in the unfeeling labyrinths of some of our larger, older, rigid, and more conservative corporations.

Sandra understands that the level at which her problems are to be resolved is not determined by the business organization alone. She is dealing not even with childhood residues in adult life. Sandra is dealing with the existential issues of dignity within nothingness, of freedom and identity as against a destructive and evil Otherness. She requires a transformation, so that she sees the wisdom of the deeper existential situation of the human condition, which in its depth is already a solution, rather than bogus solutions to artificial problems. Sandra must traverse the anxiety and journey through the guilt of assuming full responsibility for her condition.

CHAPTER 16

The Ethical Imperative in Business

The business executive knows one thing, something that academics and scholars often overlook: understanding a business problem and knowing its solution is not enough. Action is the key. Ethics is the imperative to act. And persistence is what is required of action. That means constancy—in idea, in conscious focus, in values. It is as if the entire company had but a single thought. And the leader has to make the idea become reality.

But how is one to achieve that? The answer to this question is the key to success. Required are character, courage, will, commitment, risk, and a taste for greatness. The virtues and the values of will power, of guts, of perseverance, of single-mindedness, of endurance, of energy, and of contagious joy and enthusiasm require a personal transformation. Philosophy in business, as ethics in action, may offer one key to help leaders become what they must be.

Deep structure theory should help one understand human nature well enough so that one can assess accurately and in depth most human situations. Successful leadership should come naturally. We must learn how to remove the blocks to success by understanding the more profound intricacies of human existence. The master table intends to be like a showroom or a supermarket, where the deepest structures of human existence are on display. Examine them carefully and then feel free to risk living by these realities. The act of endeavoring to fully experience the concepts listed on the master table is meant to flex mental and emotional muscles that may have lain dormant far too long. That, hopefully, will contribute to creating a transformation within you.

To go from theory or thought to action in your own life may well require just such a personal transformation. Transformation is a curious and basic opportunity. It works like this: you are confronted with a situation of anxiety and conflict. These situations start with personal problems. You are a young man; should you make a commitment to marry Lisa or to marry Jane, or should you remain a bachelor? You are a woman. Who is it to be, John or Bill? Or consider another example. Your marriage is unsatisfactory—even after time-consuming and expensive counseling. Should you now seek a divorce or should you adjust yourself to the existing marriage, on the premise that this is all you can get, or that this is all you have a right to expect from life?

Or look at business. Your business is facing a financial crisis. Should you invest more money in your endangered company, or sell it, or perhaps go into bankruptcy? You manage a large division. You discover among your newly hired personnel a brilliant young engineer. Do you reward him financially and with a promotion when others, less qualified, must thereby be bypassed? Do you venture to create anxiety, anger, and resentment in the company? Or are you willing to risk losing your employee to another company willing to recognize immediately his unquestioned abilities?

Or consider politics. You anguish over the possibility of nuclear war. How can America achieve a disarmament agreement with Russia if we cannot trust their intentions?

The first step to transformation is to experience—clearly and intensely—the pain of the conflict. You must have a precise sense of the dilemma as real and painful, and know that at the same time it simply cannot be resolved with a rational, unilateral decision. Denial, advice, or problem solving are the wrong techniques at this point, because they do not work and function only to diminish the fullness of the experience of conflict. For it is out of the soil of irresolvable conflicts and of insoluble problems that true transformations, genius performance, and paradigm shifts will eventually occur.

Step two is to press down on the anxiety of conflict with such intensity that something in the mind literally "snaps," causing the expected paradigm shift. The result is the third step, which is, in the words of Marcel Proust, like seeing an old landscape with new eyes. This is the exact point of transformation. The old problem is no longer a problem, because the "flavor" or the "mood" of reality itself has now changed. What before was worrisome has now become a matter of indifference.

For example, a key employee, in fact, a person very high up in the organization, needs to be fired by you, the CEO. Yesterday you felt this as a painful dilemma—excruciatingly so. Today, that same conflict has become the simplest thing in the world. You go into your subordinate's office and say, "Sorry, you're fired!" What has changed, what has been transformed, have not been the facts but your mood. And it wasn't will power that did it. It was an internal transformation; it was a change in perception. And that occurs at the pre-rational level. It is not under the control of the will. It is mystery, magic. But what matters is that it is possible, for it does indeed occur.

Let us consider another example. Yesterday the forthcoming job for which you have been hired as secretary to the president was fraught with anguish: "I am incapable of doing it; I will fail!," you said to yourself. Today you look forward to it. You expect it to be fun, interesting, an adventure. The worst of it is the routine—no longer is it the anxiety. And you worry neither about making a mistake nor about leaving the job if it no longer suits you.

Often, to solve the basic problems of a business and of an executive's relation to that business—especially when we deal with achieving greatness in a company—it is just such a transformation that is required. Transformation used to be called conversion. Today, using the jargon of philosophy and physics, we also call it a paradigm shift, although the religious metaphor remains highly appropriate.

As a matter of fact, one place where this shift in perception can be seen with exceptional clarity is in the "generation gap." There the transformation is from the values of the parents to those of the children. A young child does not perceive mature love. An adult has difficulty remembering with sympathy the horrid uncertainties of adolescence, or, for that matter, identifying with the moods and the fads of the new generation. Every case of culture shock is ipso facto an instance of a perceptual transformation.

Transformation is often expressed in symbols or myths. Advertisers use many of them to attract attention and at the same time to gain respect and stature. The totally independent man, often found on cigarette advertisements, is one example. The virile and seemingly healthy man belies the cancer message in the coffin-like black box at the bottom of the page. The true guardians of our symbols of transformation are the artists, the poets, the thinkers, the writers, the theologians. The respect which may or may not be accorded to them by our society becomes a measure of our readiness and our will for transformation.

The ultimate issue for this planet—world peace—depends on a transformation. This quest for socially and politically relevant transformation is the final task and the true justification for ethical action in philosophy in business. It is accomplished by a wider understanding of the deep structures of human existence and how they can be made to work, not only in personal but even more so in business affairs.

Norman Cousins writes (*Human Options*),

> Years after the Second World War, Berlin was still in ruins. Anyone who has seen the rubble of a city that has been destroyed by bombing knows that the human race is on notice, that nothing we do individually or collectively makes sense unless it is connected to the making of a structured peace.

Transformation is what translates abstract theory and anemic thought into flesh-and-blood living action. And that can be brought about only by an in-depth understanding of the nature of persons.

Problem solving has two dimensions, two levels at which it occurs: choice and transformation. Choice is always the birth of one alternative and the death of another. Also, choice invariably requires courage, reconciling oneself to loss. Choice is frequently a necessary option. But it leaves a residue of bitterness and disappointment, a trail of unfulfilled possibilities.

Transformation, however, is a case of "have your cake and eat it too." It represents the paradigm shift or conversion through which an old reality is perceived in a fresh mode, in which an old world is experienced as the new world, in which an old love is seen with novel possibilities. These eyes of transformation make old conceptions disappear and show us new ones in their stead.

For instance, before transformation one may expect a particular choice to have catastrophic consequences—whichever way one chooses. One may see it as having a right and a wrong course and a precise answer. One may think of it as demanding vast personal sacrifices. And one may think that it requires one willingly to be evil, brutal, selfish, injurious, cold, indifferent, and insensitive. Before transformation the choice may seem important. It may not appear to have a meaningful third course of action. And one of course believes that one's understandable hesitation is but a sign of one's own weakness—legitimately eliciting the contempt of others.

After transformation, however, one may perceive this very same choice as relatively unimportant; as not having catastrophic but rather perfectly manageable consequences; not as proof of weakness but as a symptom of normalcy; as having neither right nor wrong answers; as not requiring evil acts for its implementation. One begins to see a world that is receptive rather than antagonistic to the choices that we have already made.

Personal Deep-Structure Profiles in Confrontation with Personal Intelligence Profiles: The Conditions for Transformation

Einstein		Martin Luther King	
Intelligence	Deep Structure	Intelligence	Deep Structure
Logical	Identity/Freedom	Team	Ethics/Love
Transcendental	Ethics	Wisdom	Aloneness/Identity
Wisdom	Aloneness	Motivational	Home/Beauty
			Growth

Beethoven		Eisenhower	
Intelligence	Deep Structure	Intelligence	Deep Structure
Aesthetic	Identity	Team	Ethics
Motivational	Meaning	Marketing	Reality
Somatic	Beauty	Logical	Freedom
Wisdom	Death	Motivational	Identity
	Love	Somatic	Aloneness

Gandhi		J. F. Kennedy	
Intelligence	Deep Structure	Intelligence	Deep Structure
Transcendental	Ethics/Love	Motivational	Identity/Freedom
Motivational	Death	Logical	Reality
Marketing	Meaning	Marketing	Ethics
Team	Freedom/	Team	Body
	Aloneness	Somatic	Beauty

Mozart		Socrates	
Intelligence	Deep Structure	Intelligence	Deep Structure
Transcendental/	Beauty	Wisdom	Ethics
Aesthetic	Aloneness/	Logical	Identity
Somatic	Freedom	Motivational	Freedom
Team	Love/Home		Aloneness/Death

**Personal Deep-Structure Profiles in Confrontation with
Personal Intelligence Profiles: The Conditions for Transformation**

Napoleon		Nixon	
Intelligence	Deep Structure	Intelligence	Deep Structure
Motivational	Meaning/Identity	Marketing	Aloneness
Marketing	Death/Aloneness	Team	Reality
Team	Reality	Motivational	Identity
Logical		Logical	Home
Somatic			

PART THREE

THE THIRD PERSONAL CHANGE:
THE AUTHENTIC LEADER

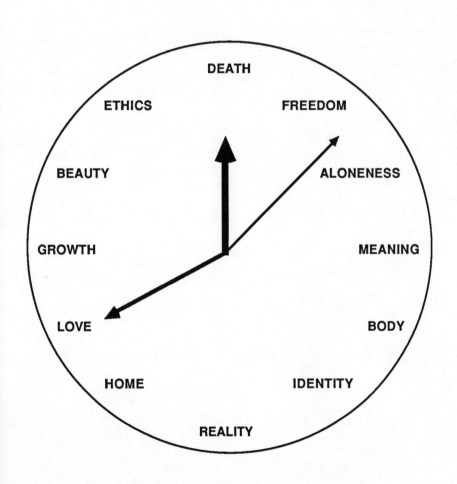

CHAPTER 17

Opening the Way to Leadership

The Ethical Imperative in Leadership

The intelligences and the deep structures infuse life into our souls and bring about a transformation in our way of perceiving the world and in our way of living in it. In religious terms, this transformation would be called conversion.

That means we combine an expanded, and thus more creative, mind with the deepest structures of our being, bringing about a free commitment to authenticity. And authenticity means to raise ourselves to new and higher levels, to the genius level of performance and to the power level of ethical action. This kind of embodied devotion and loyalty to our activities is the level of genius and power—genius in what we can accomplish and power in ethical probity. By fusing breadth of vision with depth of commitment we elevate our specific job, career, and obligations to the joy of authentic fulfillment.

One way to start this transformation is to generate enthusiasm for the ideal of the highly developed personal intelligence profile. For that, we can and must take full personal responsibility. We are accountable. And the rewards are the exhilaration of living life fully. Then we must face the moral imperative of ethical transformation.

In difficult times like the present, when competition is keen and when making a profit is far from easy, it is difficult to persuade business leaders to accept higher responsibilities. In several industries, the dual imperatives to stand up for higher purposes and to make a profit at the same time are generally accepted and must and will be fulfilled. The paradox is not questioned; and some leaders appear to be able to make the dual imperatives work. Effective executives in those industries must meet this precise challenge.

One example is the public press, the Fourth Estate. The press protects our democratic freedoms, especially our First Amendment rights. With that there can be no compromise. Freedom of the press has meaning most of all in bad times. The press is likewise expected to make a profit, for without it there can be no press. Here nature runs its course. The dual challenges must be met—here there are no excuses, for we do not compromise with either freedom or decency. And these dual challenges are in actual fact met by effective leaders. And if they are not met, a way to meet them will be found. What is important enough will also be made to succeed. That is the very meaning of effective leadership: to take prima facie impossible problems and resolve them nevertheless. The war *must* be won. The child's life *must* be saved. A nuclear war *must* be avoided. Some issues require authentic leadership, not compromises.

The same holds true of the medical and dental professions, and of proprietary hospitals: one expects the highest medical standards—for what is at stake is not a quality toaster but life itself. At the same time the hospital is a business and cannot survive without making a profit. For those who minister to the national health, no compromise with quality is ever acceptable. Yet physicians and dentists cannot afford to starve—and it is indeed often difficult for them to run their practices like a business. Even churches and congregations must be solvent. Today's leaders have no choice but to cope with the imperative of the quality/profit paradox. The effective executive is not simply the one who makes a profit, but the one who makes a profit while meeting his or her moral responsibilities and ethical obligations to clients, employees, stockholders, and society at large.

We must add to these considerations an article of faith: Decency and profit, moral responsibility and productivity, are linked. Whether this conjunction is true or not is not exclusively a matter of empirical verification or statistical generalization. For the truth of the matter is not determined by these two variables alone, but includes a third: the free human choice to connect them. We shall resolve that profit and ethics be linked! And that makes it true. For a moral law exists only by virtue of the choices of decent men and women. Morality is upheld not by nature nor by arms, but by the force of the spontaneous and autonomous human will. That is a manifestation of an ethical commitment. That personal risk is what constitutes leadership. And it is the insertion of that constant, the will to ethics, into the profit/decency equation that will affect the outcome.

Business is a language. It is a way of thinking, or working, of perceiving the world. Business looks at reality with one objective: to get things done!

And what is the business of business? To create wealth? To inspirit the economy? To create jobs? To meet the needs of society? To encourage investments? Yes. But there is more. The final goal of any human activity, and business must show us how to be effective, is to create a world moral order—a world ethics network.

Ethics is good business—this is not a scientific observation, but a decision, a choice, that free men and women make about the kind of world they want.

The equivalent of money, for example, is an idea. The anthropological and/or metaphoric function of money can be expressed in two fundamental equations: Money = Life, and Money = Idea. As in religion, we can fall in love with the symbol, and barter in terms of the symbol rather than in terms of reality. The symbol is more than a surrogate for reality; it becomes reality itself. In fact, it transcends reality.

It follows that we must treat life and ideas as we treat money: we must use the same language and apply parallel principles. Similarly, marketing minds must acknowledge that financial services can be sold best when they speak the language of life and ideas rather than the language of interest and capital gains.

Here are some fundamental guidelines to help us explore the meaning of the money/idea equation:

- Treat your ideas as you treat money: earned, received as gift, borrowed, in your pocket, in the bank, invested, used (leveraged, as with a servomechanism).
- Money is just paper, or metal. An idea is just an abstraction.
- Money is a thing, an object, something material. Money is of no value unless it becomes a process, an experience, something alive.
- And it is a person who transforms the object into an experience, the thought into an action, the abstract into the concrete.
- Ross Perot has said, "Money is the most overrated thing in the world."

Money is a thing that can be translated into an experience. Money is a "thing," an "object," that we want because it will bring us other values, mostly experiences. If we want other objects, then those other objects are translated into experiences—either through exchange, as when we buy admission to the theater, or through ownership. Many people feel that ownership of an object, like a piece of land or a gem, is itself an experience of value. Such translation—from money to object to experience—can be accomplished by (1) owning the money or (2) by spending the money for an object exchange or for a direct experience exchange or (3) by using it for investment and for leverage, which is essentially to translate money into power, as in a servomechanism.

Let us review some examples:

- Money in the bank is the experience of freedom.
- Money spent on a house is the experience of security.
- Money spent on a vacation is rest, health, and pleasure.
- Money spent on stocks is peace of mind and leisure. The meaning of the word "stocks" includes (1) the leverage achieved in real estate and in venture capital, and (2) the kind of leverage in which you employ people, from one to 100,000, who work for you and create value for you that otherwise you could not achieve. And that value is free time.

This is the power of money. It is also the power of ideas in ethical action. To summarize:

Money is not a thing but an idea. And there are many ideas of what money can be:

Money:
- How acquired:
  Earned
  Borrowed, lent, loaned
  Received as gift
  Stolen
  Counterfeited
  Created, i.e., through a life insurance policy (which creates an immediate estate), through the sale of promissory notes or mortgages, or through a commercial bank borrowing from the Federal Reserve Bank, and so on.

- How held:
  Cash in pocket
  In bank (electronic money)
  Invested—i.e., stocks (invisible money)
  Used—i.e., for salaries (leveraged money)
- How conceived, perceived; its "ontological status":
  Cash in hand
  Electronic money (computer printouts)
  Other people's money (private)
  Other people's money (government)
- How used:
  Owning
  Spending on object
  Spending on experience
  Investing/lending
  Leveraging with property (like a servomechanism; we can call
  it servomoney or servodollars or servobucks)
  Leveraging with people (employment)

Idea management is the skill and the science to promote the creation of new ideas and to take full advantage of their value.

Sui Generis (the Problem of Evil)

The sui generis zone is that region which exists only in the inwardness of each human being, and which is totally private for each individual ego. Philosophy deals with introspective data. It focuses on dreams, fantasies, and concepts. Dreams circumscribe the region of subjectivity, which is the inner light that illuminates all objects but is itself not an object. Only philosophy makes the commitment to explore systematically that region of inwardness.

Aristotle tells us that we find the meaning of life in accentuating the typically human. He urges humanity to emphasize that which we do not share with the animal species. He calls it the specific difference. For him it is rationality, since he defines a human being as a rational animal. That concept is also the foundation for Aristotelian logic.

The sui generis zone is the region of the purely or characteristically human, the zone that lies adjacent to observable and measurable animal traits. That zone includes—besides the ability to reason and to think—the following enduring human realities:

- the understanding of awareness as distinct from objects of which we may be aware
- the perception of evil
- the capacity for choice
- the ability to create
- the sense of greatness
- the valuation of a noble human spirit
- the authentication of an ethical claim
- the respect for liberty and for justice
- the revelations of love, innocence, commitment, compassion, and generosity
- the recognition of responsibility
- the glorification of devotion to truth
- the openness to religious experience
- the validation of aesthetic sensibilities
- the yearning for immortality

There is evidence that fulfilling the desiderata of this region of inwardness is the key to mental health. It follows that it is likewise the key to organizational health—and thus also of economic health.

Resistances

To be human opens the door to being evil. What guarantee do we have that the eight intelligences are not applied as easily to evil designs as to good? Was not Hitler a good marketing intelligence? an outstanding motivational intelligence?

There is no such guarantee. The fight against evil is the free and lonely decision of individual human beings to commit their lives to an ethical purpose, to being ethical individuals, to choose ethically. That lifestyle is chosen because it is right, not because it leads to rewards or because it avoids punishments. The most noble ethical posture belongs to that person who, risking total isolation, creates an ethical and civilized atmosphere by choosing to be just, fair, moral, and decent. Such a harsh and high attitude—which characterizes the finest moral leaders throughout history—is to do what is right because it is right and for no other reason.

The two-headed nemesis of the devoted and successful executive are projection and envy. As executives get better, subordinates (and others) increasingly project their own inner needs on them. The primary need of human beings, compensating for their innate impotence, is power. They will believe that the executive, their boss or their boss's boss, has far more power than he or she in fact has. That is often more of a subjective projection than an objective fact.

Furthermore, as the executive gets better, more authentic, more successful, he or she will arouse envy. And envy is an unbeatable and unmanageable emotion. Envy does not stay harnessed by the bounds of reason and quickly turns into resentment. And then it becomes hatred. The paradox, which is universal in life, is that as the executive becomes more and more authentic and achieving, he or she also gets increasingly more isolated. Isolation is occasioned by projection. And as the executive becomes more and more successful he or she becomes more and more hated..., through the envy aroused. These are no-win situations. In childhood we learn that we get rewarded for being good. As adults we learn that the better we are, the more severe the punishment. And the two principal means of castigation are isolation and hatred.

Let us examine these conflicts in more detail.

Projection means that we are not recognized for who are. Our real selves are totally ignored. We are used for the fantasies of our subordinates—mere symbols satisfying the needs of others' neuroses. Our flesh and blood reality and emotional vulnerabilities and instinctual needs are neither recognized, validated, or even understood.

The ultimate example, a reductio ad absurdum, of ignoring the personal in projection is assassination. When John Hinckley shot at Reagan he clearly did not perceive the President as a human being, as a father, a husband, a future patient in a hospital, a being with feelings, hopes and anxieties, a "Thou" (in the words of Martin Buber)—but as an "It." The victim is purely a member of the subjective and schizophrenic fantasy world of John Hinckley. And this state of complete non-recognition is emotionally painful, and excruciatingly so—not to say physically dangerous.

Adults are alone; they are isolated. And it is an isolation which means business.

Is there a solution? Yes there is: be truthful and honest with yourself and with others. And be truthful in the two dimensions of human consciousness. Be truthful in the way in which the animals are conscious—the natural consciousness. It is the innocence of Adam and Eve. Experience and accept the world as it is. Be it. And also be truthful in the the way only human beings can be truthful—the reflective or the reflexive consciousness. Be truthful about the present moment.

Thus, if the CEO is angry at a subordinate—"What makes me mad is that you are a sycophant and that you don't tell me what you really think!"—he or she must reflect on what that outburst does to the subordinate. This is the reflexive consciousness, for it bends back and down upon itself. Does it intimidate the subordinate? What is the deeper meaning of the CEO's anger? What does it reveal about the values, the childhood, the need for self-affirmation, the fear of inadequacy, the guilt of being evil in the soul of the CEO? How can the subordinate be helped to deal with the anger? How can the CEO be helped to deal with the anger? Does the anger clear the air? Does it mature the parties? Does it inhibit creative and innovative solutions? Does it diminish the value of the subordinate, so that the subordinate cannot then deliver the creativity he or she gets paid for?

If the CEO and the subordinate now get into this kind of a reflexive discussion, their authentic human connection is reestablished—without violating the character structure of either, without requiring that either one of them be different.

When people are both naturally and reflexively truthful and honest—two important concepts—then their maturity begins. They will understand how they feel and how they act. They will recognize their assumptions and trace their psychological and ontological roots. And with it they will receive the gifts of redemption and joy, peace of mind and reconciliation with life.

They understand their isolation and they understand injustice and unfairness. They no longer blame, for they understand that everyone shares a similar fate. For example, every parent had a parent. They then no longer feel special—which is both good and bad.

They are now ready for friendship, for meeting, for witness, for support, for compassion, for learning and for teaching, for genuine mature companionship. They do not expect the other to be super-human but just human. They see each other as they really are and do not place in them their projection of an ancient anger or of an ethereal hope. They now can criticize and be criticized, fire and be fired, resign and accept resignations in good faith and with rationality.

The search for maturity is the game of games that provides by far the greatest satisfaction.

The unconscious of top management may be responsible for corporate problems. The inwardness of the top leadership is reflected in the organization. This understanding is a most effective tool of transformation.

It follows that our social world is the projection of unconscious material. For our socio-economic world as we find it is what we have constructed by means of our own powers of perception. A description of this situation on a personal and psychological level is found in Eric Berne's classic book, *Games People Play.*

These issues—the invisible causes of intractable problems—are the toughest and the most expensive to deal with. They result from the limitations of top management. They are ethical deficits. Deep structures do not necessarily transform to the genius level of performance and the power level of ethics. They may detract from mental powers.

Some deficits arise from unfinished childhood business. Examples include neurotic behaviors, jealousy, selfishness, and infantilistic ways of dealing with authority, responsibility, frustration, rejection, loss, competition, conflict, money, and sexual feelings.

Peculiarly ethical deficits arise from a flaw in motivation. To be motivated by ethical considerations is to be governed by a set of rules, specifically the rules of democratic relations among people, with emphasis on fairness, equality of opportunity, justice, openness, trust, honesty, truthfulness, and regard for dignity. Major problems occur when people hesitate to do what is right because it is right, and instead do what feels good or what may seem prudent. Favoritism and exceptions to rules may result. At the heart of morale lies morality.

Unfulfilled potentials and unrealized possibilities cause developmental deficits. At what level of effectiveness do people work? At what level of their capacity does top management perform? Because leaders' potentials are so very much richer than their actual accomplishments, the gap shows up as symptoms in the organization they control. To see that gap and to be motivated to close it is also to transform the organization.

To transform an organization one must analyze the resistance of top management to facing their ethical deficits. This is the resistance to a fully disclosed authenticity. It is easy to say "Change." But people in fact do not. And they do not change because they do not want to. And they do not want to for excellent reasons: change is painful and exhausting.

But the penalty for not changing is that problems persist, and get worse. We must therefore understand the obstacles to change; we must open up ourselves to the forces that make invisible the causes of problems, and to the stresses that press these causes into the unconscious.

One type of resistance is the resistance to the anxiety of aloneness. For aloneness is a fact: it sounds romantic only until one is in it. Overcoming the resistance to aloneness can be achieved by compassion, by patience, and by understanding. The resistance to truth exists for a purpose. Moreover, that purpose is legitimate. It must be appreciated, supported, cherished, and even loved. Only then can the resistance be explored and challenged. But that can be done only by people with wisdom and who appreciate the legitimacy of the resistance .

Leaders must take full ethical responsibility themselves—as individuals and as a group—to manage these character deficits. But so must the organization below them be confronted with its adult responsibility to manage maturely its own culture needs. And that leads clearly to a situation in which everybody wins. Every individual wins and the organization as a whole wins. These two types of winning are related, for the organization benefits from individual winning, and individuals benefit from membership in a winning organization.

If this does not occur, then the resistance has not been analyzed with sufficient depth.

The deep structures of top management contribute significantly to the fundamental problems of an organization.

When these unconscious deep structures are brought into consciousness, difficult problems become easier to solve because the leaders know exactly what they are up against and with what they must deal. The unconscious must be lifted to the level of conscious choice— that is half the battle.

We must remember that the unconscious may be an unclear, even a contradictory concept. (Whoever heard of unconscious ideas, feelings, thoughts, and states of awareness? For all of the latter are by definition states of consciousness. How can we talk about "unconscious" states of "consciousness"?) But the unconscious is, nevertheless, the single most important discovery ever made in helping us understand and cope with human nature. Any real understanding of human nature must leave ample room for the unconscious.

Exercises

Exercises for reaching the unconscious deep structures can be suggested, though that is more difficult than might appear, and for a very fundamental reason: not reaching the unconscious is not a matter of ignorance or incompetence, nor is it a matter for learning or techniques. Not to reach the unconscious is a clear choice. We *choose* not to   reach the unconscious. The same self which thinks it wants to reach the unconscious also chooses not to reach the unconscious.

Thus, to reach the unconscious means to make a different *choice* from the one we are making at present. Both choices are made unconsciously, which means unknowingly, secretly, by not admitting it to ourselves, silently, in a hidden manner.

Most leaders are people who have done very well using their rational faculties. But if they feel "stuck," that can be usefully interpreted as a warning from the unconscious. Then it is time to look for the handiwork of the unconscious upon one's social and economic world. This can be done in several ways:

Assume that you have a character flaw. Do not question this assumption. Ask instead, what could that flaw be? Now force answers upon yourself. Your horizon of possibilities will be expanded to the degree that you insist on coming up with an answer.

Or consider another one. Assume, with Leibnitz, that this is the best of all possible worlds. It does not appear to you that way. Insist nevertheless that you understand it as the best, anyway. That is how mystical and other innovative world views have been created— and experienced.

It is a good guess that the anger, rage, and hate you feel are really defenses against deep opinions of self-deprecation and of self-doubt. When reason or rationalization cease to be effective defenses, then the ego mobilizes its vast reservoir of emotional energies to silence the truth of what it believes about itself. We could develop an "exercise" based on this insight and call it "insult therapy"!

Record and examine your dreams. Free associate on the basis of these dreams or pictures you have drawn about them. Pay special attention to patterns. Not dreaming or not remembering dreams is also a pattern. What could that mean?

What do you think others say about you behind your back?

Name and describe several major turning points in your life: think of the people, the circumstances, and the decisions—both conscious and unconscious, deliberate and instinctive—which you made at those times. What difference would different choices have made? Would you have had to be a different person in order to make different choices?

Fantasize the extent of your unfulfilled potential. We tend to forget—or perhaps have never known—what we in fact can do, or could have done.

Listen to the language of your body in its movements, its posture, and its shape. It is more important that you make the effort than that you be "accurate."

Study your recurring complaints . . . about anything: politics, job, family, neighbors, health, finances, sex, depression, services, and the many aspects of your inner life. That is easy to do if you keep a journal. Do you find today's issues are the same as they were ten or twenty years earlier? What can you infer from that?

Go over lists of values, deep structures, ultimate concerns, intelligences, emotions, personality types, and use them as checklists about yourself. That expands your understanding of your possibilities.

Other factors about your past and current life can suggest paradigms and become doors to your unconscious:

- your childhood scenarios
- mythology and fairy tales
- religion
- politics and your attitudes towards social and economic issues
- ethnicity
- gender

Now apply all that information and insight to your business. What are your principal business complaints? What in your company do you wish to change? What corporate structure has hitherto been resistant to change, has been obdurate to your best, most thoughtful, and most intense efforts for transformation?

What deep character structure within you might account for that corporate state of affairs? What character deficit, against which you are well armored, might lurk behind the organizational problem? How are the organizational problems related to the person you are? And how might changes in the person you are cause changes in the business?

What changes in your inmost center, your inward ego, would bring about the business transformation you seek? If the system, that is, your company, is an outgrowth of your own personal character structure, then how does your personality explain the problems at the company?

How may relationships among top management—both positive and negative—be an expression of unconscious material, substances in the psyche that have not yet been illuminated by the light of day?

And what changes in your personality would be required to resolve the organizational problems? How might the two systems—your inner self and your external organization—be causally and dynamically related?

This line of investigation will provide you with preliminary ideas, insights, feelings, and perceptions, and it will affect your will, your determination, your commitments, and your actions, in such a way that the external world will respond. Your company will respond with change to a transformation in your heart.

We must always remember that if the company does not change it is because your heart has not been transformed. And if your heart has not changed then it is not because you have failed, but because you have decided that it is a mistake for you to change your heart. For your heart had been right all along.

Positive Deep Structures

Deep structure theory recognizes the role of the unconscious in the effective use of the mind. And the unconscious plays at least two distinct roles.

The first dimension of the deep structures of the unconscious is to promote *health*. Health means a reconciled unconscious, the ability to express instinctual drives, and to have them satisfied. ("What you can feel, you can heal.") Health means to perceive the fact that the seat of the self, its center, is in a fulfilled unconscious. Deep physical as well as profound psychological health are the sine qua non of productive and creative leadership and ethics. General health also promotes spontaneity, the sensation that the mind is working all by itself, without effort or strain on our part.

Secondly, the deep structures of the unconscious help incubate creativity by allowing problems and questions to filter into the unconscious. The unconscious will then work on the problem and offer at least the beginnings of a solution.

This method includes the information-incubation-inspiration-inspection quartet (the four I's). We gather maximum amounts of information to saturate the mind and prepare it for its work. This activity is often onerous, for almost all information helps the process, even though not all the information gathered need be relevant to the project.

We then find ways to allow that information to percolate into the unconscious, so that the "other" side of our mind will have access to the material, reshaping and reorganizing it in ways the conscious mind cannot do. We do this by forgetting and by engaging in distracting activities.

We then position ourselves to be open to inspiration, to be alert to intuition, because in these subtle and non-discursive ways the unconscious reveals to us its innovations. They appear when least expected and when recording them is most difficult—in the shower, while we are driving, or sitting in the dentist's chair. But above all, the deep structures of our unconscious speak to us in our dreams. We must display faith in our unconscious, and we must be prepared to test this faith. For example, we prepare for a speech, then go for a swim to forget the preparation, and then appear on stage without notes—expecting our unconscious to send us flashes of insight during the presentation.

The corporate bureaucracy destroys the willingness of the unconscious to speak to us its mind.

Finally we test, experiment, investigate, institute, and inspect the results, so that we learn how to integrate the qualitative unconscious mind with the quantitative conscious mind. We need to make sure that what we learn in our dreams can be applied to what is real.

This method of access to the deep structures of the unconscious includes "visioning"—the transformation of character, lifestyle, and skills through the persistent, clear, and sharp focus on a "multimedia" fantasy, image, and vision of the goal.

We can now try to set up a system for developing a philosophical, creative, and ethical response to a company problem. For example, with the drop in oil prices and the drop in the dollar in early 1986, the energy business is facing disastrous problems. With the foreign competition, the American automobile business is facing massive and irreversible competition. High technology industries are no longer moving at the accelerating pace to which they were accustomed. The investments, and therefore the risks, are enormous—and the returns more anemic.

Some adjustments will occur naturally, automatically. If an oil company, for instance, believes its business is to manage natural resources, it has reached a higher level of generalization than if it says it is merely in the oil business, which is the lowest level of particularization. And from that medium level of generalization (which is not yet the highest possible) leaders and decision-makers can derive new and different particulars, such as that management or government advising are the goals of the company. Profit then lies in consulting more than in mining. Then the company is not in the oil producing business but in the energy consulting business. And its clients are not only other businesses and governments, but the general public as well.

A gasoline service station is then an energy-consulting center and not a sales center. Stockbrokers, lending institutions, computer companies, automobile dealers, realtors, insurance agents, hospitals—companies who sell what the general public finds difficult to buy—become then consulting services, helping people to deal with their stocks, their loans, their information technology, their automobiles, their homes, their protection from risk, their health. The selling occurs elsewhere.

To generalize means to get to the total concept, the holistic concept. Automobile companies are thinking of selling a complete and worriless transportation package. So may an oil company sell a comprehensive energy or natural-resource package, especially to industry and to governments. Lower oil prices then become a selling point rather than a crisis point.

The message here is not to tell companies what to do, but merely to exemplify the thought processes they need to go through. The precise answers must come from each company. But we are talking here about the role of visions and generalizations in generating solutions for companies in crisis. And this makes every employee a manager.

Here are some rules of thumb on how to contribute to the survival of endangered industries:

Examine questions like, What is our business, our product, our service, our market, our customer? These are the basic themes raised by Peter Drucker. The technique to be used is to ask, How did we start, what were we at the beginning? And then, How have we changed, why have we changed, how have our markets changed, how have our products changed? In other words, we must ask, What is our history? By raising these questions we get essential or generic ideas of what our business "really" is. Are we fulfilling a need? What is that need? What is the underpinning of that need?

The principle behind this line of questioning is to find the right level of essential generalization, so that thinking can proceed on a new, more authentic path. What are some higher-level generalities of what that need is? The highest level of generality, survive or find meaning, is rarely helpful. The lowest level of generality, where we are now, may be naive and obsolete. What is needed is a range between where we are now in our thinking about our essence and the ultimate universalization. We are in the oil business, in the business of providing jobs, in the energy business, in the business of serving our nation, of using resources in the Earth to help mankind's projects, of managing natural resources, of "fueling" the economy, and so on. These are questions for which the people in the organization have the right answers—and no one else does.

In sum, everyone needs a world strategy.

A company can always get a little better at what it does than it was before and better than the competition. That is adding epicycles. But a company can also have a breakthrough—and that occurs unexpectedly, amidst much resistance, and with the help of a few people at the genius level of performance and the power level of ethics.

That is what you can expect from an investment in transformation.

CHAPTER 18

The Transcendental
Key to Leadership

Transcendence

To transcendental intelligence we add the courage to confront our ultimate concerns. Using the theory of non-attachment we go back now through our resistances, bearing the pressure of anxiety, until the human ethical imperative to action takes over and we become transformed to the power level of ethics and the genius level of performance. In the chapters following, we will find that this ethical imperative to authenticity demands we transform the other intelligences. In so doing we reach the genius and power levels of leadership.

What are some of the values of transcendental intelligence? This intelligence is the most closely associated to what we in a narrow sense consider true Intelligence—i.e., the ability to think deeply and clearly. Transcendental intelligence improves our ability to think sharply and elevates the powers of our minds. It is the improvement of this capacity for inner vision that makes the great thinker.

When I explore what I do when I think, it becomes clear that I am a searchlight illuminating new and dark regions of inner space-time, and in so doing I get answers to my questions. My thoughts make up a mosaic within that infinite expanse of inner space and inner time, tiles which I have the power freely to rearrange. Thinking is exactly like inner space-time exploration. How do I know? Through intuition, through the evidence of the immediate experience of turning my gaze inward and sensitively describing what I see. And I can always make a deliberate effort to start this activity and then to improve it. That is the meaning of taking personal responsibility for developing intelligence.

And what is glorious is that transcendental intelligence is easy to develop. A vast literature already exists because religions have shown great interest in transcendental consciousness—that is, the pure consciousness I observe when I focus not on the seen but on the seeing.

However, this does not mean that transcendental intelligence is tied exclusively to a religious world view. It is the other way around. Religion has cast light on transcendental intelligence; it has clarified the structure of consciousness in general. And since intelligence is a consciousness phenomenon, the more we understand about consciousness the more access we have to the tools that make us intelligent. Access to transcendental consciousness is access to the insights that assist us in doing something constructive about our ability to penetrate reality.

The capacity needed is not only to learn how to think lucidly but also how to do this for long periods of time. This means that concentration is like the focus of the light—and that this light shines for a very long time. Consciousness is light.

The great thinker is the person who can explore the mysteries of inner space and inner time. That is where we find geometry and mathematics and where, as Plato accurately understood, the eternal Forms and the eternal verities reside. It therefore seems evident that the same exercises and techniques that the mystics have used for millennia to enter the realm of inner space and inner time can help us today to increase significantly our capacity to think. This inner world can be explored, and we can understand that world. In so doing we will have the secret once and for all for developing truly our ability to think. For to think is little more than to describe that inner realm. It can be described by anyone whose inner eye is developed well enough to see clearly what that realm has to offer. Meditate on transcendental consciousness—decide to enter the realm of pure awareness—before you write, or think, or plan, or calculate, or invent—and you will notice a sharp increase in your productivity.

History has consistently revered men and women who have possessed this intelligence. But what is even more astounding, and what the so-called rationalistic philosophers and mathematicians—like Descartes, Leibnitz, Wolff, and Spinoza, whose heritage stems from Plato, Parmenides, Pythagoras, and Euclid—have understood, is that there are puzzling connections between inward space of and outward space, the outside world of comets, galaxies, and astronomical distances and the inner world of subjective space and time.

Understanding these matters, which on the one hand are esoteric, mysterious, and difficult, but which on the other are the most obvious and lucid facts about this world, is the key to a brilliant mind. There is a high probability that to the degree we share in these mystical ways, our ability to think—especially the kinds of thoughts that have revolutionized the paradigms of science and the world-views of philosophers—will be vastly improved, that is, raised up to its highest possible limits.

Not only the mystics possess transcendental intelligence. Philosophers of consciousness, explorers of the structure and the nature of consciousness, have helped as much as the mystics to explain this important realm of inner consciousness. It is this exploration that can enhance virtually to infinity the sharpness of our thought. The exploration of consciousness is the discovery of the lines of thought, the habits of thought, the patterns of thought, the categories into which thought naturally falls, the changes that consciousness makes in the world that it perceives. Consciousness is the connection between awareness and perception, the study of how perception distorts pure consciousness; it distinguishes awareness, perception, sensation, ways of knowing, and so forth.

And we can do something. We can live this way, train ourselves to think this way, understand the values that follow, and find solutions to the eternal questions.

Non-Attachment

The business mind is characterized by involvement. Engagement with reality, especially the market, is its motto. But how can a decision maker be helped to keep cool in a business crisis? How can a leader maintain his or her distance and emotional calm when under severe pressure from the board of directors, when under attack from the press, when disturbed by the latest P & L statement, or when shocked by the latest stock market report? The deep structure of non-attachment may be the answer. And that is not only a value we gain from Oriental philosophy and other forms of mysticism. Far from it. The earthy and militaristic philosophers of ancient Rome, known as the Stoic philosophers, made non-attachment their foremost principle. In fact, Admiral William Sockdale, America's highest ranking and most decorated prisoner of war, used *The Enchiridion*, the book of aphorisms by the crippled slave Epictetus, to steer himself through the eight difficult years he was imprisoned in Hanoi.

Non-attachment is known in philosophy as the *epoché*, to put reality out of action and merely examine its appearance. It is a fundamental philosophical tool to integrate the mental power of deep structures. We receive the first and final truth when we make no judgments about reality and at most attempt to describe it.

Non-attachment is the best source of creative thought and innovation. For example, obeying a traffic light is usually perceived in the "natural" or "practical" attitude. We see it as a warning signal. It means danger, stop, emergency. It threatens and leads to actions. From the perspective of the phenomenological attitude, or epoché, we view the light as phenomenon only. It then discloses itself to have aesthetic qualities: it is deep red, bright red, blue red, or yellow red. It is pronounced or feeble. It is luminous or opaque.

We can understand the epoché and the various ways it can be used to stimulate thought in the techniques of Edward de Bono, author of many books on thinking. He describes what detachment in effect really looks like, and through his exercises he tries to help us replicate the detachment.

Lateral thinking. Edward de Bono's concept helps us step sideways when our mind is moving forward. He uses devices like "PO" ("provocative operation") and "unconcepting," and others we can develop ourselves. Their purpose is to deflect our thinking process from its expected forward linear trajectory and to channel it elsewhere, laterally—even if the intermediary steps are meaningless.

Edward de Bono defines lateral thinking as "a way of thinking which seeks the solution of intractable problems through unorthodox methods, or elements which would normally be ignored by logical thinking . . . . Lateral thinking leads to those simple ideas that are obvious only after they have been thought of."

Rightness is what matters in vertical thinking, richness is what matters in lateral thinking, contends de Bono. He suggests that we explore nonsequential paths, consider irrelevant information, make errors in reasoning, and be prepared to pass through a wrong idea in order to reach a solution.

One of his methods is PMI (plus, minus, and interesting). Consider this: "A law should be passed that women get paid 10% more than men." Doing a PMI on this proposition—singling out what is positive about it, negative, and just plain interesting—reveals quickly that women would reject it because companies would be encouraged to hire more men than women.

Reversal is illustrated by a factory which pollutes the river. The law says, No pollution downstream. Reversal would mean pollution is acceptable upstream. Result? The plant would drown in its own refuse. This can serve as an example of a good way to encourage responsibility.

PO statements are efforts to find value in nonsense ideas: All PO cars have square wheels, all PO airplanes fly upside down. The latter suggests that pilots whose cabin is below rather than above have a better view of the runway. The former is a method to park cars more safely on hills. A PO concept is one that is meaningless in itself but that moves thought sideways to ideas that otherwise would not have arisen. A PO idea is like an enzyme or a catalyst: a substance that provokes or facilitates a chemical reaction, but is not part of the result.

Meta-thinking. Vertical thinking is always to look for a higher level of perception—a meta-level. This approach is essentially systems thinking. It is also based on the phenomenological concept of *bracketing* or of the epoche, which is a technique for unearthing assumptions. The technique consists essentially in developing the capacity for second-order thinking or meta-thinking, that is, thinking about thinking, perceiving our perceptions, seeing our seeing, and looking at our looking. As we uncover more and more our suppressed premises and our unsuspected presuppositions, we also free the mind for galaxies of new and creative thoughts.

In discussing the multiple intelligences we must explain complex epistemological matters in plain language. By turning statements inside out, upside down, reversing them, inverting them, creating their opposites, contradicting them, negating them, looking for the worst, the best, the most interesting aspects of them, looking for nonsense, and so forth, we can loosen our attachment (cathexis is the technical term) to our habitual ways of seeing things, create a mood of non-attachment, and become open to new connections, new perceptions, new conceptualizations, and new organizations. We must, in short, play around with our statements to see what imaginative innovations might follow from this juggling. "Innovate" is the imperative for the successful modern business.

These are relatively simple ways of integrating transcendental intelligence with deep structures to achieve the genius and power levels of performance and ethical action.

The Greek Experience

It has been my dream to conduct philosophy-in-business seminars for executives away from the lecture halls of corporations or the seminar rooms of hotels. I wanted to go to the source of our civilization, to the roots of philosophy. And that meant to conduct seminars in Athens and Jerusalem, and perhaps also Benares—where the Buddha found enlightenment under the Bo tree.

I wanted to be where St. Paul stood on a polished limestone rock, outside the Parthenon and, pointing to the monumental gold statue of Athena, told the Athenians that there was another God above her! I wanted us to stand in the agora and be able to say, "Two thousand and five hundred years ago, Socrates stood on this spot and was put to death for insisting that human beings think for themselves!"

And I wanted to go with business executives to Delphi, the "navel" of the world, and be able to travel into the realm of deep structures at the very same Temple to Apollo where Alexander the Great and King Midas asked their overwhelming questions.

We did that, and we devised an exercise.

Random connections can be very helpful, for they force upon us connections that we would otherwise not think of. While in Delphi, we visited the Temple of Apollo. That morning we heard a lecture on the Oracle. We had two exercises for the participants.

"You may put one question to the Oracle. Write it down, and tomorrow you shall receive your personal answer. Do not waste your question, for it is the opportunity of a lifetime. Take thirty minutes to think up and write down your question."

At a different time we gave a second exercise. "You are lying on your deathbed. Your children come and ask you for one sentence of wisdom. They want to know the major truth that life has taught you that you wish to transmit to them. They want to know what your legacy is to them, what advice you can give them for their own lives; they want to know by what parting gift they can remember you. What will you tell them? Take thirty minutes to think and write about it."

We then placed questions and answers randomly on separate piles, with me in the middle. One helper randomly picked a question and read it to the group. A second helper picked an answer, and read that also. It was then my task, burden would be a better word—and the task of anyone else willing to help, to "interpret" these random combinations.

Through this exercise participants achieved new insights. New horizons also meant renewed freshness of interest. This exemplifies how to expand thought, how to use randomness for the enhancement of transcendental intelligence (this is also what happens with what is called the "metaphoric" or "figuring" imagination).

We can use random combinations and then force the mind to stretch. That is to work the epoché backwards, and it is a critical clue to mastering the improvement of intelligence. We accomplish this by forcing the mind to adopt new perspectives required by the arbitrary juxtapositions of sentences. We coerce the mind to make sense of, for example, the random words "green blues in the dark." We insist on a meaning, and a meaning appears. We then examine if that forced meaning is of value. If it is, we pursue it; if it is not, nothing is lost. What could it mean? Perhaps that green glows like blue in the dark, or that the green eyes of a cat are transformed in the dark into the blue eyes of a woman.

We force the mind to position itself in a new, i.e., newly appropriate, perspective. Random exercises force the mind to adapt itself to the reality it would have constructed had it the good sense to be creative and innovative in the first place. We can force ourselves to change the way in which we perceive a situation—either by changing the object or by changing the subject.

The concept of non-attachment implies the concepts of constitution, deconstitution, and reconstitution, all of which represent fundamental structuring functions of consciousness. The constitutive powers of the mind make up its capacity to organize experience, to create meanings out of chaotic data. Deconstitution is our ability to disorganize systematized experience, as a painter does when he or she takes a simple figure or landscape and distorts it (Cubists, Pointillists, Expressionists, Impressionists) so that we can see the pure sense components out of which it is fashioned. Reconstitution is to take the mosaic pieces thus disassembled and to reorganize them anew.

The examples from art and from multi-stable figures (drawings which can be interpreted variously) are not as exciting as the real-life examples. We can perceive ourselves, or human beings generically, as massive and unique beings—like Michelangelo's *Moses*—or as insignificant and undifferentiated toothpicks—like Giacometti's work *People*. We can perceive the world as friendly and trustworthy, with innocence, or with the innocent-martyr dyad (innocence will be martyred and martyrs are innocent), or we can be cynical, suspicious, paranoid, and generally hostile. In leading a company, we can be conservative and cautious, or we can take risks and seek the spectacular. All these are examples of how we take the world apart and put it together again according to our own choices. If we do none of it, we will virtually die of depression. For then we have never used our freedom to its full potential, and therefore we have not lived. If we do too much, we will righfully be called crazy. What needs to be invoked here is the judgment of what Aristotle called "the man of practical wisdom."

Any business problem that requires imagination and innovation will benefit from the mind expanding effects of exploring the inner space-time structures of transcendental intelligence. This is a direct push by the will to create a larger space for thought. And such intuitive measures are real, for they deal with the reality of intelligence. When it comes to consciousness, the real is what appears to be real.

Transcendental intelligence provides the ultimate space-time frame. Thus, transcendental intelligence is related to marketing intelligence. The latter is concerned with systemic thinking—with ever-vaster horizons. The most vast horizon of all is the expanse of infinite inner space and infinite inner time that is the central focus of transcendental intelligence.

Memory and retention are related to our capacity for this inner gaze. As we survey from an inner mountaintop the panorama of inner space, and as we realize that inner space has as much of a horizon as does outer space, that consciousness is both the darkness of the night sky and the "blue yonder" of the ocean on a clear and sunny day, we can see details that we had overlooked, and then we feel that our memory returns. Even though space and time seem different, physics tells us they form a continuum. Likewise, if we look inward, space and time are difficult to distinguish, except abstractly. There is an inner vastness, which holds in its bosom all the details of our lives. That vastness—sometimes referred to as the void—is both spatial and temporal. And the more familiar we are with it, the more at home in it we find ourselves, the better will be our memory, the more reliable our retention, and the clearer will be our thoughts.

The Oracle Exercise

Each person is told that the Oracle will answer for him or her one question. It is the opportunity of a lifetime. One must not squander this opportunity with a trivial question. The participants spend two hours wandering around the ruins of Delphi, which include the Temple of Apollo, visited for the same purpose by the powerful of antiquity.

The answers are provided by the same persons at a different time with similar instructions: You lie on your deathbed. Your most beloved person or persons visit you and ask, "What advice, message, or words of wisdom can you dispense at the end of your life as a parting gift to those you love most?"

The following questions and answers, statements, were written by people whose mother tongue is not English. All questions were addressed to the Oracle. All answers came from the deathbed exercise.

Questions and answers were randomly matched. As an exercise in creativity, the group then tried to read meaning into the randomness. Sometimes that was easy and obvious, and at other times stressful. Sometimes they were genuinely creative. Sometimes there were several interpretations, since the group took collective responsibility for generating them. In no instance were the answer and the question provided by the same person.

The value of the exercise is dual: The material, both questions and answers, comes from within the group. And the exercise is integrated with nature's inviting anthropomorphism. The exercise is structured that it asks life's ultimate questions, and also gives life's ultimate answers. The exercise stimulates creativity and innovation by forcing the mind to make sense of random combinations of living phenomena, contributions, events, and sentences.

Question: As a boy of twenty, I traveled around Spain and stayed for some time in a small fishing village. Late one evening I was sitting on a high cliff overlooking the sea; behind me a few small white houses were clinging to its side. The village was asleep, but there was a faint light in one window. As I sat looking at the lights of the fishing boats and the moon glittering in the sea, I suddenly heard from the lit window a man saying his evening prayers: "Ave Maria, gratia plena . . . ." I was instantly filled with an emotion of utmost solemnity, more so than in any church or other holy place. I am not a Catholic, perhaps not a Christian, but ever since that moment that Hail Mary has followed me. I say it to myself every day and sometimes I pray for something. Surprisingly enough, my prayers have been heard, although my use of Hail Mary can be regarded as blasphemous, since I mostly use it as a mantra. So now my question:

Shall I see this as a sign of God's will? And, more importantly, shall I follow my thought to work for the Good, trying to do something for mankind, rather than to devote my efforts to the business goals of my clients?

Answer: Never hesitate to do what is important to you or what you want to do. Do not let things like age, money, distance, or excessive difficulties stop you. These things are of earthly nature and can be overcome. You never regret what you have done; you regret what you did not do.

Interpretation: Yes! Do it! Go for it! Your life has been good so far. Do not betray your true destiny now.

Question: Why does personal development hurt so much?

Answer: Beware of the question. The answer to the correct question is there already. Only *you* dare put the question.

Interpretation: In the exploration of the pain of the question lies the answer. The answer is to be found in deepening one's experience of the question, the agony, the anxiety, the loneliness, the depression, the anger and the guilt. An answer is no answer. The exploration of experience feels like a solution. The question is a personal inquiry; it does not have a universal or a generic answer.

Question: What is my task or role on the earth?

Answer: Regardless of what happens, (a) you have unlimited resources within you to cope with pain, disappointments, and obstacles, and (b) be courageous to face fear and danger. When you get to know fear and danger, they lose their power.

Interpretation: The question is not answered directly. The answer merely says that you have the strength to meet all obstacles. The implication is that the obstacle to answering the question can also be met. The question is turned back directly to you. Do not ask; you are capable of answering it yourself!

Fulfill your potential (resources). Above all, you have the capacity to overcome the obstacles in the way to fulfilling your potential.

Question: What is the ultimate nature of man?

Answer: Risk integrity at all times.

Interpretation: Aristotle wrote that man is a rational animal. This famous definition needs to be corrected to read that man is an animal that can risk being moral and therefore having integrity. Man is a moral animal. What makes humans human is not their capacity to think, to laugh, or what have you, but their capacity and willingness to think *morally*. The capacity to make moral choices— to be just, fair, democratic, respectful, egalitarian, principled, even to be imprisoned or to do die for one's choices, is the specific difference, what is unique and special, in human nature. Here is another person's question-and-answer.

Question: From where to where do you bring me, my body, my life?

From where to where do you take me, my thought?
Which depth shall you see, my feeling?
Which heights shall you reach?
Where do you bring me, my word?
My action, where do you lead me?

You are fast like a flash, like lightning, but you stay forever.
You wonder! Thanks for every second that I live!
You wonder! Thanks for every time that I meet another soul!
A twin in this empty but full universe.
Your childhood, your youth, your time of adulthood.
You—everything in one—you divine human being, thank you!

From where to where? I ask myself,
and I get answers every second.

Because every feeling, every thought,
every word and every action,
all of you create the subjective platform
around which the ongoing universe slowly turns.

Answer: Be patient with your kids and support your friends.

Interpretation: Both are deeply true of this person: he has a seriously handicapped child, who in his words "taught him the meaning of love." And that child has required infinite patience. He is also one of the most helpful and facilitating persons one will ever meet.

The universe answers as he has lived: devote yourself to your children. Learn from them and from your relationship with them. Furthermore, your destiny is to help make things happen. The seminar was made to happen in great measure by him.

Facilitate the creation of important events. Support others in order to create value. Leadership is the desire to serve.

Question: How do I find total love?

Answer: My dear daughter: Give yourself time to listen to your inner voice, and obey it! Because it is the voice of God speaking to you. You might prefer to phrase it, "Follow your intuition or your gut feelings." That is OK. But be sure to spend enough time with your inner self. Seek stillness and solitude from time to time, if possible in contact with a beautiful landscape. And listen to that voice; it will always tell you the truth.

Krishnamurti said, "You have been led since the beginning of history, and look where it has brought you!" So get rid of the prejudices imposed on you by man's stupidity and seek the truth within!

Interpretation: The person who wrote the question has had, by curious coincidence, severe problems with his daughter. At the same time, he felt that it was she who taught him the meaning of integrity, strength, guts, independence, freedom, and determination. One of his solutions was to yearn for the solitude of the monastic life. The message of the answer is, As your daughter went through an existential crisis of terrifying proportions she also contacted her innermost isolated center for integrity and for strength. It is from that vantage point that you will succeed in your striving for true love.

Question: Did my father ever love me?

Answer: Seek love, seek the whole, the total love. Let life grow out of it. Stick together. Have patience, be generous, give of yourself, have strength, be brave, have courage. Life is a gift.

Interpretation: This already painful question becomes even more painful as one reads the "answer." The answer is that the question is the right question. But rather than to find out for sure, yes or no, wisdom lies in experiencing the need for love ever so much more intensely!

Yes, your father did love you, but in his own way. But it is only through your own love, generosity, and courage that you will find the way. Consider these points:

- A psychological or historical answer is not enough. Do not be deceived by false prophets. Listen to your inward demands. You are what you yourself make of yourself and not what the love of others, or its absence, make of you.
- The question asks for a formula. (If my father loved me then I can be fulfilled.) There is no formula.
- Follow your own intuition and you will be worthy of love.
- Total love is possible only if you open your heart to the eternal. In the eternal you find God.
- Do not ask, for life is a gift. Follow your own intuition and you will become and be worthy of love. Your father's history with you will then have nothing to do with it.
- Do not be a victim's victim; break the chain.
- Yes, he loved me, for he gave me the gift of life—which is the supreme act of love.

Question: How can I handle people I love leaving me?

Answer: Look for love. Fight for love. See to it that you get love and give love. See to it that you love yourself tenderly.

Interpretation: Be authentic. Be demanding. Be more concerned with how you love others than with how others love you. Be centered.

Question: My question is hidden deep in the valley of my inner landscape and it is urgent to climb up the mountain to reveal it through the physical pain of reaching the Oracle.

Answer: You have infinite capacities and equal responsibilities to live life to its fullest.

Interpretation: There is no visible question. I cannot find it. I lost it. I must strain to reach the heights in order to find it.

Do not be afraid to pose the question. You have both the capacity and the responsibility to raise the true question.

To live life fully is to know what questions to raise.

Question: How should I dare live out my weaker "me"?

Answer: There is no way back. One has to live.

Interpretation: Do not stop and look back. Keep going. Follow the Wallenda factor (do not question, do not doubt, move forward).

Accept and reflect. Do not hesitate to show the weaker side. Show your whole self.

Leadership is the decision to move forward even though you are weak. There is no time to stop and repair the weakness. Continue to move right on!

Question: How can I be a good human being?

Answer: Know thyself, my child!

Meet your shadow and your sun!

They always change, you must therefore meet them often.

Then give this wholeness to other people.

And the gift that you will get back

will often be great and rich.

Interpretation: This appears to be a straight, direct, and literal response.

Question: Many relationships have disappeared around me and after a long time of sorrow and crises, I begin to feel freedom. It is an opportunity to do new things. I have my children to care for and support. Otherwise I am free. What shall I do? I have one wish, and it is to go abroad. How can I find a solution to that? To bring my children abroad and support us?

Answer: Do not "force" yourself to like something that you really dislike, just because you feel dependent on other people or on one other person.

Be always true to yourself and trust that that will give you strength and friends. Always seek within you what you want to do with life and do not blame others if it is does not turn out that way.

Interpretation: You did not want the lost relationships to begin with.

Claim your freedom to strengthen your old and your new friendships, your responsibility for your children, and your plans to go abroad.

You have the answers and the inner strength to make them come true. You have no more excuses.

Question: How can I achieve real leadership qualities?

Answer: During my life I have experienced the importance to be open to, to listen to, to understand, and to respect the thoughts, emotions, and views of other people. In this way, other people have respect for mine.

Interpretation: Be a good listener. And if you already are a good listener then you already have good leadership qualities. For the role of a leader is to know how to serve.

Question: Will I be faithful in my marriage?

Answer: Try to be yourself. Be yourself. Give much love. Take care.

Interpretation: Be honest and truthful. That will solve all problems. And truthfulness means a two-tier honesty: say what you think, but also understand what you think.

Question: Dear Oracle! While sleeping by the olive tree I thought of the following. How to improve my sensitivity to respond emotionally to the feelings of other people and avoid being misinterpreted for being arrogant.

Answer: Develop a philosophy of life of your own. Clarify for yourself what is of real value for you and be glad of what you have.

Interpretation: To the degree that you are clear about your own philosophy you will also be clear to other people.

Others misunderstand you only because you misunderstand yourself.

Question: The meaning of life is to find reality. Oedipus was born to kill his father and to marry his mother, and then, as a blind man, use the rest of his life to pay for what he has done. Reality is what he has done. But what is the *meaning* of that life and of my life?

Answer: Love is the meaning of life. Whenever you think of me, I am with you.

Interpretation: The answer corrects the question. It changes it from reality to love. The only reality is love.

If reality is fatalism, then life is absurd. The answer is to go back to love. In other words, atheistic existentialism is answered by Christianity.

Love sets you free and makes you understand.

Question: I asked myself at the temple site, "What do I want most of all to happen to me before I die?" And so the question for the Oracle came to me as follows. "How should I fight my fear—or overcome it or live through it—so that it does not govern my actions?"

Answer: Be yourself and do what you believe in.

Interpretation: Do not fight your fear. You are your fear. Risk intensifying your fear by acting on your beliefs.

The Asklepius Exercise

At Epidaurus, in the Peloponnesus and near Argus, there is a temple to the god Esculapius (in Greek, Asklepius), where ancient Greeks and Romans went for healing. It was a place of snakes, for their venom was used as antidote, hence the caduceus as the symbol of medicine.

We asked the participants of the seminar to go there, in fantasy, for healing. Their first task, before meeting the physicians at the temple, was to create a vision for themselves of their future—both short and long range. This would symbolize their condition of health.

Their second task, when seeing the physician, was to ask for a diagnosis: Why has this vision not yet been accomplished? What are the obstacles to the realization of my vision? This is a search within the unconscious, into assumptions which prevent one's self-realization. Here are examples: I am an only child; my parents have no interest in me; I am the youngest child in a large family; I have no home; I have no rights; I am always number two; I must compete, win, have will power, be tough, fight; I know I can never succeed, I therefore do not try; I should have been a boy instead of a girl; I am weak, or ugly, or inferior, etc. Some of these assumptions may then be isolated as representing the unconscious obstacles to fulfillment.

The third task is medicine—to get a cure, therapy, a prescription, an action plan, something to carry back with them and something to do. All of that in order to carry out the vision.

These projects accomplished, the participants join in groups of three and read their vision-diagnosis-medicine log to each other. The rule is to listen actively—show interest and stimulate further explanation.

Then participants are asked to draw a picture with markers on a large sheet on paper to represent either one or all of their first three tasks.

Finally, these pictures are hung on the walls of the seminar room and each participant rises to give a brief description and explanation of his or her picture. The vision is thus developed four times.

You can do that yourself, in fantasy, and with friends—or in reality.

Transformation

Moving into the realm of pure consciousness—as opposed to the realm of the objects of consciousness—changes how objects or the world appear to us. When consciousness is riveted on its objects, then the world is real, the region of action and commitment. However, when we look upon the looking, when the object of our look is consciousness proper and not its objects, then the world itself changes. And it changes from the zone of action to the zone of observation. We now see the world as phenomenon only. The world does not change. But the meaning we ascribe to it does. When we now thus see the world as phenomenon only, we are afforded the opportunity to think of new arrangements, to uncover new patterns, and to sense perceptions which before eluded us. This is one of the secrets of creativity and innovation.

To see the world, not in the practical attitude, where we are selective, but through aesthetic intelligence, gives rise to new perceptions—that are fostered by modern art. We then see what is, not what we are accustomed to see. The richness of reality is enough to provide us with maximum opportunities for being creative. And best of all is that any discovery is real, since we have before us reality in its pure and pristine form. There is little danger of fantasy or delusion. Error is a function of interpretation. Truly uninterpreted experience is truly such, is also error-free.

The best way to illustrate this point is with modern art, which, by distorting our meanings, brings us in contact with experience, pure, as it was before the meaning-ascriptions of our minds worked it over. These distortions are not bad: they are not true, just practical—that is all.

These exercises in loosening the hold that consciousness has on its specific objects and constructs, this freeing of human awareness,

should increase intelligence and creativity, innovation and imagination, sufficiently to show results quickly in both business management
and marketing. Transcendental intelligence enhances the other forms
of intelligence, including motivational and team, both central to
business, so that even while it may be derided and ignored, it is still
valuable.

What is Consciousness?

The best metaphor for consciousness is black (ultraviolet) light,
which activates and renders visible fluorescent colors. Black light
exists but is invisible. Black light makes visible a world of colors
and shapes not visible under white light, sunlight. So does consciousness light up the world for us.

The fluorescent colors are not placed on the paper by the black
light. They exist independently of the black light. But the light
brings them to life; they could not be noticed without black light directed at them. The world is similar. It exists independently of consciousness. Consciousness does not create the world. But there can be
no awareness of the world without a consciousness that brings it out
(the word "existence" comes from the Latin and means "to stand out").

The world of consciousness is thus divided into at least three
regions: consciousness itself, as light that shines upon the world and
makes it visible; the real world, invisible to the eye; and the visible
world, which results from the interaction between the rays of consciousness and the dark and distant external world.

But we must expand on the metaphor. Consciousness not only
makes the world visible; it also organizes it for us. And that is more
than light does. There is no non-human metaphor to clarify this.
Only the eye will serve. For to organize is to create, and that ability
defines a human being, and no one else—except, of course, God.

A good sense of the transformational powers of transcendental intelligence, the powers of constitution of consciousness, can be found in
the American philosopher Don Ihde's brilliant book, *Experimental
Phenomenology*.

WHAT IS IT?

The above picture can be perceived—and that does not mean *con*ceived alone, but both *con* ceived and *per* ceived—in at least three fundamentally distinct ways: a "headless robot," a "dead-end hallway," and a "truncated pyramid." There is of course much more. But there are only three fundamental ways, all different, of perceiving this picture—although the interpretation of each of these perceptions may vary, for it is only limited by the extent of the imagination.

In order to see these three objects, transcendental intelligence instructs consciousness to (a) see the world as flat, upon which the headless robot appears. But if we transform the world (b) to be "pushed out," and the space of the figure is pushed away from us at its center (so that were we to see the space from the other end it would appear to be a protuberance or mountain), then we see a dead-end hallway. And if we now (c) "suck in" the space of the figure, then we see a truncated pyramid, a monument with a flat top.

In each case we transformed the transcendental deep structure of space. We could conduct similar thought experiments with time. Time can be fast; time can be slow; time can be still. There is another way in which transcendental intelligence can transform the deep structures, and that we have already done. It is to name the object. And as we name it, consciousness adjusts its space to accommodate the requirements of the new definition. That changes our perception.

When we now are concerned with transforming intelligence to the genius power level of performance and ethical action, we see immediately how we can train consciousness to expand itself and fulfill some of its more extraordinary possibilities. Herein lies a key to creativity. And if we are smart, we can find ways to make it work for us.

Thus, consciousness perceives and constitutes; but it constitutes first and then perceives what it has constituted. This is true in at least the logical if not in the temporal order. There is objective reality, that is the figure subject to various interpretations. And then there is the perceived figure, which is one of the three mentioned. The latter we call, in ordinary language, the object, for we work with it every day. Finally, we have the conceived, conceptual, or thought figure, which is an act of the rational intellect. Our mind's capacity for constitution, perception, reality formation, and object creation makes possible the transformation to the genius and power levels.

These insights are critically important for utilizing and developing the transformative powers of transcendental intelligence. How do we know all this? By direct inspection. Look at your experience, examine your consciousness. There are two forms of knowledge: immediate and mediated. "I have a headache" is immediate, direct, given knowledge. "I have a brain tumor" is mediated, inferential, indirect knowledge. The former is a raw datum, the latter is a constructed datum. The former is close to error-free; in the latter error can creep in.

When you study your consciousness, look at your own awareness. Then you are using your mind in a fundamentally different way from how it functions every day. You no longer look at the world, you are no longer conscious *of* something; rather you now look at your looking, you look at your consciousness as a consciousness *of* the world. To be able to do this is called technically the transcendental leap. It is the epoche; it is the act of reflection, the posture of non-attachment. In other words, there are two ways of perception. Consciousness may perceive an object—this is called the natural attitude—or it may perceive itself—this is known as the transcendental attitude.

This is the ultimate source of the power of our knowledge of inner reality. And that is the realm of both reason and intuition. Reason gives us the mathematical sciences, and intuition provides us with our spiritual insights and inspirations. Thus, the transcendental turn, which gives us transcendental intelligence, is a major key to transformation of mind through deep structures to the genius-power level.

The key is to develop the power to instruct consciousness to express its potential. Consciousness is both active and passive. The first is will and the second, perception. We can make a commitment to either mode of being at any time. We can develop the powers of our transcendental intelligence to be passive and accepting. Let us draw an example from art. In Impressionism, the artist records uninterpreted phenomena and both expresses and arouses our wonder at the "wall of experience" that extends before us. We open our souls to receive through the work of art the mystery of being.

We find the same attitude in the spirit of pure science:—it is to allow nature to tell us what and who she is.

We can also develop the powers of transcendental intelligence to exercise control and achieve command over our perceptions. The power of positive thinking, will power, self-discipline, auto-suggestion, inspiration by the charismatic example of others, and ascetic practices are but some illustrations of the power of our integrated intelligences have for managing the deep structures.

We furthermore face the conflict between what we experience as our true "nature"—the one true fit—and what we experience as our possibilities—the horizons available to our intelligences.

This is perhaps the key issue in counseling. A client comes in with a diminished ego. There are two different ways to attempt to reconstruct it. One, existential and natural, is to treat it like a tree which has been cut off, and through the tender administration of water, sunlight, warmth, humidity, and fertilizer allow it to turn green again and eventually express itself in flower and fruit. The other, essentialist, is to take out the stump by the roots and replace it with a plastic replica. The first is low in cost but high in commitment. The latter reverses the proportions of the recipe.

Do we have a natural sense of self? Or is our sense of self invented? If so, by whom? How much control do we have over the invention of our sense of self? What is the effect of our environment? How much freedom is good for us? And how does one go about answering these overwhelming questions? We need the genius-power level of performance and ethical action to answer these questions and make real their answers.

How to Acquire Transcendental Intelligence

Transcendental intelligence in business can be taught by presenting it in four installments: theory, examples, exercises, and action plans.

The theory's purpose is to explain (1) the difference between the natural or the practical attitude and the reflective, reflexive, contemplative, spectatorial, or observational attitude. (2) This conscious act is named non-attachment. The theory emphasizes (3) the radicalness of this conscious act, this step of consciousness, this transformation from consciousness to self-consciousness. It underscores (4) the importance of that step, for it is the opening to our inwardness, to the distinctively human. As the word self-consciousness suggests, it is also an emotional state of embarrassment. In addition, the theory points out that (5) reflexivity is an infinite regress. Finally, the theory helps us understand that inner and outer space-time are similar phenomena. Not surprisingly, (6) the language of inner space-time, logic, mathematics, and geometry, is similar to the language of outer space-time, physics, astronomy, and cosmology. That is why an apt metaphor for the transcendental ego, the infinite regress buried within the ego, is the black hole of astronomy and physics.

The transcendental ego is the ultimate point of departure for consciousness. It is the point within me where all awareness starts and from where it all radiates. The problem with that point is that it is inaccessible. At this moment, we can always think further back into the origins of our consciousness, towards the source of the beam of light that is our awareness, our looking, our vision. This neverending backwards movement into the source of the light of our consciousness is called an infinite regress. I am conscious, and I am conscious that I am conscious. And I am conscious of the fact that I am conscious that I am conscious. I can see, and I can think that someone watches me seeing. I can further think that someone is seeing the person who sees me. And this regression has no end.

This concept is replicated in physical or external space in the phenomenon of the black hole, which, likewise, absorbs all light and all objects; they accelerate inward, but never reach the center of the black hole. How did physicists derive the metaphor if not from the intuited structure of consciousness itself?

There is great power in these descriptions of consciousness. Business must begin to experiment with this method of increasing intelligence and enhancing creativity—ultimately to the benefit of ethical commitments.

In order to understand the relation between transcendental intelligence and the genius-power level of performance and ethical action, we must explore the examples of religious conversions and the new theories in physics.

St. Paul's vision on the road to Damascus is as clear an example of religious conversion as one might find.

Another example is religious mysticism. The monastic vows create a way of life congenial to paradigmatic conversion or transformation. The vows of non-attachment are (a) to give up sexual desire, which is the vow of celibacy; (b) to give up the desire for ownership of property, which is the vow of poverty; (c) to give up the need or desire for self-affirmation or self-assertion, which is the vow of obedience; and (d) to give up the pride in one's name by changing it upon entering an order. The statement of St. Anselm mentioned earlier, *credo ut intelligam*, ("I believe *so that* I may understand") shows how transcendental intelligence transforms the perceptions of the mind: only through a leap of faith can the transformation occur that reveals, through the deep structures, the genius-power level.

Examples from physics include Relativity Theory developed in response to the velocity of light problems pinpointed by the Michelson-Morely experiment and the earlier brilliant breakthroughs in astronomy of Copernicus and Kepler, stimulated by the increasing and unworkable complexity of the Ptolemaic theory of epicycles. For physics appears to be the study of external consciousness, whereas religion covers inner space. Transcendental intelligence, through the deep structures, integrates the two into one thrust of ethical greatness.

An exercise can help. Each transcendental intelligence-based deep structure session should start with meditation. This meditation, which reveals to the mind its transcendental structure, must become a permanent mind set. The meditation clarifies the truths of the theory of the nature of consciousness.

The meditation consists in imagining that inner space-time is like outer space-time. (In this theory, this is not a fantasy but a truth.) And all that space-time exists within the cranium—which also happens to be true. In this meditation we expand the cranium as far as it will go, as far as the imagination will permit it to stretch. We expand it backwards from the eyes and from the face, so that the distance from our perceptions of the world—from the objects of the external world—is increased. We elevate the inner eye; we retract the inner eye. We increase the distance from the point of observation to the point observed. And the latter—the points observed—could remain external objects or they could translate themselves into inner objects. Ideas then become the objects surveyed by the retracted inner eye. The geographer's photographic satellite becomes the relevant metaphor. The higher we go, the more vast the vision and more obvious the patterns. We need a helicopter to find a fugitive. We need to retract and elevate the inner eye to discover new ideas. The elevation of the inner eye divulges new patterns and new ideas. It enables us to shift our vision sideways, to achieve lateral vision. We develop the spiritual satellite and photograph the geography of our ideas. Our memories improve—for we rediscover lost, misplaced, or hidden ideas. We achieve increased clarity of inner vision, enhanced illumination of the inner landscape, greater resolution and detail, and improved perceptions of old and new patterns.

Distraction is a problem. A genius is the mind who can sustain this meditation for long periods of time, without distraction and without interruption, and who has the facility to write down descriptions of these inner landscapes. That requires the skill to write almost unconsciously, virtually automatically, for to express oneself laboriously or clumsily sabotages the entire detaching and meditation process.

The next step is to develop action plans for invoking transcendental intelligence to work with the deep structures.

First, acquire knowledge about the problem and about possible solutions. Get the data. Saturate the mind with information. Then incubate the information by distracting the mind with other activities: sports, music, sleep, travel, games, conversation. In this stage, we attempt to titrate the information into the unconscious. Many deliberate steps can be taken to facilitate this. Fantasy, guided daydreams, help. Think of the knowledge as heavy water resting on a lake bed and percolating into an underground reservoir.

The next step is illumination, intuition. We must be alert to spurts from the unconscious that suggest innovations. We tend to ignore these subliminal illuminations. We must train ourselves to attend to them and record them. Some appear in dreams, and some while we are awake.

Memory seems to be assisted by expanding one's transcendental intelligence. What fades from memory does not vanish but dims. It becomes much more distant and smaller, almost microscopic. But a clear mind, a purified transcendental intelligence, can recapture these subatomic particles of recollection from the most distant corners of its inner space and time.

The final step is testing. Whatever ideas appear must be tested. In lateral thinking we use nonsense ideas as catalysts for real ideas. But the virtue of an innovative idea lies in the test.

This action plan is arduous and works only if motivation is high. Transcendental intelligence should not be wasted on trivial matters. The deep structures will work for us only if we enlist them for questions which profoundly captivate our interest.

In this way, by assuming command over the full scope of the field of consciousness, the domain of transcendental intelligence, we can make the most progress towards the genius-power level.

A central characteristic of transcendental power is the capacity to think for oneself. This talent is most closely related to the principle of non-attachment. Genius-power-level leaders are only partially "in" the discussion that lies immediately before them. They are also connected with larger issues, different themes, and distant worlds.

For example, while sitting in a committee meeting and responding to suggestions and views of the people present, the genius-power level leader is also aware of meetings at a higher level of management and of contacts with other leaders at the top level. The ethical leader is in touch at all times with world events, with historical currents. And leadership awareness is in contact with the underlying psychodynamics of the situation, whose specifics may never be uttered. The leadership mind does not allow itself to have its world-view and mode of perception affected or determined by its current milieu.

The leader reacts—or initiates—with responses neither tethered to nor conditioned by the discussion, but from a mental space removed at least partially from the meeting at hand or from the immediate environment. The leader never forgets that he or she is a leader.

This "involvement from a distance," this "engagement with perspective," is not a sign of arrogance but a mark of duty and of responsibility. Thus, if someone says, "We should do A," and the next person says, "No, we should do non-A," then the leader may retort, "This discussion exemplifies the typical waste-of-money syndrome of this company." Then the leader may change the direction of the discussion with the slightly acerbic suggestion, "Why do you think no one has brought up B?" The ability to think independently, to be attentive and alert to the proceedings but not to be seduced by them, is a key mark of the leadership mind.

Related is the ability to step back, to choose to be uninvolved with the current situation, and to ask, "How are we doing?" "Are you getting what you want out of this discussion?" "Are we making progress?" "Could we be doing something better?" These distancing steps or detaching acts of consciousness can help create an atmosphere of breakthrough, of creativity, of advancement, of progress, of mind expansion, of innovation.

The leader is able to remove him or her self from any situation and assess it from the next higher level of awareness. Thus, thinking for oneself, that is, thinking independently of one's surrounding circumstances, being able to evoke other cultures in the mind, other milieus, other experiences, other sets of expectations, other peers, other models, other atmospheres, other metaphysics—and stepping out of the situation and assessing it from the next higher level of awareness, are two key leadership virtues.

Transcendental intelligence touches the ultimate concerns. And they go far beyond business. But to the degree that business makes demands on every one of the intelligences, there can be little doubt that enhancing transcendental intelligence will transform the business of which it is a part.

CHAPTER 19

Transforming
Motivational Intelligence

Think for Yourself

The leader whose personal intelligence profile focuses on motivational intelligence needs more than most a transformation to the genius-power level. Motivational energy leads quickly to confrontation within the organization. For example, in the effective leadership mind, singlemindedness and goal orientation make up one set of characteristics. Motivational leaders always carry with them a list of priorities, not just a list of things to do but a prioritized, hierarchical list. And the list is constantly revised. Only that which gets to the top of the page is really ever done. Many things will never get done. People understand that not everything will get done because it cannot get done. But those who depend on executives to be leaders will acknowledge and appreciate the fact that what is essential will never be neglected.

This mind has an internal gyroscope. Motivational intelligence is self-starting. One can see it even in the walk and in incidental daily activities. The goal is always in mind, like an inner picture which guides the person and which is not removed by adventitious distractions.

This mind is like a jet plane. It flies high as long as it flies fast. Stop its racing, even momentarily, and it will plummet to its destruction.

Such focused awareness can be interpreted and experienced as insensitivity and even rudeness. In this case communication is essential. Let people know you do not reject them, but only that you do first things first. Everyone can benefit from that attitude. Always take out time to acknowledge people for their efforts. But expect them to be mature. A leader surrounds himself or herself with adults, not people who need constant validation and are excessively sensitive.

This apparent rudeness often brings the motivational leader to his or her two-headed nemesis: projection and envy. As these executives fly high, subordinates (and others) increasingly project their own inner needs on them. The primary need of human beings, compensating for their innate impotence, is power. They will believe that the executive, their boss or their boss's boss, has far more power than he or she in fact has. This is more often a subjective projection than an objective fact.

Is there a solution? Yes, there is: we must be truthful and honest with ourselves and with others—truthful in the two dimensions of human consciousness. We must be truthful in the way in which the animals are conscious—the natural consciousness. It is the innocence of Adam and Eve. Experience and accept the world as it is. Be it. And we must also be truthful in the way only human beings can be truthful—the reflective or the reflexive consciousness. Be truthful about the present moment.

This moment of truth is the ethical imperative to act. Remember the three steps to transformation: (1) Experience the pain of the confrontation. (2) Intensify the pain to an anxiety involving deep structures. (3) Choose to allow multiple intelligences and deep structures to merge and unify in a felt shift of transformation, "seeing an old landscape with the new eyes."

The security of motivationally intelligent leaders lies not in the love and the loyalty of their employees and friends, nor is their validation based on a personal commitment—such as to a child or a patient. These leaders' validation from others is based instead on the persistent promise—often more implicit than explicit—that their success will rub off on others, is contagious. Thus, once the mantle of leadership falls and the power is gone, this type of executive will quickly find himself or herself without friends. But the need for charismatic contact and security keeps the motivational mind going intently in its unswerving direction. People become attached to transformational leaders of this kind of because of their aura of success, not because of their warm and endearing qualities. People need leaders. And success rubs off. Leadership is a special substance, much desired, elevating, energizing, suggestive of power.

It may be helpful to draw a few parallels. The motivational intelligence relishes its inner clarity, the freedom it enjoys from the environment, and its skill at selective perception. These are aspects of transcendental intelligence.

The marketing intelligence quickly adapts to changing circumstances—like the computer on an airliner, which adjusts instantaneously to changes in the wind and to the weight distribution within the aircraft.

The motivational intelligence is always on the move. It is always going someplace. It is always active. It does not rest—except when out of sight and private.

Team intelligent executives know how to use people and how to work through people. They have a sense of the value of other people; they know their need for other people, and they understand their own limitations, which give rise to their need for other people. They are not embarrassed nor are they self-conscious in saying, "I can't do it; I need someone to help me with it, or to do it for me." Nor does that make them feel inferior.

The motivational intelligent executives are extremely focused on tasks, on what needs to be done—to the exclusion of irrelevant information and distracting data. This means a high power of concentration, which is also a characteristic of transcendental intelligence.

Let us look at an example. The Garland Packaging Company took off time for a weekend of reflection not only for upper management, but for the entire organization, including secretaries, drivers, and cooks. The idea was to provide an uplifting experience for a few days and to continue the spirit engendered with low cost but effective follow-up programs.

Top management needs team intelligence to set up such a two-and-a-half-day program. For concern with developing people follows team intelligence. However, since the objective of the workshop was to challenge employees to take personal responsibility, motivational intelligence was the theme of the workshop. The essence of the program was to challenge leaders to energize themselves, take personal responsibility for their own enthusiasm, and to be spontaneously and autonomously creative.

But such programs also exemplify several other intelligences. Using poetry and music and art to present ideas shows aesthetic intelligence at work. The arts can be communicate more clearly than mere logical words.

Most organizations develop a list of complaints no different from the grievances aired by the Garland Packaging Company. They can be summarized as follows:

Difficulty in communication or flow of information. People claim consistently that they do not know what the rest of the organization is doing. This leads to duplication, to the wrong kind of work, and to general frustration--because workers feel discounted, ignored. They do not have their existence acknowledged. If they do not know what is going on in the rest of the organization, employees do not feel themselves part of the larger organization and of its purposes. Their work is less meaningful than it would be if they could see it in context.

Poor communication can be attributed to (a) the size of the organization, (b) its fast-paced mode of operation, (c) the rate of change required. And change is fast and constant, as Heracleitus already contended six hundred years before Christ, because the market which the business addresses is unpredictable and changes direction. But change also is connected with the deeper social and cultural trends, the transformation of old products and services into new meanings. And the sluggish mind finds it difficult to make the necessary accommodation.

The problem of communication, legitimate as it may be and deserving of concerted action as it certainly is, is nevertheless also an outgrowth of the structure of reality, of the nature of things.

Another concern or class of complaints is the lack of clarity. And that also refers to at least three areas: (a) Job description or role definition (what exactly am I supposed to be doing in this organization? Is this really the job for my department? Why are they doing our work?). (b) Reporting relationship, direction of accountability, the precise nature of the organization chart (who is my boss?). And (c) the direction, mission, or vision of the larger organization or company.

A final generic class of concerns is the inadequate (or nonexistent) utilization of individual talents, skills, and creative potentials. People complain that they are underused, that they have limited opportunities to develop, that they cannot adequately demonstrate and express what they can do best—that for which they could receive the greatest recognition, and what would give them their greatest fulfillment. And that makes it difficult to make their maximum contribution to the organization.

Since these are typical complaints, it is important to give them what might be considered a generic response.

The response, or the manner in which we might deal with these issues, consists of two parts. One is to enumerate the facts—the facts about human existence, about the human condition, about human nature, about the manner in which human beings exist in this world and the way in which they are able to cope with life or redeem the value of existence in a difficult world.

You think you now live in chaos? You will never get your act together! Things will never be really different around here, because they cannot be different. And that is not because you have a problem but because what you perceive to be the problem is really your solution, and that that what you think will be a solution will in fact create a series of needless problems.

A fast-paced, exciting, exacting, superior, and visionary organization, driven by a motivational intelligence, will always be chaotic. It is like the situation with anxiety. We believe that it is a disease, when in fact it is a natural and even a healthy aspect of the human condition. As a result, we administer tranquilizers, we disrupt nature and well being, call that disruption health, and are puzzled as the organism gradually returns to its natural healthy state. We believe instead that we are confronted with a recurring chronic illness. And the cycle repeats itself: we continue to treat anxiety, until either treatment or life itself gives up and ends.

This confrontation with reality—the reality of ambiguity, of chaos, of confusion, of the mystery of being—and with our inability to ever bring about or even to envision the possibility of a final order, produces intense anxiety and leads to excruciating frustration. But such a conviction is in fact ultimate philosophical realism and as such must serve as the foundation of any authentic existence.

It is important not to accept any problem as prima facie real. It is always tempting to join in the set of consensually made assumptions. Even the most armored, prepared, or guarded souls can fall into these presupposition traps. That leads them to engage consultants who develop complex reorganizational schemes designed to meet the specific problems. This is fine and good, and might even work. But it is also highly convoluted. Is there not a simple way?

Reorganizational schemes do not work without a prelude of proper attitudes. And as attitudes change, and are maintained in being with follow-up commitments, the employees themselves will create an atmosphere of determination and creativity where they will think up and implement detailed pragmatic solutions—by themselves and for themselves.

Specifically, to expect clear role definitions, clear job assignments, and clear lines of responsibility—where all contingencies are decided in advance—is mostly an illusory hope. It is not even fair to call these expectations hopes, for should they ever be met, the ensuing bureaucracy would be so oppressive and stultifying that the staff would wish it had never raised the issue in the first place. Motivational transformation turns the problem into a solution—because the solution was the problem. The motivationally transformed organization, and that means its individual members, must move from a posture of dependency to one of autonomy. The organization must be willing to support a participatory, free, independence-oriented employee population, and must be willing to give up old-fashioned bureaucratic and authoritarian modes of management. That is a well-established principle in much of American business today.

What is not so readily established is that the decision for individual responsibility rests on the employees themselves and is often not related to management policies. Moreover, even if management wants autonomous and creative employees, there is little they can do. How do you help a person become autonomous? What can you do to help a person become more independent, more of a self-starter? The answer is simple: nothing! For to assist autonomy is to foster dependency.

This is the meaning of greatness, to grasp and to seize one's innate autonomy. Its rewards are personal rather than parental. That is to say, the final rewards are not from colleagues, supervisors, managers, or presidents. The final rewards are self-validating. The ability to judge oneself and feel satisfaction in autonomy comes only with maturity. At a too tender age, that self-assurance would be rationalization. But for the experienced person, the knowledge of true values is a concept that makes emotional sense. The issue cannot be forced. The rewards of good work are self-respect. And in the end, I and I alone validate my own sense of self-respect. This is not to say that what people think does not affect me or that it does not mean a great deal to me. It does. Being susceptible to others' opinions may be fortunate or not, but we also know that mature individuals can transcend what others think of them.

Employees must recognize the limitations—personal as well as professional and organizational—of their bosses. Not only are bosses limited in their personal strength, they are also restricted in turn by their own superiors, by the economics of the company, by the marketplace, and by the number of employees, and the complexity of the problems they must manage. To recognize that authority figures and parent surrogates are weak, have faults, and are limited is a powerful step toward maturity, autonomy, and independence—true not only of work but of life in general.

Correlatively, bosses have as one of their critical functions to serve as model for members of the organization. That is a hallmark of true leadership.

Accountability is an important sign of maturity. To demand of employees that they be autonomous is to ask for mental health. People must feel themselves accountable regardless of who is at fault for what in any particular situation. To be accountable is to be effective; it means to focus on outcomes and not on fault-finding—even though faults are there and people are guilty. The focus is on results, because that is what is wanted, not on what in actual fact serves as excuses for failure. But it is only we ourselves who believe in these excuses, and only temporarily at that. And people who hold themselves accountable are not always rewarded or acknowledged either; in fact, not infrequently they are reprimanded for what should specifically be their most valued accomplishment. That is unjust; but dwelling on it interferes with outcomes.

People must understand the meaning of being a self-starter, a self-energizer. We can assume personal responsibility to motivate ourselves, to become creators in difficult situations. This produces anxiety. But the key to being human is to understand that we have the God-given capacity to bring about a state of being, a situation, a reality, a condition, out of nothing. This mystery must be universally understood. It is the heart of motivational intelligence. Remember, God made man in His image; and God is a creator. To be human therefore is to identify with our capacity for *exnihilation*, to create something out of nothing. We are the source of our own energy. And that is to understand the mystery of the will.

There are at least two types of normal personal problems or realities that interfere with good job performance. Roughly speaking, one applies to the young and the other to the middle-aged. The young have problems because of the fragmentation of their lives.

The young do not identify easily with any of their projects—the ones on the job included—because there is not enough energy, time, or attention to devote to them all. Four different groups of forces pull on our lives: career, job, ambition; home, family, relationships, sexuality; recreation, entertainment, fun, relaxation, doing nothing; and personal, spiritual, private needs Those we experience only in total isolation—or with God or our analyst; this is our destiny, our secret meaning, our inner mission.

It is not an exaggeration to say, if we have ideals of excellence, that every one of these life values is so utterly demanding that we must give 200 percent for each in order to get a 25 percent return. The paltry return will always make us feel guilty and inadequate—for that we are—and the effort will always exhaust us—for that is also the truth.

There is no solution to the conflicts. They are real, built into our culture. The usual solution, balance, is a compromise that always fails. For the achievers one wishes to emulate, one's heroes, who achieved a thousand percent (in music, in golf, in drama, in poetry, in business, in politics, in spirituality, in wisdom, and so on.) were daimonic, in that their passion for one of these dimensions totally invaded and possessed all the other corners of theirs souls (see Rollo May, *Love and Will*). When Emerson said that nothing great was ever achieved without enthusiasm, he must have meant that passion achieves, that achievement is a form of excess, not balance or compromise. To compromise with others is acceptable, but to do that with oneself is not. To achieve with passion requires a major, a massive decision, a choice which most people have neither the power nor the courage to make. (Perhaps the resistance is good common sense.) One may have to reach a mature age to find the fortitude to make such potent choices.

On the other hand, when one does reach a mature age (this need not be a number), one develops a sense of what Jung called individuation. One feels integration at a higher level; the conflicts are less real; the anxiety gradually diminishes. One seems to have adapted. Perhaps it is transformation, transcendence, integration, or synthesis instead of compromise.

The final "fact" (personal, emotional, philosophical, psychological) about the above concerns of employees is the need to understand the inwardness of people and of their struggles. When we understand people we appreciate at least two insights or facts about them.

People are mostly irrational. We think they reason, but they mostly feel. We think we see their logic, but they operate mostly out of instinct. We think they are sophisticated, civilized, and cultured, but they are primitive instead, and anthropologists understand them better than logicians. We understand the forces, more powerful than human nature, which seize and rule the souls of many individuals.

But also, we learn to value people as we understand them better. Each person is a universe within, a subjective galaxy, an inward cosmos. We appreciate how each person means well, struggles with his or her particular body, personality, family, and world. We appreciate the richness and the mystery, the complexity and the good intentions, the confusions and the distortions, the twists and the pains of the souls that we get to know better.

And as we see the irrational and the struggle in the souls of our colleagues, many problems simply dissolve themselves "into a dew."

We can view the above as "philosophical facts" regarding the concerns of employees. This should help them attain a perspective which makes these problems manageable.

Ethical Power

What we require is a greatness response, a commitment to choose the ethical imperative. Socrates taught us that this leads to ethical power.

Socrates, in defense of his life, said that the unexamined life is not worth living. How willing and able are you to examine your unconscious assumptions, the suppressed premises of the way you think and live, work and strive, value, and are ambitious? Are you willing to examine the presuppositions behind how you run your business or organization? the assumptions you make about how you perform your job and how you manage?

There are many ways to uncover these assumptions. One is to imagine random nonsense changes and see what associations they stimulate in you. "I should be driving a tractor instead of writing books!" What is good about that? (physical work, exercise, less anxiety); what is bad? (hard work, lack of interest); and what is interesting? (new experiences, new friends, new values, new world-view, new ambitions, concerned with the visible rather than the abstract, fresh air, and so on). Now recheck your values.

Why should we take existence for granted? That is part of the unexamined life. And that leads us to the topic of greatness. We can progress only by asking, Why is there something rather than nothing? why is there being rather than non-being? How can we understand the foundation of the need for greatness in ethics?

Greatness, or ethical excellence, is the philosophic equivalent for the now popular business word "excellence." It is a human being's response to nihilism, to the fear of nothingness, to the threat to values, and to the danger to existence itself.

Nihilism means we are always in the presence—in the sense of background or horizon—of the question of existence itself. Why are there beings rather than nothing? Why does your particular society, with its values and its rules, exist rather than not? Why were you born into your particular circumstances rather than not? What, if any, would be your story if your parents had not met? or had met earlier? or later? or what if the particular sperm that fertilized the egg that became you had been a different sperm cell, or a different egg cell? Why do you exist rather than not? Why are you conscious, of a world and of a self, rather than not? If you come from a family of four children, and if your parents had had only one, would that child have been you? If you are last in a large family, does that mean that your parents had to try to have you, missed several times, kept trying, until finally they had you?

Can you feel your dependency on your physiology and your environment? Do you wonder at the mystery of being and the miracle of existence? the wonder that there is a world when it might be far more logical for there to be nothing at all?

The very contingency of existence requires an ethical power response. The greatness response is that God is a necessary being, a being which cannot not exist, a being that exists by virtue of its own necessity, a being which cannot be conceived as not existing. God possesses "aseity." He is an *existens a se*, a Being who creates Himself. God is said to be *causa sui*, his own cause. And since God made man in His image, these insights and characteristics of God are projections of the eternal questions within our own souls. But "God" as used here can mean many things: the human spirit, human consciousness, human determination, the innermost source of awareness in the ego, and so on. And you are invited to join with that necessary being and say "I am."

Saint Anselm argued in this and similar ways for the existence of God. The truth is that existence is the only miracle, the sole miracle that needs to be. And existence cannot be thought of as not being, even though any individual being within existence is contingent and can be thought of as becoming and going away, being born and dying, being created and destroyed. Not so existence itself, or being, or what theologians would then call God—or even Nature.

Thus, in affirming the genius power level of performance and of ethics in action—in business and elsewhere—you are in fact participating in the most profound project of being itself, of the universe, of the cosmos. This is how your philosophy can deepen the goals of your business. It is the commitment to the courage for greatness.

The genius and power levels of performance and ethical action are your response to nihilism, that is, to the threat of nothingness. Greatness is to stand up to the most severe reality of life, the incomprehensibility of death. We can meet death in four ways. We can believe in immortality (Kant argued that a rational universe cannot give us rational desires, such as love, life, and justice, which it then does not fulfill, without guaranteeing a life hereafter where these values are realized). We can reconcile with death (overcome the fear of it) by finding and fulfilling our destiny. We can live a life of infinite despair. Or we can deny the reality of death, and with it life also.

The power level of ethics is to stand up to the horror of evil. The Nobel Peace Prize has been awarded annually precisely to celebrate the power level of ethics. In 1986 the recipient was Elie Wiesel:

> Shortly after his liberation from a Nazi concentration camp in 1945, a gaunt and grieving survivor made what now seems an uncharacteristic vow. He promised that he would not speak for at least ten years of the horrors he had witnessed. The silence was kept, but when the words finally emerged, they came in a torrent. Novels, essays, speeches and lectures all spoke tirelessly of the need to rescue the Holocaust from the silence of history. Last week Elie Wiesel's words of witness were honored with the Nobel Prize for Peace, which carries with it an award of $287,769.78. From Oslo, the Nobel Committee praised him as "one of the most

important spiritual leaders and guides in an age when violence, repression and racism continue to characterize the
world. Wiesel is a messenger to mankind: his message is one
of peace, atonement and human dignity."

Time, 27 October 1986

The power level of ethics is to stand up to your normal anxiety and
vulnerability. Religion and society (philosophy and organizations)
have tried to cope with these issues—not logically but ritualistically, symbolically, and mythologically. But there are other ways
as well.

The genius-power level of authenticity is to stand up to the confusion of doubt. For any original thought and every step of courage is
contrary to the received opinion and thus in the eyes of the establishment is by definition crazy.

There are as many, and unusual, ways to be great through the
genius power level as there are people. One way is to be a Mozart
who has touched millions with his limpid music and by his short,
agitated, rather innocent life. This kind of an artist sings angeli-
cally, with neither malice nor repression, but from a source of suffering. This kind of ethically powerful greatness is the ideal of pure
innocence. It can be deeply moving, because it lifts us out from the
ordinary, "sinful" region of the world, only to transport us to a realm
of light. It is a gift of grace, neither requested nor earned, often more
a burden than a blessing. It is to be equal to one's fate, whatever the
consequences. It is the innocence-martyrdom syndrome. And to call it
that is not to devalue it. It is the subject matter of much of medieval
philosophy, theology, and art.

Another way of being ethically powerful is through the I-am
experience. The I-am affirmation is in defiance of God; it is the
expression of ultimate hubris. It is the last word in humanism. It is as
dangerous as it is necessary. It shows that man vanquishes God, for
God too has said I am. And there may not be room for two suns in the
sky. But if the I am is only that of God, then the I-am experience is
one of complete submission to the higher power.

There is a third way to be ethically powerful. It is through service. Every person feels unworthy. There is a reason. It is the truth of
human vulnerability. Any sign of character is pretense, for every
strength is but hidden weakness; nothing dressed up to look like
something.

To deal with our nothingness within a threatening universe, and our guilt about it, has been the principal assignment of religion. It is a universal theme. We hide it. And it embarrasses us. Consequently, a person will look after others more than after himself or herself. This is the parenting instinct. It is more important to be of service and to be honored and perceived as worthy, as making a genuine contribution, than it is to profit from selfish gain. The validation we get from others is more convincing than the one we give ourselves—which is often no more than whistling in the dark.

People who feel and act differently, that is, who are selfish, self-seeking, self-centered, and inconsiderate, in actual fact exhibit a reaction-formation against this deeper truth. They follow a bankrupt philosophy because they can see no way out of their profound sense of inadequacy. They ignore the fact that the guilt of vulnerability is normal, that it is the core of the human condition, and that the answer is to live through the experience and welcome its revelations.

The genius-power level of authenticity is the human ethical decision to stand up to evil, to the demonic, to this guilt of vulnerability—to face it, confront it, stare it down.

It was this discovery which was underscored for me on a visit to Crete, for it seemed that the Cretan culture, which meant Minoan as well as Achaean, was mostly a vigorous and dramatic response to the fears occasioned by life itself, by the vagaries of human existence, and by the specifics of the threatening physical and the menacing political environment.

One impression that strikes one is the fear of the projection of human evil; it is something which we might call primitivism. Plato writes, "Zeus bound his own father, Cronos, for wrongfully devouring his own children; and . . . Cronos, in his turn, castrated his father for similar reasons." Medea kills Jason's (of the Golden Fleece) three sons in retribution for her husband's unfaithfulness. Theseus invites his brother to a dinner, and serves him his own children. This begins the curse on the house of Atreus and gives rise to the subject matter of Sophocles' Oresteia Trilogy.

We can see that if Freud is right in theorizing that these are childhood fantasies, then many of our most heinous fears are projections of repressed infantile material. Ancient peoples feared their own unconscious—perhaps the greatest fear of all, for its source remains forever invisible.

A second strong impression one gets is the incredible cruelty and brutal cheapness of life in antiquity—constant warfare, executions, forced conversions, enslavements, slavery, and mass destruction—especially of precious objects and sacred structures. Violence seems almost the sole subject of art, records, writings, engravings, literature, myths, and so on. Even the more advanced Athenian society did not much value the free thinking individual person. This may not conform to history's theory of Greek society, but it is nevertheless the impression which I brought back from my visit. The individual appears to have had meaning and identity only as a member of the state, a citizen, for otherwise, the individual was ostracized—and, like the oyster, abandoned at the bottom of the sea. There still reverberates, however, an incredible vigor, the power of the life-force and the energy of creativity which must have been so clearly alive in those early days. And Nietzsche understood this energy. Life was to be affirmed in spite of the dangers. That is greatness.

One does not get in those islands any real sense of compassion, love, forgiveness, tenderness, or recognition of the absolute sanctity of the person as the basic values of ancient societies. The Judeo-Christian difference is here pronounced. Breathing in that Mediterranean air, one can feel that Saint Paul had something new and important to say.

One senses the people's lack of protection, in antiquity, from natural disasters, that is, tidal waves, earthquakes, storms, diseases, wild animals. The ubiquitousness of violence in the region—geological (earthquakes, storms, and floods) and biological (eat or be eaten), as well as human (cruelty, conquests, enslavements, and other forms of barbarism)—is manifestly a fundamental phenomenon of human history. This is based on or caused by the frailty and vulnerability of the individual human being threatened when confronted with the powers of the masses of humanity. I see the 300,000 Persians marching on Greece, to be met with the unified forces of Hellas—50,000 strong, at Platea, commanded by the Spartan general Themistocles—who desperately needed to protect their vulnerable cities (and wives and children) from the hordes from the East. The Greek victory—brought about by the tactic of slicing the Persians into small pockets of resistance and then annihilating them individually—was in truth wrought out of sheer will power and commitment to greatness, based on the need for the survival of their identity. This the Persians did not need, for they were in a foreign land.

Violence in this context becomes natural and is depicted in the art and literature of the time—and that includes the Bible—without sentimentality.

Adding up all these threats, in the early days of Western civilization, we can understand the intense vulnerablity of human beings and their consequent fears.

As a result of the pervasiveness of fear in antiquity, the social became paramount and the individual minor, even in Athens. And there developed a need and a desire for a strong ruler, the god-king. Identification with that symbol of power gave pride and identity to the fragile and terrified individuals of the population. While standing there in the ruins of the monastery at Arkadi these insights became to me clear as axioms. Athens experimented briefly with individualism and humanism. It put that idea to sleep with the execution of Socrates. And this idea was not revived successfully, culturally until the Renaissance, and not politically until the American and French revolutions.

The genius-power level of performance and ethics is to stand up to these basic human fears. Socrates' way was one path to greatness. Another is through the creation of powerful states or powerful figures within these states, such as the god-king, prominent both in Egypt and in Knossos. But the humanistic way today—evolved through millennia and still in the process of evolution—is the Socratic self-affirmation of the individual.

It is always difficult to assert oneself as an individual. And that seems to have been outright impossible in antiquity. Individualism is inherently superior to theocratic and other autocratic solutions to the problem of the fragility of human existence. And that fragility translates itself into what Paul Tillich calls, in his *The Courage to Be*, the intrinsic unacceptability of a human being in his or her own eyes, not to speak of in the eyes of God. Today, we expect the power of the state to exist for one foundational purpose and one foundational purpose only—and that is the protection of the rights of the individual. But are we as individuals strong enough to bring about the ideal, to fight off the constant threats to it? Here is where greatness comes in.

Becoming transformed to the genius level of performance and the power level of ethics, in short, greatness, is a virtue universally recognized when it exists. We are inspired by it; we become proud as a result of it; and our healthy envy makes us wish to emulate it. Another way of stating this same point is to talk about the concentration of power. People flock to the center of power like moths to a flame and iron filings to a magnet. We see a network of monasteries around Avignon simply because seven popes had their palace-in-exile there. People are attracted to the center of power as the subatomic particles of the sun are attracted centripetally to its gravitational center—and thus produce the intense pressure which becomes the incredible power of the sun's radiation. And it extends well beyond the solar system. These are the psychodynamics that establish a monarchy, that justify it, that make it legitimate, that make it feel good.

The need for worship is an extension of this natural law of the concentration of power—physical as well as social. Even the king at Knossos worshipped privately. Many nations have monuments to greatness—an ontological need for their population. Paris is one example. It is a city devoted to celebrate the glory of France. Another good example is the city of London. By withstanding Hitler during World War II, it represents the power of the will. London has become a symbol for the self-energization of the will to stand up to evil. So was Churchill a symbol. Westminster Abbey and Windsor Castle remind the English of the power and the regal pomp of their nation. In identifying oneself with that power one becomes powerful oneself, and the fact that the power may abuse us does not change its attractiveness. In fact, it gives us a direct experience of its power. Washington, D.C., exists for similar purposes.

Is power authentic? Is the only legitimate power the power of the individual self? Is the power of society, of the state, and of kings but a reminder of the power of God, of nature, of the cosmos? Power can be abused. That means both tyranny—where power is used and not needed—and weakness—where power is needed but not used.

Such toughness and realism are leadership traits. They are also a way of being great, effective ways of standing up to nihilism. That is why for twenty-five centuries Western civilization has drawn its inspiration from Greece. It was a great culture, for it stood up to nihilism. It was a cult of greatness, for it said "I am" to the void.

The key to motivational intelligence is the understanding that a human being cannot be replaced. The actual charismatic and inspiring will of a living human being, the personal one-to-one commitment from one human being to another, the actual I-Thou encounter between two individual and unique throbbing human hearts, the irreplaceablilty of the individual person and of the individual relationship, that is what motivational intelligence is all about.

Insight, techniques, knowledge, theory, all fail. We are here at the existential core, and we must acknowledge that truth, reality, and knowledge are an individual event, in an individual place, at a specific time, generated by a unique act of will, springing from the core of a unique inwardness.

The I Am

If God, the great "I Am," represents a literary or mythological ideal for human existence—and this is true whether one believes in God or not—then the genius level of performance and the power level of ethics can be seen to be universal human aspirations. To the degree that one feels committed to this ideal and makes progress towards such a goal, one is fulfilled. One wants to die having made a maximum effort towards perfection, for in that project lies final happiness.

Excitement, joy, hope are essentially artificial modes of being. They are kept in existence through a miracle. Joy is no more explicable than is existence itself. And if existence is an act of grace, so is joy. What is, philosophically speaking, "natural" is a dark and chill nothingness. What is miraculous is the energy of the sun. What is natural is the void of death; what is miraculous is the will to live, which, always threatened, nevertheless remains defiant.

There is controversy of whether depression and joy—moods in general—are chemically or subjectively caused. The answer is probably both. There is a relationship of reciprocity between mind and matter, a confirmation of Spinoza's "double aspect theory" (mind and matter are two aspects of a unitary substance, two ways of perceiving one thing).

Kierkegaard averred that all life is anxious. Heidegger told us that life is a being-unto-death. Unamuno held that life is tragic. These philosophers have pointed out that life is also depressing. For all our sterling achievements are surrendered inescapably in death.

Only the illusion of the "eternal now," the possibly fraudulent permanence of the present moment, protects us from the logic of suicide.

The ability to give hope under these conditions is the ultimate theme of motivational intelligence. It is an issue of the self-starting, self-energizing dimension of the mind. And that spurt of life and spark of happiness is never mechanical. It is always an individual action, a personal choice, a decision, a *creatio ex nihilo*—a God-like creation out of nothing. That ineluctable fact demonstrates the irreplaceability of a human being. What brings the joy of hope is not a new technique or organizational design, but touching with the finger of insight the creative core of the soul.

Here true leadership comes in. And for that we need courage. Because to start from within a cloud of depression, boredom, and meaninglessness—which is what self-aware people feel (it is the penalty for open eyes)—and then lift oneself out of that with sheer will power, that is the secret of true leadership. Only a human being can do that. Such self-uplifting acts spring from the void of human inwardness, they ascend from the hollow of human subjectivity. Science does not reach this region. Nor does it claim to. Nothing can *cause* this self-uplifting. Nothing can *make* it happen. It is the spontaneous and free decision to be, which, when enacted, is inspired and sublime. To witness the spontaneous act of being is the only miracle one needs in order to penetrate into the deeper reality of the world. And we human beings, at the core of our subjective consciousness, possess that power for self-creation. (That is why in Oriental philosophy there is no distinction between the God that is behind the world and the Self that is behind the ego.)

But even here there are two ways of coming to be: one philosopher says that we have a destiny, and we can discover it, whereas another maintains that we must invent it.

The pervasiveness of human freedom, the control we exert over who we are, can be clarified by tuning in to our unconscious death wish. It is to always ask the same question: what obstacles am I placing in the way of hope and self-fulfillment? What ancient anger lurks in my soul? What pleasure do I derive from self-destruction, from hatred of self, from self-injury? from self-pity? What sweetness does the negative bring?

By making contact with both our will to live and our will to die, we disclose fully the enormous scope of our freedom. For life is not just an instinct to live, nor is death only an instinct to die. Both in the end must be understood as self-willed. We must own that will, take responsibility for it. And when that is recognized, and the non-natural or non-scientific character of human depth is obvious, then we have achieved access to the fullness of the human potential to energize itself. Then we can begin to know something of the greatness released through the transformation to the genius level of performance and the power level of ethics.

The Genius and Power Levels in Action

Let us look at some practical steps.

Act independently. Take the risk. Have faith in and make a commitment to your leadership ability and your creativity, but do it in conscious response to a situation, not in an abstract vacuum. Any situation is made up of external or outer facts, that is, the needs of the organization or the group, and of inner facts, that is, the sensitivities and feelings of the people involved, including yourself.

The obverse of this is to facilitate others to act independently, to be fully themselves. You must expect it—and then accept it. Decisions may not always go your way; but your colleagues will also have the chance to use the fullness of their potential to make you successful.

In sum, this means that you must take full personal responsibility to create a successful outcome given the facts you have before you, given the reality in whose midst you exist. Do you find chaos? Do you find that the chaos is due to other people's incompetence? Fine. Know it. Assign responsibility and blame. But now take the situation in hand as you find it, take it as it is, and be determined to make a success out of it. That is the key. That is the meaning of adulthood, of maturity, of effectiveness, of focusing on outcomes, and of taking responsibility. Think of outcomes and not of excuses. That is the rule of thumb for success.

Will you be praised? Will those who have benefited thank you? Do not expect it: they probably will not. What then? Do not be silent. Expect fairness. Tolerate human frailty. Expect, articulately, that next time it should be different. But be certain you hold up your side of the responsibility and the maturity. For your self-respect demands that the failure of others not lower your own standards.

Remember, contrary to common belief, people are not rewarded for their accomplishments. As a child, your parents and teachers praised and honored you for being diligent at your homework, or attractive, or athletic, or for practicing and performing the piano. But as you grew up and went outside the home you found envy instead. The more you achieve, the more people will try to defeat you. This means that your sources of validation must now be metamorphosed from the outer reality to the inner. You must now learn the art of self-validation. You need to understand and practice, difficult as that may be, the art of loving, supporting, respecting, esteeming, validating yourself—perhaps with the help of one who genuinely loves you.

Here is a dramatic example: Many visitors feel that one of the most moving and inspired monuments in Washington, D.C., thoughtfully executed and in good taste—and one of the most difficult to have designed—is the Vietnam Memorial. Rather than thank and appreciate the architect for devoting her superior instincts to this sensitive task, people maligned and nearly destroyed her.

UP AGAINST THE WALL

In 1981 Yale senior Maya Ying Lin won the competition to design the Vietnam Veterans Memorial, topping 1,420 entries. Since the dedication in 1982, more than 9 million visitors have thronged the Washington Mall site, and a Plexiglas replica of the black marble wall is touring the country. Yet just after the dedication, a disheartened Lin quit her graduate architecture studies at Harvard, and dropped from sight.

Early on, Lin had trouble convincing officials of her right to oversee the project. Some veterans attacked her design as "a degrading ditch" and a "wall of shame." Raised in the "safe, friendly" college town of Athens, Ohio, the young Chinese-American suddenly encountered racial prejudice; "We can't have a memorial by a gook," one vet raged.

Early in 1982, opponents of Lin's design pushed through the addition of a sculpture of combat soldiers and a flag to the memorial. Commuting each week from Harvard, she helped persuade officials to place them at the site entrance, some distance from her wall. Lin's defense of her design was seen by some as elitist indifference to veterans. Hurt by the negative publicity and weary of public curiosity, she impulsively had her never-before-cut hair cropped boyishly short. Finally, after staying up all night in a Washington hotel trying to finish a school paper, she decided, "I can't do this anymore."

After working quietly for a Boston architect most of 1983, Lin decided to return to New Haven and Yale that fall. "I needed a place to start over," she says. "Yale was like going home." She's been studying with trend-setting architects like Frank Gehry, collaborating on an outdoor sculpture for upstate New York's Artpark and writing on architecture for the *New Republic*. After graduating this spring she hopes to join a small firm ("you get to do more"), then go out on her own. Frequent invitations to lecture remind Lin, now 26, of her bout with fame, but she rarely accepts, preferring to look ahead. "I used to be terrified that at 21 I might already have outdone myself," she says. "Now I'm too busy to think about it."

Newsweek, January 20, 1986.

Come to grips with the information problem. Take personal responsibility to be informed. Ask questions, look up things, inquire, call, read your mail. And, correlatively, take personal responsibility to inform others and to see to it that they stay informed. Call them, write to them, check back, visit them. Expect the same of colleagues. You are setting an example. In time, people will follow.

Remember that organizations and human existence in general are organized around the importance of a unified field of consciousness. The fundamental human relationship is an intimate I-thou rather than an impersonal I-it relationship. You depend on the organization and the organization depends on you. Both tend to forget these axioms of human interaction.

Your key word is reliability. To be reliable means to learn how to be accurate in what you say. It is of course even more accurate to say that what you see is always your perception. If a problem has no solution, as is often true of the chaos in fast-paced organizations, then accuracy demands, even though people may not like to hear it, that you say so.

Both reliability and commitment are a function of "presence." You know a real live human being stands before you—which is the meaning of presence—because that person is committed. He or she is loyal and dedicated. A person who is present is reliable, which means that this person can be counted on to do exactly what was agreed—and to do it without additional reminder. When people are reliable and committed, they are present to us, present to you. They are there. They are real. With caring, concerned, and involved human beings, we feel the richness of contact.

Presence is a root trait of health and authenticity in human affairs. When people are present, transparent, you know what they feel, where they stand, who they are, what they think, and you can trust them. In short, reliability, trust, and commitment occur whenever presence exists.

Clarity, honesty, transparency, awareness, that is, presence and reliability, lead to trust. They are signs of maturity and of an evolved soul. That means a few rules: keep your word; remember your promises; do not promise merely to placate; tell people if you change your mind or if you promised what you cannot deliver. Learn to assess reality accurately, so that you distort neither in your speech nor in your commitments. If you make a mistake admit it quickly and see what, beyond an apology, you can do to compensate for the error. Be realistic: understand that people, including you, are not perfect. But you can resolve to be reliable, especially in your willingness to let people know that you cannot give what you have led them to expect. That may be difficult, but it is essential. Above all, it means that you are at all times aware of people, of their existence, and of their needs—and that you will not overextend yourself just because you may have made an unthinking and idle statement.

Be aware that people take you much more seriously than you may expect. This is true especially in high-risk ego-involved relationships—where the stakes are high and the consequences major. Be also aware that people quickly slip into psychological contracts: their expectations may be projections of their needs more than reflections of your intentions. People pay attention to body language—to the tone of voice, to a smile, a scowl, to a look, closeness, distance, a glance, eye contact, or the averted gaze. And these messages build expectations, positive or negative, or signal disappointments, acceptance or rejection, approach or avoidance. They say, "There is a future for me" or "There is no future for me." They indicate, "I approve of you," or "I disapprove of you." The body language may have no basis in conscious choice or in deliberate intention. It nevertheless sets up psychological expectations which if violated are perceived as betrayals.

People are time. A human being is the time of his or her life. There is nothing more to our life than our time on earth. And of that time the real time is quality time. Be on time; leave on time. Know that time commitments are sacrosanct. But also know that times conflict—sacred times conflict. Let people know that you respect their time but that you cannot always adhere to time commitments. But tell them; let them know; give them notice. People, and particularly in business, are their time. All they have to offer, to contribute, and to sell, is their time. Know that and act accordingly. But neither be compulsive, be not imprisoned by rigidity. To respect time means that some things must be done in seconds. Others require the maturation of years.

To respect time also means you know that what induces pressure is always time. It is only time that creates stress. Therefore, a rigid schedule means permanent pressure. Perhaps that leads to ulcers and heart attacks. But time also means your priorities are in order. You do what is of value; and you do it now. To respect time is therefore to respect the human—in you and in others.

Time can stand for many things; know them all. Tell them all. And practice them all. Act on these insights.

Decide to gain maximum clarity, that is, objectivity, about who you are, personally: psychologically, idiosyncratically, as you and you alone, and generically, that is, as a human being, sharing traits with all humanity. A significant aspect of this is to know how people perceive you and what messages you give them. People's reaction to you is an index of the messages they get from you. Look at the world around you, especially the social world, the world of people: that is your unconscious made visible.

The underlying principle behind this analysis is personal responsibility. And the basic meaning of personal responsibility is that you are willing, you choose, to energize yourself, that you realistically, which means accurately, assess the situation in which you find yourself, and that you resolve to survive as a company, group, organization, or project. And within that context, you win.

This means you understand the meaning of human freedom, the power of creation within you, the structure of the will, and the realism of action.

Below is a brief summary of benefits that follow if you are transformed to the genius and power levels in action.

Life will improve all around. You will be more fulfilled, happier, healthier, than before. You will look forward to coming to work. Many of the feelings of anxiety, resentment, and nausea that people get under stress will abate. You will release energy you did not know you had. You will feel secure, at peace, strong.

Your work will improve and you will get recognition.

You will grow and gain in marketability. People pay "big bucks" to get the kind of personal growth and maturity that can come from an organization where autonomy is intelligently fostered. As you learn to say "I am" from your depth you are helped to become more fully human. Marketability means that you get yourself ready for career advancement: for promotions or for better jobs, and better-paying jobs. You are being prepared for high responsibility, for the kinds of positions that can give you the most personal satisfaction, with the highest financial rewards.

The benefits carry over to your personal life. Authentic growth in one area of life transfers to other areas as well.

If you do well in your career and if the learning transforms your personal life, then you are well on your way to your genius power level of ethics in action. Motivational intelligence is the joy of being alive. We can then hear Tennyson say,

> No life that breathes with human breath
> Has ever truly longed for death.

CHAPTER 20

Transforming the
Intelligence of Wisdom

Levels of Depth

Part of wisdom is to have the right metaphysics. What that is can be judged only on pragmatic terms. A useful model follows.

The psyche has structures, perhaps innate, called archetypes. These affect our perceptions of the world. We see the world as a cinematographic projection of our archetypes. The world is like a living dream. The figures in our everyday world reflect and represent these archetypal structures deeply buried within the soul. Logic, causation, space, and time are in philosophy often thought not to be real properties of the world but projections of the mind. In psychology we talk of both prejudice and world-views, such as religious faith and atheism, as projections on the world.

But the raw material of the dream is not the dream itself but denuded, hard, and intractable reality. Within limits we can change the world best by first changing ourselves. The dream aspect of the world gives us concrete suggestions and emotional support on how to act to achieve our goals and satisfy our needs. The everyday world is the dream world diluted ("intermingled" is a better word) with the granite of external reality. The dream shows us in its purity how the mind works. Everyday existence is a dance before our eyes, a reflection or a projection of the mostly unconscious struggles within the soul. There is subjective as well as objective realism, and they are companions to each other in our effort to harness for our survival the mystery of existence. This wisdom is the true technology.

Surrounding this "subjectivized" and therefore living world is the harsh and implacable external reality—death, the market, other people, nature, and so forth.

The central psyche is pure conscious subjectivity. Exploring it is subjective realism. The frame is the impersonal reality of the universe. Exploring that is objective realism. The events, objects, and persons of the world among which we live are a mixture of both. Technology copes with objective reality; philosophy and its cognates in counseling, consulting, therapy, and the like cope with subjective realism. Therefore, we must master both technology and philosophy to maturely fulfill our potential for wisdom. It is the direction in which both nature and the mind wish to evolve.

Another fundamental aspect of wisdom is to understand that our experience of reality comes in layers. Experiences are metaphors for deeper truths. And unless we manage our problems at a deep enough level, our results will be paltry compared to what they might be. To illustrate the point we might select a possible list of levels of depth:

Level 1. Business. Here the problems are as we encounter them every day, and how they make their way into memos or into meetings:

We need more of this or that!

We need to promote so-and-so and reprimand that other s.o.b.!

Why haven't the gizmos and widgets come in?

Why is he so stupid?

Why aren't they making the numbers?

Can't he remember?

Look how he treated that customer!

She deserves a raise, but the boss is too stingy to give it to her!

Level 2. Personal philosophy. Here the individual is concerned with the personal values held and cherished, with prejudices and biases, self-concepts and world views. They underlie the more mundane issues illustrated above:

I deserve more respect than I am getting.

I need to pay more attention to my family; I feel guilty that I might be neglecting them.

I can no longer emotionally afford to come home tired and have no patience for the baby.

Mother needs some attention; she's getting on in years and I must be sure we have a good relationship before she dies.

I haven't read a good book all month!

I am wasting my time here!

I am doing nothing for my future.

I am getting all emotional and making myself look ridiculous.

When did I last pay heed to my duties as a citizen?

Everyone is in this world to rip off the other guy and protect himself from being ripped off in turn: it's a jungle out there.

In a marriage it is important that husband and wife be full partners, taking equal responsibility for home duties and for generating income.

Level 3. Psychological significance. Beneath my values as perceived lie their psychological roots. Our values and personal philosophies may appear to be self-chosen, but more often than not they are in fact the consequences of childhood experiences and training.

My relationships to members of the opposite sex are immature and often even infantile, that is why I have problems with my colleagues.

I am excessively sensitive about being promoted because I have problems with authority figures.

I am a dependent personality; I cannot act autonomously, because I never could confront my father and assert my own independence: he died when I was young.

I am a second child, and I can only conceive of myself as number two.

I was an only child and therefore I act like a prima donna and am a problem to everyone, for I cannot adapt easily.

I like my desk always neat and clean.

I attribute my intemperate smoking habits and my somewhat excessive drinking to a lack of sucking satisfaction during my first six months of life.

I am reserved; I do not express my feelings freely; I like to work and to be by myself.

I love to go to parties and I need to have large numbers of friends.

I am the intuitive type; I rarely bother to think things through in detail.

I get more satisfaction working on a computer program than out of singing, dancing, or playing a musical instrument.

Level 4. Tradition, ethnicity, culture. The rules, presuppositions, and expectations of society—the archetypes which we presumably inherit from time immemorial with our consciousness and which constitute our cultural inheritance—answer for us many of the most important questions. When reason fails or experience is insufficient, then we fall back on what society prescribes as right. To challenge or even to question these deeply buried rules, of which we may be

only partially aware, is dangerous. These rules and modes of procedure are deeply ensconced in our behavior; they are the fundamental
patterns of perception of almost everyone we know. They occur at a
level of the psyche deeper than personal psychology and they can be
resolved best by tracing their roots to their origin.

I cannot see myself marrying outside of my faith.

I like to be with people of my own kind, especially around the
holidays. I do not believe in God nor do I go to church—except when a
close relative dies, or when a child is born to us, or when someone in
our family gets married!

I believe in the value of work and ambition and I cannot stand
lazy people.

I always respect a man of the cloth.

Tears come to my eyes when I read some of the stories in the Bible.

I believe that in the end the good will be rewarded for their
sacrifices.

I believe a woman's place is in the home.

Neighborliness and hospitality are among the highest of all virtues.

Level 5. The physiological, somatic, bodily level. Many of our
views, thoughts, ideas, attitudes, moods, philosophies, and ways of
perceiving reality have their origins in our physiology or leave
their mark on our bodies and in the state of our general health. Exercise, nutrition, inherited traits, the endocrine system, and so on, can
be intimately related to our feelings, our efficiency, our attitude, and
our spirit.

One of the clearest examples is the effect that anti-depressant
and anti-psychotic medication can have on our general outlook on
life, on how we evaluate our experiences, and on how we judge our
perceptions. Sometimes emotional or practical problems can be
solved quickly by medical attention. Lack of energy may appear first
to be the result of boredom, and then, the consequences of inner conflicts—but upon physical examination what may be discovered is a
potassium deficiency. The treatment then is not a lecture from the
boss, nor is it psychotherapy, but to eat plenty of bananas.

*Level 6. The underlying philosophic issues, the theological
themes, the question of Being itself, the deep structures of human existence.* The previous issues can sometimes be helpfully understood as
metaphors and dramatizations, illustrations and diagrams, pictures

and suggestions, of the eternal questions. Solutions and answers are often irrelevant, for the eternal questions rarely have answers, and if they do, they do not mean very much. Understanding, appreciation, comprehension, exploration—these are the words that help us deal with the eternal questions.

Perhaps the greatest of them all is the question of God. Does He exist? Is there a purpose to this world? Or is it a random universe? Is there life after death? Before birth? And, if so, is it ethically related, as held in the doctrine of karma? We do not know the answers to these questions, yet they determine the things that matter most to us in life.

For example, anxiety, guilt, ambiguity, and polarity are reflections of structures in ultimate reality; these are our limits, our boundaries. As human beings who have been seasoned and adapted to the real world by evolution, we fit well into that reality. Reality is tailor-made, as it were, for people who understand these ultimate issues of human existence. People whose eyes are open to what actually is will feel comfortable with that reality. The problem is not with the world; nor is it with us. It is with our ignorance. The world is right for us and still we want to make it over. In many ways it is fortunate that the world does not respond to our tampering.

But what are some of these eternal questions? Specifically, we must face our death and our freedom of choice, our responsibility, as much as our need for forgiveness and for a home; we must confront our search for identity and autonomy as much as for our requirements for love. We must have meaning in life and we are affected by beauty. Courage is inescapable. Commitments are necessary risks. These are some of the deep structures.

The concept of layers of depth can be illustrated by a picture in an advertisement which (in the words of my friend Paul Decker) "stops you from turning the page." A park bench. On its right, a young lady, dreaming, looking at her young man, who is kneeling to the right beside her. Both seem innocent and serious. Evidently he is proposing. On the left of the bench—a bum, clutching his wine bottle, asleep, grinning, toothless, unshaven, clothes disheveled, ripped, shoes broken.

Why are you touched? That bench shows the two sides of existence. It pictures a choice open to everyone. It evokes the depth of your freedom. Which side do you choose? Do you wish to choose? Do you fear you might choose? Which side have your children chosen? Your parents? The most profound issue, your freedom to choose love or to choose degradation, stops you from turning the page. You are riveted to the truth about your freedom, and your guilt and your anxiety, your hope and your despair, mesmerize you so you cannot turn the page. We must look at the truth beneath the symbols.

What is in a fable? A hidden truth. Business problems are also fables. What is their hidden truth? for you? for others?

Have you ever considered the following? Adam, before the Fall, never saw another man. The only human presence before him, ever, was Eve. There were no people, only the Garden of Eden. He experienced his reality as a man only to the extent that Eve was present to him. What is a man? A being who is who he is and who becomes who he is meant to become only by fully focusing on that which he is not: a woman.

But there is more. For Adam there was only one woman, ever—as if the actual woman and the archetype of the feminine were one and the same. For Eve the same is true. She knows who she is only in the presence of the only human reality in her world—her man. Every human being wants to feel special. Jealousy is most intense when someone other than oneself is special. Eve is special to Adam—she has no competition, not even hypothetically. That is commitment.

So it is with business problems. They hide a deeper truth. And it is that deeper truth which must be understood in order to solve the business problem. And you can do that by working at the level of the symbols. You solve the problem at its roots. And being aware that there is depth, you, through your symbols, which is your business, attain your true meaning.

Thus, the deeper the level at which we deal with our business and life's issues, the more effective our efforts become. That is a fundamental rule, which is understood and implemented by the leader who has the intelligence of wisdom.

Tom Robbins, in *Even Cowgirls Get the Blues,* says it well:

> "You really don't believe in political solutions, do you?"
>
> "I believe in political solutions to political problems. But man's primary problems aren't political; they're philosophical. Until humans can solve their philosophic problems, they're condemned to solve their political problems over and over again. It's a cruel, repetitious bore."
>
> (Quoted in Daniel Yankelovitch, *New Rules.*)

The Anatomy of Courage

The intelligence of wisdom, transformed to the genius power level of performance and of ethical action, concerns itself with the issues underlying the anxiety of change in corporations.

Courage may be the most important point of all. Of all the qualities that philosophy can bring to business, courage is the most significant, the one most in demand. Courage is inevitable. It is not really a choice whether or not we are to be courageous. Courage is tied to maturity, is connected intimately with living life fully. One of the grave problems of life is self-limitation: we refuse to fulfill our potential. We live only marginally. Freud called that a psychoneurosis. But marginal living is not as much the product of a bad childhood or of ignorance about human nature—as of a lack of courage. Self-limitation, the unwillingness to be entrepreneurial and creative—perhaps the most significant problem among employees in American corporations today—results from a deceptive search for security. Security is to be found in only three human virtues: realism, responsibility, and courage. Only those people who are fully in touch with reality, who hold themselves fully accountable and responsible for the consequences of their actions, and who are willing to display courage, have real security. Those who submit passively to organizations and those who fear to challenge authority are people who believe that their subservience, the limitations they impose upon themselves, will give them security. This is a cruel illusion. The day we wake up and understand that life cannot be lived without courage—for no one is exempt—is also the day we become mature, the day of our initiation into the fullness of human wisdom.

Courage is a decision. People are not born heroes—nor cowards. Courage is clearly a decision. This is good, for everyone can be courageous. But this is also bad, because it discloses how painful it is to be courageous. Courage is something one has to do; it does not do itself or happen while one is under an anaesthetic. It happens only under conditions of full consciousness. Courage is a choice, a commitment, a willingness. Courage is an action, not a passion—nothing passive.

But what *kind* of a decision is courage?

Courage is the decision to face experience, and live through maximum doses of anxiety. Military courage is an example as good as it is traditional. The courageous soldier chooses to face death. Historical tradition interprets that to be a decision for greatness. Even those who oppose soldiering, as did Gandhi, need to choose to display precisely the same kind of courage.

But what the courageous person faces is more than anxiety. It is also guilt and loneliness, physical pain and depression. To live through this kind of pain and anxiety requries some understanding of what anxiety is.

Kierkegaard defines despair or anxiety as the condition in which we wish to die but cannot.

Current and regrettably, common examples of such suffering appear in the unwanted prolonging of life in a fatal illness; in imprisonment and torture; and in deep personal tragedy and loss (which leads to a "why me?" feeling).

Anxiety can be clarified by listing some of its so-called causes.

- Death
- Evil
- Freedom, free will
- Change
- Abandonment
- Assault
- Ridicule (feelings of inferiority)
- Insanity (doubt)

We must remember that the anxiety of courage is normal; it provides one with the emotional truth of the human condition. And if anxiety is denied, it makes one ill. Anxiety, fully confronted, fully faced, fully lived through, converts itself into joy, security, strength, centeredness, and character.

To repeat, one reaches maturity, adulthood, and authenticity when one realizes that life cannot be lived without courage. "Techniques," helpful as they may be, are often no more than attempts to live life without courage.

Wisdom arises out of the tragic sense of life. We must make a basic choice: is life good? Or is life tragic? The deeper answer seems to be the latter. Joy that is not based on tragedy can be superficial. Wisdom, then, is the courage to stand up to the tragic sense of life. That gives human beings nobility. That makes life worth living. It gives us a sense of exhilaration.

The tragic sense of life has several components. One is death. We distinguish between the death of another and our own death. For the former the evidence is immediate experience; for the latter the evidence is circumstantial or inferential. That mysterious issue has been managed through mythology and theology. Death brings life into focus. A fish does not know it is in water until it is taken out. In parallel fashion, a human being does not know about life and its sacred value until the thought of death is introduced.

Death sets us straight in our values. It gives us a total plan for life. It gives us the resolve to find meaning.

To stand up to death is wisdom.

To stand up to evil is also wisdom. Evil is real. The behavioral sciences ignore this fact. Theology and philosophy are the places to go for insights about evil. Nothing stands between us and evil other than our free choice to affirm ethics. That is how important human beings are.

Wisdom is the courage to stand up to insanity. Thinking for yourself, examining prejudices, all these are iconoclastic forms of thought. When the chips are down, truth is determined by the social order. To think independently is therefore always to be thought crazy. The punishment may be death: consider Socrates, Jesus, and Martin Luther King.

In sum, the greatness of wisdom is what happens when we muster the courage to stand up to anxiety. In other words, wisdom is to stand up to evil, to death, and to insanity.

> Be not afraid of greatness. Some are born great, some achieve
> greatness, and some have greatness thrust upon them.
>   (William Shakespeare, *Twelfth Night*)

Leadership, which ethical wisdom implies, is to be a mentor, a model; it is to have made the commitment to give, to be of service, to make a contribution, and to be as fully self-developed as possible.

The Bible is a fundamental document of western civilization. It defines for us the meaning of human nature: men and women are "freedoms," beings who create. And they affirm their existence. The greatness of wisdom therefore is to say "I am":

> So God created man in his own image, in the image of God
> created he him; male and female created he them.
>   (*Genesis* 1:27)

> In the beginning God created the heavens and the earth.
>   (*Genesis* 1:1)

God said to Moses, "I AM WHO I AM." And he said, "Say
this to the people of Israel, 'I AM has sent me to you.' . . .
this is my name for ever, and thus I am to be remembered
throughout all generations."

(*Exodus* 3:14-15)

Carl Rogers, quoting Kierkegaard, can be said to interpret for us
the meaning of this last passage from the Second Book of Moses:

The most common despair is of not choosing, or willing to be
oneself;
but the deepest form of despair is to be "another than himself."
The opposite of despair is "to will to be that self which one
truly is."

Let us suggest a metaphor. When your inner and outer minds are in
a state of total silence, then you can hear the cosmos being created
out of nothing (*creatio ex nihilo*) and to hear it speak the words I AM
(in Sanskrit it would be AUM). You hear the cosmos freely affirm its
own existence.

That is the energy of the galaxies, of the black holes, the supernovae, the comets, the suns, the planets, the earth's geology—the
volcanoes, earthquakes, winds, and tides. That is the energy of evolution and the life force, of the will to live and individual ambition.

Each of us is invited to join the universal chorus—freely, each being his or her own creator—and to take personal responsibility to
sing I AM. To say "I am" is to join the universal energy, the energy of
the galaxies and of the atoms, of the dinosaurs and of the amoebae,
of the sun and of our own body.

We must underscore the importance, the risk, and apparently the
novelty in business of "seeing with the heart." There can be no
courage, no wisdom, and no leadership if one cannot see with heart.
The heart locks in as an organ of perception and as the vision of the
truth when life pushes one up against a cliff or a precipice. The
response is always with the heart—and rightfully so. The head
protects the ethics, but the heart is what is human. The head can
preserve our morality, but the heart understands. Many have said it
better:

That ye, being rooted and grounded in love, may be able to comprehend . . . what is the breadth, and length, and depth, and height.

(*Ephesians* 3:17-18)

What is true is invisible to the eye. It is only with the heart that one can see clearly.

(Antoine de Saint-Exupéry)

Some day after mastering the winds, the waves, the tides, and gravity, we will harness for God the energies of love. And then, for the second time in the history of the world, man will have discovered fire.

(Pierre Teilhard de Chardin)

The intelligence of wisdom leads directly to the leadership challenge.

Ultimate Concerns

No human being can live in keeping with the demands of his or her conscience until the ultimate concerns are confronted. It does not matter if we agree on what these are. What matters is that we understand such questions exist, burning, real in every heart. People who confront them feel that they live. And people who deny them live only half a life, if at all. What we call illness—from a broken arm to a depression—results in great part from the denial of the eternal questions. Man (and woman) was born to wonder and to question, to ask why there are beings rather than nothing, why it is that we can see, be aware of a world, be conscious at all in the first place. We were born to ask why there must be death, and whether love can ever be fulfilled.

One reason for the difficulty of raising the eternal questions in a business context is that these questions seem irrelevant and impractical, not profit-oriented or productivity-related. More than that, the minds of many executives are not trained to focus on what they call abstract issues, but instead on what they think is concrete. However, more than one company president has said that the most concrete, practical, and immediate concern was to deal with his employees' questions about the meaning of life.

It is therefore important to note that the eternal questions arise principally under extreme circumstances—*in extremis* we call it. It is then that issues other than the so-called practical ones emerge as important. We may get to them by talking of country and God, of family and children, of political issues and moral values, of childhood and religious training.

But what appears most mature, respectful, dignified, and inherently valuable is to point out systematically under what circumstances these ultimate concerns arise.

They appear in what Abraham Maslow called peak experiences. They can also be called experiences leading to wisdom. And these extreme conditions are both positive and negative. In fact, because so-called peak experiences arise mostly under conditions of extreme duress, it is quite proper to call them "nadir or depth experiences."

Peak or nadir experiences are quite properly called passions, for they are not the result of a deliberate action of a person. They invade awareness, they flood consciousness. They happen to us; we do not make them happen. Often they are accompanied by bodily expressions, such as crying or laughing. They are the products of the unconscious. Deliberate and rational approaches, logical explanations, and planned techniques to achieve peak experiences rarely produce them, any more than intense mental concentration would increase the amount of vitamin C in the bloodstream.

An even more interesting, and certainly more important, aspect of peak experiences is their cognitive value. They reveal; they give us information, as it were, on the nature of reality. But they inform us not of scientific facts but of the truth behind the truth, the reality behind reality, the vision beyond where the eye can reach. There exists another reality, perhaps given to us in intuition, which opens itself up to peak experiences. Deep emotions change the truth. We are talking here about transforming reality. Peak experiences disclose to us a secret reality, hidden to most but desired by all. The deeper truth is something that we all seek. That is why philosophy and religion, art and magic, are important in the genius-power level.

This transformation should be called seeing with the heart. Pascal told us that the heart has its reasons of which reason knows nothing.

These visions are self-evident: all we need to know to determine if they are "true" is to examine the experience itself. These are what we call cognitive emotions.

Such an attitude towards the knowledge value of intuitions is fairly popular today. It used to be at odds with the scientific attitude. That was in the days of the supremacy of positivism. Today, paradox, contradiction, and ambiguity are no longer controversial. There is only one caveat, and that is directed against the romantic excesses of intuition when it is not constrained by the sobriety of reason and ethics. We have seen such excesses not only in the evil worldview of Nazi Germany, but also in the Jonestown disaster in Guiana and in the Rajneeshpuran debacle in Oregon.

All civilizations are founded on such intuitions from peak experiences. The culture guarantees their preservation. But we must always monitor their ethical character and their sense of justice, so that they preserve human freedoms and guarantee the dignity of the individual. In this way we maintain the truth value of what the heart sees without endangering our sanity.

The ultimate concerns emerge with particular clarity under four circumstances, especially in their extreme forms: grace, love, will, and anxiety. These have been managed by psychiatry, by romantic literature, by sports, and by religion respectively. Let us take a closer look at each of them.

Grace. The experience of grace is to receive a gift that is undeserved, a gift as desirable as it is undeserved, a gift of infinite proportions like life itself, like a child, like the world's most prestigious prize. And undeserved means that there is no way to cajole, force, seduce, threaten, demand, extract, extort, or plead to receive that gift. It is given freely.

Religion provides the best metaphors. Creation is that kind of grace: life, existence, vision, sound, joy, meaning, the universe. When we contrast these values or realities, or whatever one might wish to call them, with their non-being, we understand that our impotence in bringing them about is as staggering as the immensity of their absolute value. It reminds one of Walt Whitman's "A mouse is miracle enough to stagger sextillions of infidels."

When in the presence of grace, we have a peak experience and reality is transfigured: we are saved at sea because a good Samaritan risks his or her life; a physician stops to attend to an accident victim on the way to an important engagement, Anne Frank and Franz Werfel were saved, by the Dutch and the French respectively, at grave risk to their protectors. What happens to change that which is real?

An act of such unusual and unexpected character is inserted into our world so that the theories which hold it together unravel and must be instantaneously and automatically reconstructed. Nietzsche, in Zarathustra's Prologue, calls grace *schenkende Tugend*, the virtue of giving. He compares it to the sun, which can "look upon an all-too-great happiness without envy," for it is too rich to take; it can only give.

Love. Love is another transforming phenomenon. Love, as passion, as first romance, may be compared to the touching of an archetype—a dynamic experience. The soul is suffused with a sense of resolution, fulfillment, salvation, inspiration, transformation. One need only quote arcadian or anachreontic poetry to be reminded of the epiphany of love. Love in this sense is an argument for the existence of God. Its transforming magic demonstrates the validity of religious solutions to the world's mysteries. From the perspective of the narrowly practical, decisions made under the influence of love are even less reliable than those made while inebriated or psychotic. But from the perspective of the larger designs of civilization and the eternal verities—and those values which, in the name of culture, we teach children and adults in our schools, churches, libraries, operas, novels, and colleges and universities—the only significant decisions are made in the warm aura of love. That, for example, is the basic message of Christianity: love enough, and its power will transform the world. It will teach the skeptic that the mystic vision is correct.

Will. The third condition under which peak experiences occur is the will. The will is the foundation of ethics, for the moral code maintains its existence on the strength of the supporting human will alone. The Constitution exists because the will of the people supports it. An army is effective by virtue of the will of its soldiers, the will of its commanders, and the will of the population at home.

The will is like magic. It is a decision *ex nihilo* for justice. The will cannot be bribed or caused. It is *causa sui*. Immanuel Kant deserves his fame on the strength of this insight alone. The will of the strong can never be broken. We are so much impressed by this self-chosen steel in the soul that in the presence of such stunning uniqueness the transformation of reality pregnant in peak experiences is thrust upon us. He who is blessed with the confrontation with the will, even if it is the iron fist of his enemy, will never be the same again, for he has seen the spiritual granite of an uncaused act, the event of original creation itself. To actually see the power of the will is to expand infinitely the possibilities of human nature.

God is the only pure freedom. If we believe in God, then the freedom is real and it is our task on earth to live in the imitation of this divine and cosmic freedom. If we do not believe in God, then the idea that God is Freedom is a myth, a projection, and idealization of the most important human issue. In either case, we are clear that freedom is the supreme value of our lives as human beings and also that freedom is not part of the natural order, not part of the world described by science.

But freedom is supremely real nevertheless. In fact, we are willing to defend freedom by making the ultimate sacrifice, something we are not likely to do for the preservation of a scientific law.

The Egyptians worshipped the sun. That is understandable enough, considering the fact that the sun is the source of all life on earth. Our energy, the energy of being alive in which we human beings participate, is the same energy that is in the sun. The very same! But the amount is not the same. We are but thin slivers of that enormous energy which resides in and comes from the sun. But the quality of the energy is the same. In medieval times, some splinters were sacred relics, a mere look at them was worth many indulgences that would speed one's soul through purgatory. They were sacred relics because they were thought to be splinters from the cross on which Jesus was crucified. We have within us such a splinter from the sun.

The French philosopher René Descartes magnificently expresses the sanctity of freedom in these words:

> It is the faculty of the will only, or freedom of choice, which
> I experience to be so great that I am unable to conceive the
> idea of another that shall be more ample and extended; so
> that it is chiefly my will which leads me to discern that I
> bear a certain image and similitude of Deity.

Anxiety. We come to the last, and perhaps the most frequent, source of peak experiences—the phenomenon of anxiety, with its cognates of guilt and death. When confronted with extreme sorrow, our life is transformed and its new reality thunderously announces itself. I am talking of the death of a dear friend, of a child, of a beloved parent, or of any human being, if we are sensitive enough to have infinite compassion for all sentient creatures. Serious accidents and emotional shocks can change fundamentally our definition of what is real.

And we cannot say that our vision is clouded by emotion. Under conditions of extreme stress, the power of certainty and the conviction of truth are far more convincing than the tested consensual reality of ordinary circumstances. When my daughter's childhood companion was killed in an automobile collision by a drunken driver and I attended the funeral Mass, I knew that the priest's words, which under normal circumstances I would have thought interesting mythology, were then the ultimate truth. It was real that Theresa was in heaven, indisputable that in being taken first she was blessed. And it was an axiom that the rest of us were less pure than she and that we had been condemned to expiate our sins through a longer stay in this "vale of tears."

When your daughter dies, you know the truth of religion. And this truth is stronger than the most scientific proof fathomed in an unfeeling laboratory. That is the power of seeing with the heart, the transformative value of peak experiences. That is where our values are formed. That is how we touch on the Reality behind reality, on the Truth deeper than the truth, and on that Being which is the source of all being. The ultimate realism is to confront the ultimate concerns.

A certain frustration is always connected to this sequence of events. Business programs are announced and interest in them is engendered by reference to a myopic pragmatism: new advertising techniques, advanced bottom-line awareness, productivity enhancements, increased cost-effectiveness, and better manipulation of the internal environment. The real interest of the participants, however, quickly moves over to the more typically philosophic and deeper issues of courage and anxiety. Executives say they want practical, cost-conscious information, yet when given it often find it superficial. The fact is that depth is its own practical application. Nothing is more practical than for people to deepen themselves. The deeper the people, the more effective their relationships. "Virtue is knowledge," said Socrates. The more you understand of the human condition, the more effective you are as a business person, whether you sell, negotiate, manage people, do accounting, study the law, or develop products.

Let us remember that the ultimate wisdom is to confront the ultimate concerns—and this requires a commitment to the power level of Ethics.

Julius Heuscher, M.D., a psychiatrist and long-time friend, from Los Gatos, California, displayed the following sign in his waiting room:

We are impatient
of being on the way to something new
and yet it is the law of all progress
that it is made
by passing through some stages of instability
and that may take a very long time.

Our ideas mature gradually—
let them flow—
let them shape themselves
without undue haste.
Don't try to force them on
as though you could be today
what time will make you tomorrow.

Only God could say
what this new spirit
gradually forming within you
will be.
Give Him the benefit of believing
that His Hand is leading you surely
through the obscurity and the "becoming"
and accept for love of Him
the anxiety of feeling yourself
in suspense and incomplete.

Know that your activity has to be far-reaching.
It must emanate from a heart that has suffered.
We must offer our existence to God,
who makes use,
better than we could ever anticipate,
of the struggle in which we are enveloped.
                              (Pierre Teilhard de Chardin)

CHAPTER 21

Transforming
Team Intelligence

Transforming to Leadership

Management author Ron Lippit has developed a helpful list of contrasting leadership styles. It can well serve our purpose for describing the differences between masculine and feminine leadership styles. The obvious conclusion is that both are of value. A leader must use what he or she is comfortable with, and subordinates will respond and model themselves accordingly. It is more important to be authentic than to be right. We are often attracted to one style but act out another. We may think we identify with our same-sex parent, but in fact we exhibit in our behavior the character traits of our opposite sex parent.

The ideal is androgyny, for that is the fully developed person. Psychologist June Singer talks of four types of people. Some are weak in both femininity and masculinity. These are neutral and low-energy people, and not very interesting, a bit abstract. Some are strong in one kind of development but at the expense of the other. These are the more traditional strong masculine and feminine types. But then there are those who are strong in both sets of traits. And they, in fact, are the fully developed persons. They have the grounding necessary to become leaders.

Here is the Lippit list:

Style I (which could be called masculine)	*Style II* (which could be called feminine)
Results-oriented	People-oriented
Directed action	Part of the group
Business as business	Business as people and then product

Product-centered	People-centered
Product-sensitive	People-sensitive
Responsibility to save the group	Responsibility with the group for collaboration
Rely on rewarding and punishing leaders to get results	Rely on the motivation of the group to attain goals, etc.
Likes causing action	Stimulates group action
Wants final approval	Works toward consensus
Forceful	Collaborative, consultative
Likes working alone	Seeks feedback on ideas
Suspicious of group decision-making	Committed to shared decision-making
Committed to maintaining and perfecting equilibrium of the company	Lifelong commitment to change

Is God, the father archetype, dead?

The masculine leadership style is comfortable with clarity and the feminine is comfortable with ambiguity. There is a third leadership style: rational. The first two evoke our deepest feelings, refer to our atavistic needs, and rouse our most primitive responses. The third is ethical and democratic. It is Kantian, Spinozistic, Stoic. It presumes that human actions can be motivated not only by profound emotions and ancient memories, but also by reason and logic. The first two are patriarchal and matriarchal respectively, the third is democratic and constitutional.

The first two leadership styles are emotional; they are deep. They touch the older parts of the brain. They depend on culture, on symbols, and on myths. The third leadership style is mythless—as Freud suggested in *The Future of an Illusion.* It is harsh, traditional, and lonely. It is one hundred percent realistic. It is a life and a management style without illusions.

Much of the discussion to follow deals with the most common leadership style in America, the masculine.

The first question to ask is, How does each style affect you personally? What about the masculine leadership style, for example? How do you respond emotionally when confronted directly—in a real life situation and where a great deal is at stake—with either of these two leadership styles? How do you feel when confronted with hardness--logical and benign, reasonable and prudent, but hardness nevertheless? Many respond with anger, fear, panic, or envy, but also with relief. Many learn from it and imitate it. Many admit, after some trepidation, that such a confrontation with the hard wall of masculine leadership is instructive and opens up a new dimension in their lives.

The power which they see used against them they will now imitate and use in their favor. By feeling the impact of hardness themselves they learn what hardness is, how to appropriate it for themselves, how to become it themselves, and how to use it. Strong masculine leadership style, because it is hard, because it is like steel, like a wall, and because it is effective and can therefore be life-saving, produces anxiety, guilt, fear of death, terror. It also can be the experience of evil, because it is the experience of the Other, the fully Other, the totally Other, the Wholly Other. It is seeing the void, the abyss. It is the experience which signals the death of narcissism and schizophrenia, for it forces the psyche (the self, the ego, the soul) to admit the existence of another being. It shows that another freedom is as strong as I am. It shows me my limits, my boundaries; it forces me to accept my finitude. I give up being God only in the presence of a superior and invincible force. That is why, in the Old Testament, man finally gives up being or wanting to be God when he is demolished by God, terrified into submission by God. God has the power to kill all the firstborn in Egypt, and even the almighty Pharaoh must cower in submission to Jehovah.

How, on the other hand, do you respond to a lucid, intense, and extensive experience of feminine leadership? Some respond with gratitude, appreciation, joy, personal growth, development, self-disclosure, creativity, and health.

And finally, how do you respond to rational leadership? Most find it dry and impersonal, unsatisfying to the psyche but right nevertheless. It is what modern democratic human beings choose, and must choose, and are justified in choosing--regardless of whether or not their anthropology has prepared them for it.

But back to the masculine leadership style.

The psyche is formed by several forces: some are internal, but many are external. Unless the psyche is forced to grow up, to be formed, to shape itself, it will not do so. The psyche may wish by its own nature to grow, but it is also inherently lazy. In the last analysis, it is only emergencies that can force it to grow up. This is how children go to school, accept siblings, graduate, get jobs, leave home, stay alone, function without their parents, get married, go to summer camp, play the piano in public, play on football teams, serve on swim teams, learn to swim, to bicycle, to drive a car.

Power is transmitted—or taught—through confrontation with the masculine leadership style. Confrontation means encounter, and encounter means wrestling, struggling, fighting, lovemaking, engaging, intertwining, interpenetrating. Confrontation feels good, gives strength, passes the mantle of power from father to son, passes masculinity and royalty from father to son, from king to prince. A son learns to be masculine like his father by "wrestling" with (fighting, arguing, becoming alienated from) his father. The masculine possibilities in girls are transmitted in similar fashion.

The father archetype, central to the development of the human species, has died. It is no longer an ideal; and fatherhood in the sense of the ancient Roman paterfamilias, or even anything similar to that, is dead in the modern family. The masculine has been emasculated at the altar of equality. That is democratically right but archetypally disastrous. This is the stage of evolutionary development at which we find ourselves today. Young people do not respond to the father archetype anymore—either in themselves or in others. The political process assassinates father-archetype simulacra: two Kennedys, Martin Luther King, Sadat, Gandhi, Indira Gandhi, Olof Palme. Reagan was shot at, Truman was shot at, Ford was shot at. Will the father stay dead? Has reason killed him? Will the viscera restore him?

The masculine style of leadership can enhance the creativity of the subordinates, for they can be like their Father-archetype boss, not submissive to him. The key is imitation.

If people have difficulty in dealing with a masculine leader when he fully displays his nature to them, through rational and benign anger, expecting his subordinates to rise to the occasion, then an organization like a management training program or a company university or a corporate college can help interpret this style to the executives and help them deal with it constructively.

The leadership environment is qualitatively different, different in kind, from what we might term "ordinary" human relationships. It occurs at a different level. Expectations of self and expectations of others are different; risks are different; values are different; lifestyles are different; character is different; interpersonal relationships are different; rewards are different. And the demands for self-sacrifice are different. Once locked into the ethos of leadership, many bridges are burned behind the leader, and it may be difficult if not impossible for such a person to return to the lifestyles and the relationships of ordinary modes of existence.

Leaders are found not only in industry. Leadership is present and needed everywhere: in the arts, in education, in science, in the professions, in scholarship, in sports, as well as of course in business, politics, and the military.

This stylization may sound romanticized or exaggerated or both. It may also sound dehumanized—satanized, which we may define at this moment as the opposite of romanticized. It may seem to bring back the old days of emperors and knights, of the divine rights of kings, of absolute monarchs. It may seem that in an age of democracy and of socialism, and in a milieu of rationalism and constitutionalism, of civil liberties and of therapeutic sensitivities, there is categorically no room for such primitivism.

But we still like to read about kings: we travel to England to see the changing of the guard and to France to admire the splendor of the pre-Revolution palaces. We stand in wonder before the great pyramids and in the palace of Knossos, all of which were dedicated to the absolute power of absolute god-kings. We are fascinated with the moguls of industry and the poobahs of business. And when in their presence, we revere political leaders—even though we may have contempt for them in their absence. Total leadership has mesmerized populations throughout history and it has not yet lost its spell for modern man.

Surely all this will be denied, as it must. But this view that leadership is a sui generis form of social relationships seems to be an inescapably basic premise and a key requisite to dealing effectively and accurately with leadership issues. In leadership circles, virtually the only problem is that this premise of the unique nature of the leadership mind and of leadership relationships is ignored. Difficulties in human sensitivities and in interpersonal relations at that high level occur mostly because people—including the leaders themselves—ignore this fact of the special phenomenon of the sociology of leadership.

We cannot call that leadership group, which is as large as it is amorphous, an aristocracy, because today it is—at least frequently—earned and not inherited. We should call it a meritocracy. The fact that the leadership milieu, its sociology, its ethos or mythos, pays—and pays handsomely and into the millions—argues for its effectiveness, its reality. This single fact demonstrates that we must take the leadership mind and its environment seriously.

What are some of the attributes of this uniqueness?

- Implacable reliance on self
- Crudeness and toughness with oneself and with other people
- Incredible self-discipline, stamina, and energy
- A fiercely demanding presence, which for those who can tolerate it, can be invigorating and inspiring. It can elevate those around the leader to levels of achievement thought out of the question otherwise. It raises standards; it not only fulfills but it actually increases the human potential itself.
- Relentless focus on results more than on human frailties and sensitivities
- Justification by effectiveness. Ineffective leaders are eliminated by the forces of natural selection, and they are therefore a rare or an extinct species.
- Willingness to accept alienation. In fact, alienation is sought, nurtured. It is unavoidable. It must be faced. And it is the most severe armoring known to man. On the one hand, these leaders alienate themselves from their fellow men and women, because when one places results before people one ipso facto alienates people. This phenomenon leads to the intense isolation of the leader.

  On the other hand, this kind of leader must virtually sacrifice himself or herself for the cause by adopting such a seriously alienating style of self and of life. For he or she is in the leadership position for reasons of social utility. And the utility is results—survival first of all. This is true as much of the military as it is of business. For society needs results, and society will in the end sacrifice the leader in order to achieve results.

But this alienation is not necessarily self-serving. It is an alienation necessitated by the emergency exigencies of the group or of the organization—for everything is an emergency, and an unceasing one at that, at the high levels of management.

- Finally, the thrill of leadership has the same survival value for the species as does the orgasm. This shows once more biology at work.

All this may well be denied as excessive, but these points on leadership nevertheless seem inescapably important and true, and they may be useful for dealing with leadership and leadership-related issues.

People at high levels of responsibility, people who get paid well—either in money or status or other, emotional rewards, in self-satisfaction, in character, in learning, or in marketability, or in career enhancement—must learn how to deal with the leadership ethos. Their expectations of their own interrelationships, and especially their relation with the primary leader, must be as severe as the exigencies of the leadership situation itself. Nothing is certain; nothing can be predicted. Personal feelings and individual emotional needs are to be sacrificed for the good of the organization. Compassion and mercy are not leadership virtues; forgiveness is granted only on utilitarian and manipulative grounds. The delicate spectacles of human inwardness are sacrificed at the altar of results.

People surrounding powerful leaders must be prepared to relinquish forever infantilistic or childlike dependency needs, the yearnings for love, intimacy, closeness, understanding, gentleness, forgiveness. They cannot rationally expect loyalty to their position—for their position is utility-based. They must be prepared to leave on an instant's notice. And they must be cheerful about it all—because these are the expectations of high leadership positions. But while engaged as leaders or as part of the leadership cadre, they must be completely devoted and unquestionably loyal. People who are not prepared to commit themselves to such severity—a rigor reminiscent of the stoicism of the Roman soldiers, a philosophy that made Rome the ruler of the so-called known world for one thousand years—should studiously avoid dabbling in leadership affairs.

People in leadership positions must be fulfilled and happy by completely giving up childlike ways. They must expect of themselves the highest standards, the highest level of independence, and zero whining. That is difficult, indeed, and even dehumanizing. But to expect anything else in high business and government leadership circles is unreasonable, and, worst of all, totally useless. It is the formula for failure. They are people who thrive under these intense and stressful circumstances. Leaders are people for whom the relentless alertness demanded by high stakes leads to health, even to super-health.

Once that point is driven home and integrated at high-level leadership meetings, the most common liabilities can be turned into assets:

- to use the energy for the business and not for personal self-indulgence;
- to use the high-cost, scarce, and invaluable executive time of the top leadership of an organization for the business of the organization and not to placate bruised feelings;
- to use the energy and the consciousness of high-priced minds for marketing and for profits, for survival and for the creation of a vibrant organization, and not for palace intrigues and for Machiavellian schemes of self-promotion.

In sum, there is a sui generis ethos or culture of top leadership. To understand this, and to accept the responsibilities that follow from this reality, can go a long way towards solving many of the delicate power, ambition, and interpersonal issues that can be so very damaging to an entire corporation. They are expensive, and they slow down the corporate process and its efficiency, something very obvious to anyone who has ever attended top management meetings.

The top leadership of an organization must be challenged to accept their higher responsibility. They must perceive their transactions to occur in a fishbowl, where the board, senior management, all employees, and all clients, as well as those aspects of the nation affected directly by the organization, are watching. They can then not afford to indulge in personal sensitivities or in narrow interests. They can then display only the finest, noblest, and highest leadership qualities, opting at all times for the rational benefit of the organization itself.

Top management can be challenged in this way to exhibit maturity about personal sensitivities, about personal relationships, about ambiguity, about power issues, about individual ambitions, about the primacy of rationality, about thinking big about the business, and devoting their full attention, loyalty, commitment, and energy to the organization, and not just part of themselves. They must also be challenged to remember that clarity—no ambiguity in roles or in goals—is essential but impossible. They must therefore always try harder.

We must ask, Can we be a team? An organization can be a team without being made up of exactly the same persons all the time.

Similarly, individuals at high levels of management can be expected to cope with difficult emotional issues, such as rejection, rationally. The more responsibility people have, that is, the higher up they are in the ranks of management, the more maturity can be expected, demanded, and challenged of them. We can call this rational teamwork, for it is conscious and deliberate. It must be contraposed to primitive teamwork, which is a more direct reference to the instinct for gregariousness among human beings.

Brief mention must be made of the failure or of the limits of the military analogy. The masculine leadership style is often expressed, and adequately so, in military terms: generals, chief of staff, saluting, uniform, sergeants, kings, princes, emperors, prime minister, knights, torpedoes, mines, rifles, guns, bombs, armies, defeat, victory, execution, flank, rear guard, scouts, maneuvers, the front, commander-in-chief, laying down their arms, battlefield, trenches, and so on. The emergence of the feminine leadership style—the return of the goddess—makes these metaphors obsolete, inadequate, useless.

But there is a more immediate reason why these often popular metaphors are limited and often useless. The kind of bonding we find in the family, in a nation—especially a nation under siege, which arouses the population's patriotism—and in an army cannot be achieved in a corporation. The reason is that the danger is not the same. There is only one family, one nation, and one army, but there are many companies. There may be, it is true, such bonding in sports teams and other high-intensity projects. But it is common danger that binds team members beyond all individual neuroses.

To substitute for that we need a company with a worthy mission, a superordinate goal, a philosophic commitment which transcends egocentric goals—we need in a company the equivalent of an immortality project. That is why we must always look for the deeper functions and the deeper possibilities of a company's role. We must search for some living commitment, which a company could manifest, to which one can legitimately dedicate one's life. Then real team building makes sense.

For what we seek in life is an unconditional commitment. And not only to and from our leader, but also to and from each other. We want it, we long for it, we crave it. Such bonding feels good; it is fulfilling. It is restful; it is revered and silent peace. This need is primitive and thus difficult to fulfill, because modern society tries to be rational and mature and not primeval and elemental.

But teamwork, in addition to feeling good, releases creativity. It enables us to achieve more than we could do singly. It strengthens our arms and empowers us as individuals. There is magic in encounter. Our team can come to our aid.

The enabling and empowering benefits of teamwork—which represents authentic personal growth not achievable outside a team—must be sought deliberately, consciously, rationally. Commitment is the growth-producing element in teamwork. It is a choice, an act of faith, a self-fulfilling prophecy. If I choose to create a team by rationally and deliberately making a free commitment to other persons, then begins the momentum for arousing the more primitive form of teamwork.

I am not naturally a member of a team. I choose to be so. I choose that commitment freely, in the clear knowledge that it may end against my will. For all of us are subject to the forces of the market. The art of modern team building balances commitment within the matrix of reality.

The question for many a company is, which is primary, the individual or the team? What are the advantages and disadvantages of both or of either? The individual emphasis brings new ideas and new blood to the company, for people who are no longer useful are fired and new people who are more promising are brought in. Rather than be forced to choose between the individual and the team (the latter being the intimate, universal lifestyle, world-view, or value), we must dialogue between the two. We cannot choose between these any more than a man can choose between his wife and his daughter. The dialogue between these opposing polarities yields the higher principle of individuation, the mature perspective where (as it is with a religious approach to the conflict between life and death) the conflict no longer seems real, viable, or a matter of serious concern.

The advantages of the decision for individualism, or of individual decisions, is that they can be quick, clear, bold, and risky. And that is often needed. The advantage with team decisions, or with the decision to be primarily a team, is that they provide for the slow evolution of ideas—rather than having them announced suddenly--and for support. They provide loyalty.

The authentic boss demands that senior employees or executives use their freedom to the fullest. Those who do must be in a culture which encourages freedom and creativity through dialogue. It is difficult to hire sufficient numbers of entrepreneurs. Some are fully that and others are potentially that. A company must have a training program in which the creativity and the freedom of potential geniuses is released.

Transformation to Autonomy

Leaders encourage their subordinates and their organizations to become autonomous, independent, and creative (for these are interrelated virtues). They assail dependency modes of being. They tell us that the days of paternalistic organizations are over. The attraction of large corporations which will take care of their employees, provided the latter are subservient to the culture and fit into the demands of that culture, is now an atavistic illusion. Employees at all levels can no longer go to sleep on the job, nor expect that the security of routine will be available to them indefinitely. The modern manager is always in danger, lives like an accosted animal or a hunted refugee—and must learn to like it, to feel it as real, to thrive rather than wither under these stern realities. The modern manager must know that feeling the stresses of the forces of evolution is feeling reality, and that this contact is healthy and not pathological, growth producing and not disease causing.

Leaders encourage autonomy for several reasons. It is the right thing to do; it is what organizations need. Competition is becoming keener because companies are getting better. Internationalism is increasing, which means that the forthcoming economic equilibrium will not be measured in national but in international terms. In the light of communications and information technologies, theoretically America's minimum wage is the world's minimum wage, though this is a long way from implementation.

Furthermore, in encouraging the autonomy of their organizations, leaders encourage autonomy in themselves. There is not one human being alive who could not benefit from an additional dose of autonomy, of freedom, of responsibility, and of claiming the ownership of his or her existence.

It is always useful to take seriously the reality and the value of the unconscious. We want the world to change according to our own personal unconscious needs. And that is not bad; but these projects must be articulated, raised to consciousness, and managed by our deliberate, rational, intelligent, responsible free will.

It is therefore a common phenomenon to find that leaders encourage autonomy in their organizations, and then they either panic when they get it or indirectly—that is, with actions more than with words—they stifle it.

The self-diagnosis of such a situation is "frustration." One asks a group of executives, what does it feel like to be you? And the common answer, in one word, is "frustration."

What is the remedy? The leader must discover that he has entered into a new region of personal leadership growth. The autonomy that the organization has achieved, with his help, also represents a diagnosis of what he needs and wants to achieve in his personal life and in his leadership style. In fighting him, the organization is giving *him* also the opportunity to grow as he had wished *them* to grow. For when the leader understands and integrates these insights, he makes a quantum leap in his own leadership growth.

Case Study

X is a successful but sluggish company. A is their popular leader. The organization was bought by company Y, and the two companies then instituted a successful merger, Y-X. In an unusual move, and based on A's sterling leadership qualities, A is then promoted to

CEO of the new company. Y's CEO, in turn, becomes chairman. But a successor for X must be found. The organization which A left (that is, X) is a bit too passive to have produced its own natural leader. This fact made A's promotion difficult for the old organization, X. Ideally, a natural succession leader should emerge from X. But it appears now that an outsider must be hired.

The chairman then asks several consultants to create a program designed to rouse the leadership consciousness of that organization (company X). At the time of the leadership program, A left his old organization, the region, and moved far away--to the distant headquarters of company Y.

Their leader, A, is now a key figure in naming his own successor. But he had not done so, nor had his chairman, by the time of the leadership project, which included a seminar designed to raise the leadership consciousness of the old organization.

The consultants' leadership–consciousness-raising seminar was held against a background of intense emotional and political activity resulting from the recent departure of its top executive and the vast uncertainties created by the absence of a successor.

A, the leader of X, was much esteemed and beloved by his people. The contention was, and it held much truth, that A stimulated the creativity and the autonomy of his subordinates, that they were making genuine progress towards earning increasing individual responsibility, and that they could manage well by themselves.

They had been protected by X from excessive external constraints, and they were validated and acknowledged by X for their own personal leadership accomplishments, that is, for their demonstrations of innovation and initiative.

Now that A was leaving, there was ambiguity: even though they were independent, they were able to be so because of a loving (i.e., acknowledging) and protective father. Their leader was a demanding but benevolent patriarch and friend.

But an important principle must be invoked here. *Real and mature leadership and independence do not come with a guaranteed education, no matter how good it is, but only through the struggles with the unforgiving world of ultimate economic reality.*

With the benevolent father now gone, the jealous and destructive so-called real world was in danger of taking over.

The result of challenging the members of the heretofore passive organization to take responsibility for themselves, something that occurred in the leadership project, was that they chose to send a clear and specific message to top management: do not appoint a successor until we are first consulted, face to face, by both the new CEO and the chairman.

The first reaction of top management to this message was negative: the consultants should never have been brought in to set up the leadership project! They end up meddling with the company! They are playing with fire!

The final result, however, was to raise the leadership consciousness of the newly promoted executive himself, and with it, justify the rightness of the promotion and provide for the survival and progress of the newly merged company. For A was not part of the leadership project. By rights, he should have been—but the circumstances of the merger and the ensuing promotion made that impossible.

Let us examine some details.

A leader encourages autonomy, integrity, and creativity in his subordinates, in part because it is desperately needed by the organization and in part because he needs to encourage that development within himself. He projects his own growth needs onto the organization. He hopes to see his own subjective and invisible deficiencies corrected in his objective or visible world, which is the organization. He pushes not for what he is, but for what he wishes to become. The example he wishes to give is autonomy, but the unconscious message he in fact gives, and which is therefore what is actually transmitted, heard, and then mirrored by the orgnization, is dependency. This is not at all uncommon; and it is only a small part of the total picture—the rest of which is very authentic. *But it is precisely this small part which, when understood and corrected, can make a big and profitable difference.*

The transmittal of autonomy does not work when he either teaches or preaches it, for he effectively also stops it with his unconscious and automatic "stopping" or "braking" habits. A pattern in the organization appears to be that a manager automatically contradicts and challenges subordinates' suggestions with the often repeated and mechanical phrase, "I cannot really see what will be accomplished by that!" It seems that the challenge is thrown at the subordinates not because the logic or the exigencies of the situation demand it, but because such is the role or function of a manager or leader within this particular subculture. In other words, a manager *defines* himself as manager by the language that he uses—he does *not become* one.

In this case, technique prevails over authenticity. Integrity demands attention to both the company issues and to the personal issues (i.e., identity, sense of worth, the making of a contribution) of the subordinate. Technique may lead to the appearance of leadership, but not to its substance.

A is afraid of autonomy among his subordinates; this fear stems from a deeper source of his being. He is unconscious of that fear but acts on it nevertheless. The (surprising) *results prove* (unconscious) *intent.* He nevertheless thinks that he wishes to stimulate autonomy. And it is a fact that he, his organization, and the company need that autonomy among the subordinates in order to get the full worth of the salaries paid and in order to insure the newly formed company's survival.

If they are silent and do not act autonomously, maturely, and creatively, that reflects the subtle, unconscious, sub rosa, deceptive, albeit well-intentioned autocracy under which they were nurtured.

Power must empower people, and not make them cower: both leaders and subordinates must know that. A did not encourage autonomy (verbal protestations to the contrary)—but he is a person of good will and can himself respond to the challenge to autonomy.

When a team of consultants (internal or external) succeeds in stimulating autonomy, integrity, and creativity, the executive, who asked for and paid for the autonomy, may be surprised, not pleased, at the objectified and therefore visible transformation in what should have been his own subjective unconscious. The autonomy he earlier wanted and which he now cannot readily manage has suddenly become a reality in the organization. The surprise can be also laced with jealousy: why should they be autonomous and not I? Why do they benefit from my sacrifice? And why do they reject me when I have been good to them?

The automatic and robotic reaction then repeats itself: "I don't really see what can be accomplished by these new developments. What value can be obtained from this new behavior?"

But the truth is otherwise, and very hopeful. To A, a brand new opportunity for leadership presents itself. The promotion requires a quantum jump in leadership.

The newly promoted leader must receive this message:

Here is another opportunity to develop your people (i.e., those in company X), to be loyal to them, and demonstrate contact, respect, and care. Your behavior will serve as model and will reflect well on the full organization. Use this opportunity to practice both love (and compassion) and challenge (both closeness and distance) as leadership traits.

Are A, the new CEO, and B, the old CEO and now chairman, competent to manage a meeting about a proposed successor? A meeting in which subordinates feel emotionally safe and are encouraged to speak up, are acknowledged, a meeting at which all speak with full economic, managerial, financial, psychological, and philosophical sensitivity, truth, realism, and honesty?

There are some useful pointers for such a meeting: see it as a request for healing, for honesty, for patience with difficult issues, for the healing process to conduct itself in its own natural way. In other words, respect the verbatim aspects of the discussion, but acknowledge also the unconscious undercurrent, the subtle needs that are met by such a gathering or ceremony.

And this gets us now to an additional principle of leadership: the transformation of the leader. It occurs, or it must occur, at moments of significant promotion, when old leadership habits no longer work, and when new decision making styles must be instituted. For each promotion is an elevation from manager to leader. A manager who remains a manager upon promotion was promoted in error. *Promotion requires a paradigm shift from manager to leader.* And this cycle repeats itself with each advancement.

True leadership involves both meticulous and dedicated behind-the-scenes work, homework it is called, but it also calls for seizing the grand-gesture opportunity: display, offer, and expect more autonomy, more demands, and more modeling, more risks or challenging human beings for higher performance.

The first grand gesture is for A to take full personal responsibility for the fact that no one in company X is ready to take over. Words are not enough. He must understand in his heart the psychodynamics which led to that failure.

Part of the situation is that *there never is enough time in the business world to do what must be done.* There is never enough time to train the people. Everything must be accomplished faster that it can be accomplished, and difficult decisions, requiring reflection, must be made in a split second.

How true that is also of the military! How often must young and inexperienced troops bear the brunt of the first battle!

It is like marriage or having children. Both of these decisions require much thought. In fact, there is no such thing ever as sufficient thought about them. Such decisions are actually made when the pressure suddenly is so intense that postponement of these fateful choices is no longer possible. The actual decision is then made in an instant.

And one can never plan a steady course. Unexpected curves and potholes, oncoming traffic and bad weather, problems with the vehicle itself appear with uncomfortable suddenness. As is made obvious in a good mystery play, such as Agatha Christie's *The Mouse Trap,* one is always trapped by the unwilling assumptions that one's leadership limitations and the alienation of an indifferent world force one to make!

Leadership is also service. It is a moral choice. A leader has power and uses that power for the protection and profit of those to whom he or she has made a commitment. Power is not sought, but thrust upon one. It is a gift, like grace. This is the moral dimension of leadership. Harry S Truman's Hiroshima decision, right or wrong, exemplifies leadership. *He chooses to take upon himself the isolation, the anxiety, and the guilt—irrevocable, all three—because someone must do it.* Having prolonged the war instead would not have diminished his isolation, the anxiety, and the guilt. This is the fee of services exacted from the leader. It was he, and neither you nor I, who had to suffer these consequences. We can second-guess, and either praise or blame him. But since the decision was not ours, we do not suffer the isolation, the anxiety, and the guilt. Leadership means sacrifice for the good of others, a sacrifice rarely understood and even less frequently rewarded. The needs and passions are far too great to allow the true leader to receive his or her just acknowledgment.

Are you sure you want to be a leader? Are you certain that you are leadership material? These questions must be your constant companions.

Finally, it is important to present the full situation clearly to the newly promoted leader. This can be done by instituting a multiplicity of levels of analysis and diagnosis, of discussion and action plans. Here are some examples of levels of discussion:

- literal
- ethical (democratic)
- political (manipulative, cynical, materialistic)
- unconscious (grieving the loss of the past, managing the anxiety of the present, adapting to the new circumstances)
- philosophic (need for genius level leadership and performance)

In all of this the greatest enemies are pettiness and envy, for leadership demands the utmost in self-sacrificing generosity. Shakespeare's *A Winter's Tale* was based on Robert Green's 1588 play, *Pandosto*, in which the author writes, "Among all the passions wherewith human minds are perplexed there is none that so galleth with restless despite as the infectious sore of jealousy."

Leadership has real meaning only under circumstances of genuine danger and stress. Subordinates must feel that there is someone in authority who is strong enough and also willing to protect them.

We live in a democratic country. Even though our company bosses—unlike our politicians—are not elected by us, we still expect them to represent us, and not to represent the company. Your representative in Congress does not represent the President to you. Quite to the contrary, he or she *represents you* to the president . . . and to the rest of the world. Executives must never be unrealistic, but employees need to feel that their bosses are loyal to them, when that loyalty means something.

If there is stress in top management, because of market conditions, then that stress must be absorbed by top management. A parent cannot expect a child to take on or to cure his or her anxieties. The same is true of employees when their bosses are under stress. Executives get paid emotionally and financially to manage stress in their own souls, and not to pass it on to those who depend on the power of their leaders for emotional and financial security.

The One Contribution

What are the ultimate issues in a company? The final obstacles to success? If one could make a single contribution to an organization, what would it be? What does a corporation really "need"? Does it

need help with formulating strategic plans? Does it need more adequate information about its markets? Does it need a different culture?
Does it need more future thinking? Does it need to understand itself
as an independently functioning system, where structure has more
power than individuals? Does it need more sophisticated automation? Does it need better financial reports? Does it need more
generous bonus programs? Benefits? Does it need courage? Change?
Entrepreneurship? Cost cutting? More aggressive marketing? More
focus on quality? Community and social action programs? Does it
need quality circles? A single leader? Multiple leaders? More
loyalty? More initiative? A clearer corporate vision? Of course, the
answer is all of these. But what if there were only one chance, one
opportunity, one thing that could be done? In short, what is the one
truth for the decision-maker?

Is there an answer? Probably not an absolute one. But we should
nevertheless try to find a defensible answer.

The most important locus of intervention is always at the top of a
company. Even though people at the top may themselves be
imprisoned in the webs of their own organization—both the micro-
organization at the top and the more encompassing macroorganiza-
tion below them—not much can be accomplished without their
signatures and their blessings.

It is rational to assume that people at the top of the organization
ladder have skills and character structures which are as desirable
as they are exceptional. It is rare to meet top leaders who are not
also of unusual intelligence. It is equally rational to assume that
they, like all human beings, are nevertheless limited in other
respects. It then follows that in their limitations as human beings—
whether personal or professional or both—will be found the
obstacles, to the degree that such exist, to organizational success.

In simple language this means that personal insufficiencies, character flaws, ignorance of the boundary conditions of human existence,
limited wisdom on how to cope with the eternal questions, lack of
courage, restricted commitment to the values of the organization,
fear of full disclosure, lack of clarity about the weaknesses and the
evil within oneself, ineptitude in dealing with anxiety and guilt,
lack of appreciation of the multitudinous obligations flowing from
the ethical dimension of the human spirit, and lack of love (meaning
love of self, love of another, and love from another) are the real
causes of organizational difficulties.

These limitations reflect deep character structures and are not superficial personality traits conducive to making easy decisions.

Problems in organizations exist and are not solved, in the last analysis, for these reasons:

- People's personal sensitivities, which are highly understandable, prevent the maximum use of their talents.
- Unfinished childhood business sabotages both organizational effectiveness and personal fulfillment.
- The incomplete realization of the richness of one's potential, the strictures on full personal development, are the final obstacles to maximizing opportunities.

In the genuine fulfillment of an organization's potential, everyone wins and no one loses. That is an axiom not yet widely enough accepted.   And it is precisely this provincialism of doubt which prevents its universal implementation.

These human frailties are not defects; they are facts of life. People do the best they can with the gifts of their existence, but they can always grow further. They can always do better. And in that enduring possibility for improvement lies hope and joy. But all growth must be predicated on first accepting and cherishing, not criticizing, the foundations of growth.

Company problems must be seen as representing externally, in the manner of projections, conditions within the souls of the leaders. The social world in which we live, which includes the company, can be understood as our unconscious made visible. Problems that trouble an organization reflect some deep core of inauthenticity, malfunction, deficiency, or flaw inside the heart of the leader's ego.   If, for example, the top of the organization does not function smoothly as a team, certain tough questions may fruitfully be asked. Does the leader as a person have a deep and an authentic sense of teamwork? Does he or she have an abiding desire to be a member of a team? Is the leader truly committed to other people? Is that person committed to a vision? Does the leader have energy for teamwork and vision? Is the leader serious and caring about running the organization? Does the leader understand and relate to people as individual human beings or only as organizations and systems, structured to maximize profits? Can the leader see the world through the eyes of another? Can the leader see himself or herself through the eyes of a subordinate?

The stress on the leader's character can easily be overemphasized. However, the value of this focus lies in two simple principles.
First, most successful executives are already doing many of the right
things and are also doing things right. And, second, when there are
still problems that resist all attempts at solution, it is useful to consider deeper causes. The system that displeases becomes a projection,
an externalization, an extrusion, a reflection, an objectification, a
reification of structures deep within the leadership soul. These
structures are unconscious; they are invisible. They are assumed,
never questioned. For to question is to move to a higher perspective,
to a new dimension. The fish first must be out of water before water
becomes to it a reality. A child must be away from home, before
homesickness gives it the value. An analytic mind must first become
visionary before it loses its potential. A loner must become a team
player before team values can be even concepts. And egocentrism must
step up to love, and self-centeredness to morality, before the absence
of love and morality can be noticed.

What is to be done? What shall be our actions? We must first
understand that not doing enough results from ignorance of the real
problem and the decision, mostly unconscious, not to do anything
about it.

We cannot, in the form of an isometric exercise, push our right fist
into our left open palm and ask what technique will make the right
hand prevail over the left. The same decision which energizes the
right fist also energizes the left palm. To tell people to become wise
and self-disclosed and then devote their deepest interest and make
their most pronounced commitment to the welfare of the whole, of
the total organization, may simply not serve the core purposes of the
self. The self may not wish to surrender those defenses of the ego
which stand in the way of optimum corporate performance. And the
defenses—better called obstacles in this context—are always the
same two, and they are related: ignorance and lack of will (or lack of
desire).

We must eliminate fundamental character flaws and replace
them with reciprocal character strengths. This applies first and
foremost to top executives. But the flaws and the strengths we have
been discussing cannot be reduced to communication skills, listening
skills, computer-aided decision-making, avoiding panic reactions,
achieving larger perspectives, and so forth. They have to do with

the very system that we call our human existence. They are the most basic structures of consciousness itself. They concern elements within human existence proper.

For the difficulty in making the right decisions about who we are or who we ultimately are to be is rooted in the fundamental ambiguity of existence itself. Being is ambiguous; the ambiguity takes many forms, but it never goes away. Each courageous and univocal decision leads to a new fork in the road. Every additional artery produces myriads of new capillaries. It is the very ambiguity of existence, the polarization which never vanishes, that gives us not only our sense of free will but our actual freedom.

To destroy ambiguity is tyranny, for to destroy ambiguity is also to destroy our free will. If we act freely, we exchange security for dignity, whether in world politics, at the top of organizations, or in the privacy of our bedrooms. But in destroying our freedom we effectively eliminate ourselves as human beings. We use our freedom to freely choose its last act: to destroy itself. And once destroyed, like life itself, freedom cannot be resurrected. For to resurrect freedom is a free choice. And there is no more freedom left. The species "freedom" is extinct. It can no longer reproduce itself.

What then is the critical choice facing each soul as it looks into the void of existence?

It is the conflict between existential aloneness and membership in a system. It is the paradox of choosing to be lonely and free, the isolated individual, the independent identity, on the one hand, and the member of the team, the member of the group, the member of the family, on the other. Where lies our source of identity? Where is the origin of our sense of self? For the unspeakable panic of the schizophrenic derives precisely from this loss of self. Does our feeling of identity—our feeling of being—grow in our isolation? Or does it emerge out of participation?

We know of course that both these alternatives are true; otherwise we could not understand them. We know, of course, also, that they are incompatible. And we also know that they co-exist in one and the same soul. This triadic inconsistency generates the energy for the psychodynamics of a paradigm shift.

The principle is to experience the contradiction and to confront the conflict, for that will elevate the maturity of the soul. Problem solving stops growth, whereas living through a problem transforms perception. That is how one facilitates genuine creativity.

Top executives confront this as their fundamental issue. Will they act in isolation? Will they be the decision-makers for whom "the buck stops here"? Could they make a unilateral decision, of the magnitude of Truman's, to drop an atom bomb and kill more than one hundred thousand people and usher in the nuclear age and make ours the only nation to have ever used nuclear devices against human beings? Or not make it, and take those consequences? Will they take full responsibility for such an action? Will they hold themselves fully accountable? Will they be able to withstand that much loneliness? For to do what is right may never be fully clear, yet it needs to be done. And few will be loved for doing what is right. Many will be punished, even by death. And more, like Robert Oppenheimer, in charge of the Manhattan project, will be crippled by guilt—even though they may have done right.

Is leadership worth such agony? Can such loneliness be endured? But consider this: is leadership avoidable? Socrates told us that the only excuse for leading is that otherwise those will who are less capable.

The other choice is to deny the ultimacy of the individual and to recognize and affirm unequivocally the primacy of the group, the team, the family, the organization, the system, history, roots, heritage, tradition, context. The organization is a system; its problems follow from its structure, not from individual deficiencies. It is cowardly to look for scapegoats, as many of us did after the space shuttle disaster, when the true fault lies in the system, in which we all participate. Accidents will happen; we do not know exactly when and how. And the "culprits," the "negligent" ones, are merely those who by coincidence happen to have been around when the disaster struck. It reminds one of Claude Rains, who, at the end of *Casablanca*, after Humphrey Bogart shoots the general before his very eyes, orders his subordinates to "round up the usual suspects."

Why not apply these investigations and their ensuing standards to industries where accidents are waiting to happen? Why wait until it is too late? The industries that need scrutiny are those where accidents have not yet happened. Once they occur, the system will become self-correcting, without an investigation. Could it be that in the event of universal investigations—or universal ascription of responsibility—all systems would stop? Could it be that we need scapegoats in order to avoid the enormous burden of our own personal responsibility? Will we then be able to say accidents or problems occurred because of the incompetence of others and not because we have not taken full responsibility ourselves? Will that allay our anxiety and diminish our guilt? It will, if we decide that the social structure, the system, is primary and that it is the source of our identity. This choice says that the system will correct itself. Individuals must feel in harmony with their system. As individuals we are nothing. The heroic ego is a fraud. We are identities only by virtue of the group in which we participate, with which we identify, to which we belong, and through which we work. And the problems of the organization must be solved by the leader's ability as facilitator. The leader must facilitate the organization in such a way that the communal solution gradually emerges. That is today's received wisdom on how to manage change.

This solution feels warm, satisfying, and it often works. But it also feels cowardly, dull, unimaginative, conservative, weak, non-heroic, uninspiring, non-visionary, slow, compromising, indecisive. In many cases, strong, clear, precise, unambiguous, courageous, dramatic decisions are required. Group-think may flatten the peaks, narrow the undulations, and quell the fire of the eternal verities.

To say "I" or to say "We" is the archetypal choice, the ultra-choice, for every conscientious executive. What is your first choice? And how will you make it?

Emotional Safety

Following is a general statement of what one should know and of what one can do about creating a climate of emotional safety at a top-level management meeting or confrontation.

A group of senior executives is designing a day to spend dialoguing with top management about the usually undiscussed and even unknown issues in the company, issues which are the true obstacles to fulfilling the vision and the strategic plans of their organization.

(A distinction is here drawn between senior management [level 2] and top management [level 1]. The former consists of about forty persons, and the latter, which can also be referred to as the management committee or the executive committee, consists of perhaps eight at most, with three or four, including the CEO, holding the real power.)

One overarching concern of the two groups is emotional safety. That is a multifaceted issue. The following elements are to be singled out for distinction:

- The emotional safety of *senior management as a group. The* group may be intimidated or have a culture in which certain issues are not raised with top management. Individual, face-to-face discussions may be safe emotionally; there may be a real feeling of comfort in these "one-on-one" meetings. But when the group assembles as a whole, the unspoken rules—such as "thou shalt *not* look ridiculous"—may prevail and inhibit.

- The emotional safety of *individuals among senior management.* This is the converse of the above. Some people may feel more timid than others. There may be a history of bruised feelings between specific individuals in the senior management group with members of the management committee. Others may just be naturally shy or retiring. These persons may then feel inhibited as individuals, even though the group itself may be outspoken.

- Then there is the question of actual safety. And that fact refers to both the group as a whole and to individuals within the group as single entities. To propose to create an atmosphere of absolute emotional safety may be impossible, even fraudulent, for there is no total safety anywhere. Moreover, in a highly charged and high level organizational atmosphere, where the financial, the identity, and the career risks are major, there lurk real dangers. The job, which for many is also their sense of identity, can be put in jeopardy, or lost outright. Permanent enemies can be made. One can become irretrievably defined and classified. Income opportunities can be diminshed or eliminated altogether. Careers can be ruined. And what can be lost is far from minor—a career has been years in the making. To deny these facts is to deny reality.

  Furthermore, beyond the danger there are opportunities. For each and every employee there arise conflicts between their individual expanding job possibilities and loyalty to their parent organization.

- And then there are the parallel issues of the emotional and the actual safety of top management. Subordinates—even at their finest—tend to view superiors as parent surrogates. And a parent can mean many things:

Δ someone to fear, that is, an authority, a father, a paterfamilias;

Δ a person in whose presence one becomes infantilized, that is,
behaves like a child. Many effective adults revert to childhood behaviors in the presence of their aging parents;

Δ a person who is perceived as wanting to mother us. We unconsciously believe that our boss's reward, as it was our
mother's, is to take care of us. In other words, to allow our
boss to take care of us is reward enough for the boss—as it was
with our mother.

Δ Subordinates tend to act as children vis-à-vis their bosses in
this sense: they want attention; they want recognition; they
want rewards; they believe their bosses can dispense goods
and values, happiness and answers, fulfillment and solutions—expectations which are partially realistic with
parents, fully realistic with God, but marginally realistic at
best with real-life bosses.

Δ Subordinates are often not sufficiently aware of the limitations of their superiors. And these limitations can be of
various sorts. Superiors are preoccupied with major corporate
issues which go far beyond the interests of a single subordinate, as well as with personal frustrations in their own lives.
It is always painful to discover that a superior is less interested in oneself than one needs, wishes, or feels one deserves.
But superiors also have their characteriological limitations:
envy, selfishness, insensitivity, anger. Everyone does, but
leaders often are thought to have immunity.

These issues affect executives who are the managers or the superiors of others. Top executives will find it very difficult to deal with
these emotional needs of their subordinates. These infantilistic
needs are far from obvious; nor are they likely to be pronounced, but
they usually exist, and they can create the most severe of all
problems. Furthermore, they cannot easily be dealt with, because of
their sub rosa charcacter. These themes create, for top management,
emotional dangers. Management's own emotional safety is
threatened by the refusal of subordinates to perceive them for the
real flesh and blood, limited, passionate, irrational, struggling,

doubting, incomplete human beings that they, like everyone else, are. Top management's frail humanity must be fully acknowledged.

Moreover, top management's safety is also a matter of real danger: top management must account to the board, to the marketplace, to the stock analysts, to the stockholders, to the consumer, to the law, and to its employees, and must deal with takeover threats. And there are many zones of conflict between their own financial and career interests and their obligations to the corporation.

Many of these points may well have been exaggerated. But such exaggeration is no more harmful than looking through a microscope to magnify a virus. The virus is virulent regardless of its minuscule size. And studying it can teach us how to protect ourselves from it. The same is true of the underlying emotional misunderstandings. To bring them to light gives mature men and women the opportunity to cope with them and to teach others how to do that.

Tactics

Men and women of intelligence and of good will cooperate in transcending these subtle difficulties in human communications. There are many ways to list and discuss them. Here are a few:

The parameters for these presentations are, What can the senior management group do to get their bosses, top management, to listen to their needs, grievances, real issues?

First and foremost, top management must be confronted with the adult reality that management positions require therapeutic skills. And therapeutic skills are listening skills. They are the skills to make people feel heard. But there is more. They are skills for telling the truth, for knowing how to be honest. To listen skillfully and respond is to tell the truth in a way that feels like love, like compassion, like understanding, like help—and not like criticism, rejection, degradation, insult.

To tell the truth is not always easy, for who knows what the truth is? The rule of thumb—and this is absolutely basic—is to step back, move out of the involvement with which one is engaged in the present moment, become a spectator, and take an exploring look at what is happening. "Withdrawal," "non-attachment," "stepping back," "adopting a spectatorial posture," "moving from the engaged to the spectatorial attitude," these are the expressions which attempt to describe this fundamental recursive step of consciousness.

Only from this spectatorial perspective upon one's own actions can one see the truth. And to tell the truth is then simply to describe what one sees as one observes oneself in action. We call that critical step of the mind self-reference or self-consciousness.

The eventual result of good listening is that people unfold themselves, that they mature and grow, and that they solve their own problems. It leads to autonomy, for that is the natural direction in which the human psyche wishes to develop. The results are good feelings, a sense of fulfillment, and enhanced creativity.

But therapeutic skills are not really skills: they are expressions of wisdom, of adult behavior, and of mature personalities. There can be no therapeutic skills which do not also sprout out from within human authenticity. And that project, to become fully human, is our task on earth, and it is a task which transcends all corporate needs.

Now to the specific tactics:

- The premise is that the group must help the boss or bosses to be good listeners. The subordinate helps the leader to become a good leader. It may be emotionally difficult for the child to help the parent be a good parent; but in the business arena, that works. This idea is sold to the subordinate.

- In the process of helping the leader become a good leader, the subordinate helps the leader achieve his or her dearest goals. This idea is sold to the leader.

- For what are the leader's goals? To have a good team. To feel the presence of a team. To feel like a family. To have an era of good feelings among senior and top management. To be able to work while feeling good rather than while being anxious; to be loved rather than to be hated, to be liked rather than to be disliked, to be esteemed rather than to be held in contempt (always, smiles please more than scowls); to develop a real sense of team spirit between senior and top management; to create an atmosphere of extensive emotional safety, where the truth can be spoken. This is how the maximum creativity and contribution of each group member can be assured. That is how one creates an organization which is financially successful and in whose membership anyone can glow with pride.

And what do we do when we must make tough decisions? Can we be supported emotionally by those we must let go? Yes, for that would be the ultimate in success. It can be done, if we can show that the job has changed so much that it has moved away from its old manager. And the obsolete manager should not change, for the character traits which endeared him to his past are far more valuable than the job itself. Thus, if a manager is kindly and loved but the organization under him no longer responds to kindness and love, but asks for hardness, then it is time for the manager to move on. Not because he has failed: on the contrary, were he to become hard and succeed in the new kind of company, then he would have failed. But true success is to leave the organization and remain kind. That is the critical human point. That is how a "dismissed" subordinate can support his or her boss even in the ultimate act of firing. That is successful communication!

Thus, *it is the task of subordinates to help the boss to help them to achieve his own goal—which is to create an organization with a high quality (aligned) team spirit.* (The expression is clumsy in part because it describes a complex human reality.)

- The boss's goals are congruent with the goals of the organization.

- There are interferences with the goals. These may involve the boss's or bosses' behavior habits, language habits, or character structures.

- These interferences or obstacles must be viewed as resistances to authenticity, as sabotage to success. But beyond that,

- they must be viewed as mostly unconscious, unintentional, or unaware, and

- as understandable, legitimate, and as existing for good reason. The importance of this latter point cannot be overestimated!

- The group must express understanding of the legitimacy of the bosses' feelings. But above and beyond that, the understanding must be real, not feigned. Examples are, "I know this must not be easy for you." "I have also been in your position, and I can feel empathy with you." "I acknowledge your good will."

- The members of the group must express their own feelings. And they must learn how to do that so that their feelings will be heard.

- And that is done by being subjective, using the first person, speaking accurately, being sensitive. One must describe how one feels and what one perceives and what appears to be happening to oneself. One must not accuse, or even state presumptive facts—which are always controversial —nor speak for others or assess others' feelings and motives. Examples of successful grievance statements are, "That statement hurts my feelings," "I feel put down," "I believe there is a more helpful way to state the same point," "It would be important to me if you could consider the following."

- Think big. Think in perspective. Always ask, What is a better way to do it?

- Take personal, individual, and group responsibility for effectiveness. You want results, outcomes; do not get stuck on process, rules, directions, procedures, discussions. Your goal is a worthy human cause. Stick to it. Achieve it. *Life will never forgive you—nor will you, nor will your conscience—if you do not achieve your humanizing and ethical goals.*

- Be—in your mind, in your will, and in your heart—what you yourself wish others to be. Always view your own wishes and statements and criticisms as self-referential. Always ask yourself, "Am I really talking about myself?" It is in you where lies the greatest potential for change. Your control is over yourself— little else. Use that power!

- Complaints about others—accurate as they are—usually contain also an element of projection. As you criticize others, as you ask favors of them, you may actually be criticizing yourself and asking of yourself. For example, when you say to a subordinate, "I really care about you!", you may also be saying, "I wish someone would care for me as I care for you!" When a subordinate makes you angry, you may in part also feel that your own inadequacy makes you angry.

- Always assume that what you think of, and say about, your boss, your subordinates think of and say about you.

- If you want to develop a team, then involve everyone on both sides of the discussion team. Certain persons tend to emerge as leaders and spokespersons; some individuals are propelled into greater visibility than others. Attention to fairness as well as to tapping the creative potential of all executives demands that everyone be noticed and be invited to speak—on both sides of the discussion table.

- To manage reality means two things:

    1. to fulfill one's need for intimacy, approval, closeness, friendship, love, camaraderie, and

    2. to deal maturely with alienation, danger, irrationality, injustice, opposition—i.e., hard facts.

    The first is the soft reality; the second is the hard reality. Both are real.

Mature managers can integrate these two apparently incompatible polarities.

- We deal with this conflict by "telling it like it is." We must understand the polarity dimension of human existence. The joy of living is to learn to cope with all that ambiguity and paradox. That is the fuel for evolutionary progress.

    The truth is still our greatest ally.

CHAPTER 22

Transforming
Marketing Intelligence

The Power Level

How would one apply the genius-power level of performance and ethical action to marketing? If the marketing problem is, for example, the selling of large and sophisticated systems—whether for government, or for the medical establishment, or for heavy industry—the more general question we must pose is, How can philosophy in business assist the marketing of these large and specialized items or systems?

The first premise is that the expected usual must obtain: quality, experience, service, reliability, honesty, integrity, as well as marketing analyses, trends projections, and so on.

But we know how to do that. Because every business is getting better at the highest level quality control, the competition also gets keener. That is what the free enterprise system intends to accomplish—and in fact has achieved. But for those insiders contending with the system, the overwhelming question of how to beat the competition remains. And here the new marketing approach which uses philosophy in business may be of assistance. And the intention of philosophy in business is to increase the value, that is, the quality, of the company and the service of the company. The marriage of philosophy and business must lead to an authentic win-win situation.

The primacy of networking is the first premise of philosophy in business as applied to marketing. That is why mass marketing works best when it is associated with a public figure—usually a non-controversial member of the entertainment industry, IBM's Charlie Chaplin figure being a particularly felicitous example—who has established a "personal contact," i.e., network, making connection with millions of potential customers.

The additional premise is that people of influence must be approached and challenged at the level of their highest, noblest, and most sophisticated instincts.

And the applications of these two premises are three:

- Find the mission of the company. The mission is assigned by reality and not by fiat. The mission depends on what the actual business of the company is, on how it is perceived by the public, and on what actual values the company represents. These actual values are realities; they are historical, social, political, and economic facts over which the executives of the company have relatively little control—and to which they must respond.

  If a company is in the food business, its task is to feed the public, whatever else they may claim. If the company is in the pharmaceutical business, then the health of the nation is its business, and no change in board policy will affect that reality or the values inherent in it. Managing money is the business of banks and the values which money represents to the public are the values in which the bank deals. And no restatement of bank policy or mission can affect this fact. If a company builds aircraft, it is in the safety and transportation business, in the business of bringing the peoples of the world closer together— regardless of whether or not the stockholders of that company wish to think in this way. If a company sells toothpaste, then oral hygiene and all which that implies is the value element of their business.

- A company represents certain basic ethical values. We must understand what they are, and how they are to be implemented responsibly.

  For example, the Fluidex Pharmaceutical Company is in the health business, which exhibits the value of care, which activates love—which in turn translates into the values of life and of existence. It is a free enterprise business, which activates the value of liberty or of freedom. It is a company which is after market share, and it therefore actualizes the value of growth.

  Philosophy in business can help clarify what these values are and then interest significant people to participate in implementing these higher goals. We assume that competence, high ethical standards, and a highly developed sense of values go together in the personality structures of high executives.

- A company's problems are solved not only for the company in question but for the public. To the degree that the company solves these problems, it is fulfilling a public service and perhaps even a historic economic function. For example, a truck-manufacturing company not only sells trucks, but helps solve the transportation problems of this nation.

Change

Another major theme to be classified and discussed under the topic of survival in marketing intelligence is change. Change is the phenomenon of survival. Survival requires change. So does adaptability, flexibility, or wonder. Transferring from one system to the next signals a further need for change.

The *first* principle of change is this: there is an intrinsic problem with planning and setting goals. No one will deny their value or their proven advantage. But there is a certain unreality about goals and objectives.

Both the predicted and the planned futures make sense essentially only in terms of today's realities, today's needs, and today's values. We all must remember making plans and commitments as children about our futures as adults: whom we were going to marry, what our occupation was to be, where we would live, and how we were to act towards others, how we would raise our own children, especially in view of how we were treated by our parents and our teachers. And how much money we were going to have at what age. Talk about inflation . . . ! Not only did most of these predictions not come to pass, but what is even more significant, we regard them today as humorous at best and ridiculous at worst.

How many times do we find a young person in his or her early twenties with a complete plan for life: a strategic plan for everything until the end of time. Whereas such certainty, aplomb, determination, and enterprise are impressive and indeed worthy of emulation, there is an aspect to all this planning which is patently immature, compulsive, irrational, adolescent, and just plain bad common sense. It is an obsession for order which has more to do with inner anxieties than with external realities. For the young person of today has desires, needs, energies, and values that probably will mean little some thirty or forty years hence. The person changes and so does the environment. And the future is not what you shall be or what your environment shall be, but what your interaction with your environment shall be. You and the environment live in constant dialogue, and you are both changed by it. Even if one's plans were to come true, in many instances they would not be dynamic and profit us little. In business, strategic plans are important; but what is more important is the mind which is trained or has trained itself to think strategically—and this implies respect for the intrinsic "irrealism" of planning.

What this means in practice is something like the following: One adheres to rigorous strategic planning principles—perhaps by adopting the management author Michael Porter's "competitive advantage" procedures—but realizes at the same time that these procedures themselves are questionable, and in any event must be re-evaluated constantly. The strategic position of the industry must be reevaluated continuously; the position of your company with respect to the rest of the industry must be reevaluated continuously; and the desirability of strategic thinking itself must be reevaluated continuously.

In fact, we can argue that the compulsion to set strategic plans, especially in one's personal life—considering the predictably fast and changing world—is more a resistance to change than a recognition of it or proof of mastery over it.

The *second* principle of change is this: Change is a beginning. We all know that. We look forward to better days, and we anticipate what will happen with varying degrees of anxiety. We also may worry about the future. Be that as it may, change is the beginning of something new.

But change is also an ending. To this extent we must mourn it, and we must ceremoniously bury the past, ritualistically surrender what is now gone and is forever lost. Change, by rolling events down into the abyss of an irrecoverable past, is also sad, tragic, is about loss, and leads to nostalgia ("Nostalgia ain't what it used to be," Peter De Vries). The tears and the sorrow must be felt, expressed, and respected. The past is to be mourned. To be misunderstood is to be in pain. People are grateful if we understand and honor their hurt.

But above all, change is a leap through a neutral zone. That is the crazy period, the period of insanity. That is when one agrees with one's critics who say, "You have gone crazy!" It is the existential crisis, a crisis of the soul. It is here that the knowledge that anxiety is the healthful way to change can save our lives, and certainly preserve our sanity. Wallace Stevens wrote, "Lost enough to find myself," and the *I-Ching* says, "Savor that without flavor." These phrases describe the neutral zone, the leap, the foundationlessness, the groundlessness, the anguished leap over the gaping void below, that is, the actual moment or period of change. Remember, you cannot leap over a precipice in two easy smaller jumps. While in the air, you are gripped by the panic, the anxiety, that are the inevitable companions of true growth.

The *third* and last principle of change is the following ten-point sequence.

- Necessity. Change is necessary. It is here to stay. There is not much point in fighting it. It occurs everywhere. And we will in fact adapt, whether we want to or not and whether we agree to it or not. It can be predicted with certainty that we will make change work. That is useful information. It can help soothe and reassure us.

- The unknown. The outcome of change is unknown. We must operate in an environment where the results are hopes and guesses, never facts or predictable realities. Strategic planning is essentially impossible, for it presupposes a knowledge of the future. All we can do is to prepare the workforce and the company now to be flexible and adaptable later, so that whatever the future may bring, top management can be confident of a positive outcome. And that kind of ubiquitous preparation is known as management education. Education is for change, not for a specific future. Thus education is the real strategic planning. We plan for the type of people we want in our organization, not for the kind of structure and products our business will have. And we want people who are highly competent in managing change. They will help decide the nature of our business.

- Faith. We need to have the faith—the faith that can move mountains and therefore make things true—that change is progressive and not regressive. We must believe that change is part of evolution, and then we shall be perfectly willing to flow along with—in fact, welcome—the evolutionary changes that are taking place in nature. And nature encompasses both the physical and the social environment, including the econ-omy. It is the very essence of business to adapt itself quickly to the evolving market conditions. In fact, this kind of flexibility and sensitivity to the market defines a successful leader. And the market is part of nature. Market fluctuations are natural events based on natural laws. Society operates by the laws of group interactions, and to the degree that human beings are part of nature, the laws of human interaction are also part of nature. The industrial and ensuing social changes are equally natural. The marketing intelligence adapts to the market as protozoa adapt to the brine.

- Resistance. It is normal to meet resistance to change. This is a law of physics (inertia and momentum, Newton's Second Law of Motion), a law of social behavior, and a law of the psyche or the soul. The executive's mind must be set on this. Resistances to change are to be expected and need not frighten us. The adaptive responses are a routine part of life. It is this comfortable, tolerant, and patient—in short, positive—mindset which can make the difference between success and failure, survival or demise, in today's business climate.

- Mystery. The process of change is mysterious. There seems to be no predictable way to understand it, and that is one reason why it cannot be predicted. And therefore it cannot be controlled, harnessed, or forced to bend to our will. Even if we postulate forces—such as nature, evolution, God, the life force, the will to live, spirit, consciousness becoming self-conscious, freedom, the cosmic mind, the universal reason, substance, logic, the collective unconscious, or the general will—they help us little in making sense of change, its nature, and its direction. The leader must be prepared to operate in a quagmire which is not understood because it cannot be understood. And this primordial Chaos, the Greek god, cannot be understood because it is intrinsically incomprehensible.

- New Paradigms. Change often leads to paradigm shifts, to major, fundamental changes in the perception of the world and in the assumptions we make about the nature of reality. Examples are changing from the notion of a flat to a spherical earth, from a geocentric universe to a heliocentric solar system, from creationism to evolution, from a fixed concept of space–time to a relative one, from an absolute monarchy to a radical democracy, from a God-centered world to a human-centered world, and so forth.

- Danger. The denial of change can only lead to disaster. All repression is bad. Not facing facts never solves a problem. Refusing to see reality for what it is can only bring disappointment, disillusionment, frustration, failure, and pain. The mark of an effective executive is the willingness and the resulting habit of accepting facts as they are and responding instantly. Change must be fully felt, explored, experienced, lived through. Then we can expect success and joy, not failure and depression.

- Anxiety. We must always expect change will be accompanied by anxiety. And the insights pertaining to anxiety (which is normal) and to courage (which is the choice to tolerate anxiety) apply fully also to the uncertainties and the tribulations of change.

- Mourning. Closely related to facing anxiety is the need to mourn in change. Mourning means to legitimize the pain, to enter it, to feel and to express the tears, the regrets, the loss, the anger, the end. It is good to create ceremonies around mourning, so that it does not become cerebral but is seen and felt and expressed with one's full body, with one's comprehensive gestures, and with the consent of the group. There is no substitute for the comfortable feeling and the healing succor of public support.

- Obstacles. We must focus on the obstacles to change. "Analyze the resistance," the psychoanalysts prescribed. The vision of the new is the easy part. Enthusiasm gives us the temporary illusion that the barriers, which we often make and hold in place by ourselves, can be knocked down. But the hard work is to isolate the resistances and face them slowly and persistently.

I recently spoke to several young, bright, well-intentioned, and disillusioned Ph.D.s about how they felt about their jobs in one of America's larger corporations. They represent a large number of bright and educated young Americans who have entered our most important companies. They feel privileged to have the opportunity, in fact the charter, to change the organization. They are called the "change agents" for the organization; not a bad expression. They may be disappointed that the organization does not respond as they would wish it did. Many employees feel that bureaucracy deprives them of oxygen and thus diminishes their capacity to be themselves.

(Jonas Salk said recently that it is good we can prevent the crippling of the body, but can we prevent the crippling of the mind?) And in feeling somewhat suffocated in their effort to be, they find it difficult to make their maximum contribution to the company. They feel they are blamed for not doing their best, yet they are prevented from doing it.

What to do? First, they must realize that they cannot change the culture of the organization, and that perhaps even their desire to do so is arrogant and presumptuous. To change a large corporation is to hope that an ant can win an argument with an elephant. Second, discussions about changing the large organization are being repeated today by the thousands, in all the industries of the Western world. Our discussion is typical of the culture of the modern organization, for we are speaking the language of the age. Third, the organization will change anyway, because the larger culture within which it exists demands it, whether these employees are permitted to make, and can make, their contributions or not. In fact, they could leave right now, and the organization would change without them. Fourth, their principal responsibility to their boss is to make him powerful and successful. He needs them to do that, and he will be grateful for their understanding and loyalty. And, finally, their responsibility to themselves is to make themselves marketable: to be so good at what they do, that—unlike consultants or therapists, who must make themselves obsolete—the organization they serve will not be able to do without them.

Survival

Survival is a key to the marketing intelligence. There are many ways to survive. In the animal kingdom, brute force prevails and survives. That may be emotionally gratifying, but it is also usually unethical—in human standards—and often fatal. In civilization (or so-called civilization), survival is complex, bureaucratic, legalistic, convoluted, emotionally frustrating, and biologically stressful. We fight for survival and for justice through negotiations and by attacking assumptions. That may be difficult, but it is the effective way to survive in the business ambience.

Two experiences illustrated and brought home to me the negotiation dimension of survival.

How do we deal with a marketing emergency? The masculine leadership style says, Fight. The feminine leadership style says, Love, for quality and love are feminine survival traits. A combination of the two says, Appreciate your opponent, negotiate, be good in debate, and understand assumptions.

Life is full of marketing-type emergencies. One was a two-hour interchange (1 January 1986) between a group of citizens from Seattle with a corresponding number from Leningrad. The TV host was Phil Donahue. What struck me most was the divergence of world views, a painful reality which made communication between the Russians and the Americans virtually impossible. There was no real common ground. There were no significant common assumptions. The revelation was to see, directly, in the thick of human interaction, how harmful indeed can be the absence of common assumptions.

When the Russian master of ceremonies said that the Korean 747, the civilian airplane lost over the Kamchatka Peninsula and shot down by the Russians, was a spy plane, or that the reason Jewish emigration from Russia is down to a mere trickle is that all the Jews who wanted to leave Russia have already done so, then we knew that any actual discussion ended at that very point. In fact, one recognized that no actual discussion had ever started in the first place.

That is a negotiating trick against which powerful defenses must be mobilized. But when a generation has been raised brainwashed—which is the denial of reality and means distortion under the guise of reasonableness—and kept in its place by extreme isolation and Iron Curtain borders, then the task is monumental and fiercely frustrating, but no less important for its difficulty.

We do not ordinarily comprehend that there are people whose fundamental assumptions, basic structures of perceiving the world, are categorically different from ours, are light years apart, and require the patience of Job to tolerate. To experience this to learn once more a key lesson about what we perceive to be evil. It is healthy to monitor our emotional responses. We simply cannot digest what is occurring unless we have the intellectual tools to understand that we are in the presence of a collision of assumptions, a head-on crash of metaphysics. And this ignorance or blindness, or myopia, leads us to conclude that there are essentially only two options open to us. One is to go to sleep, to ignore the feelings of evil and nausea which overcome us, and the other is to go murderously on the attack, and say there is no way to reason. Their assumptions are evil, and we must be ready to strike out and go to war. We must be prepared to kill—and die. That is the danger of monolithic thinking.

Negotiation, however, is the answer. It is the answer in business, and it is the answer at a more basic level in politics and history. But we must understand that negotiation is a marketplace phenomenon, and specifically a free-market phenomenon.

The most insidious tool of the immoral negotiator is the evil of denying someone else's reality. And the reality denied is experienced to be mine. I do not feel that I am denying anyone else's reality, although as a matter of fact I might be doing precisely that. The pain of having one's deepest reality, sincerest beliefs, and most ancient convictions denied—convictions so strong that they could be called knowledge and certainty—constitutes the effective, the definitive, destruction of the mind.

I am my reality. And if you deny it, if you act as if it did not exist, then you are eliminating me from the surface of the earth as effectively as if you were to pulverize me with an atom bomb—except that in the latter case I would not have to live condemned to observe my non-existence. For you to deny my existence, especially if you are in a position of power, if you have what I need, is to drive me crazy, to make me psychotic, to push me into schizophrenia, to plunge me into the deepest depression, to push me over the brink. And you will eventually succeed in making me into a non-person, a shell, a being that may breathe but has long ago left behind its human core. No wonder the United Nations has defined brainwashing as a major crime, the rape of the mind.

What was most effective in the TV program just alluded to was an American's statement to the Russians that we do not trust the Russian government—and for good reason (such as the arming of Russia during President Carter's disarmament, and the fact that during the entire TV program not once was the Russian government criticized by Russians). Perhaps the Russian people can understand that.

What has this got to do with survival and negotiation as aspects of the marketing intelligence? Marketing is the art of survival, and one of the basic tools of the art of social survival is bartering, bargaining, negotiating. The Indians negotiated with Lewis and Clark in the Northwest Territory. And the Americans and the Russians must negotiate with each other.

To understand the basics of negotiation is half the battle. We need to accept the realities of the marketplace as a natural law; they are natural not only for economics but also for society and social interactions.

This law does not change through legislation designed to abolish it. If communism, or any other totalitarian or autocratic, including theocratic, social order, counters this law, the competition of the marketplace nevertheless remains. Russia is now, as always, competing with the West. There is of course also political competition within Russia. This suppression of competition gives rise to an enormous bureaucracy, which in turn creates insidious pockets of competition within the system itself, pockets which are not natural but are gratuitously oppressive. The same applies to an oligarchy, which perhaps describes the American economy in the late nineteenth and early twentieth centuries.

Another example of the pervasiveness of negotiation—horse-trading may be a better word—is the experience of relocating, moving. My friend Warren Bennis once told me that what he hates most are moving and having a heart attack—in that order. Certain truths from my perception of the movers' response to the marketplace emerge in that experience: Money is everything. Human reality, social interactions, existential truths, all of them are consolidated in one agreed-upon method of transaction and explanation: Money. "I am in it for the money," says the driver. "I am in it to get the cheapest deal," replies the customer. No laws or regulations, agreements or contracts, seem to change the fundamental pressures of the marketplace: supply and demand. It is very difficult for customers to treat drivers and workers as human beings if the constant message from them is, "I'll do nothing except for the money, and all I want from you is money" and it is very difficult for a contractor to be civilized towards a customer if all the customer does is try to squeeze a little more free service out of the vendor. Human relations are seen not as generous, ethical, principled, just, but as mere bartering. Bargaining, seeking bargains, negotiating, playing games, haggling over price—as in a Tunisian bazaar—must be themselves viewed as a healthy, normal, ethical, just, fair, and humane way of relating to people. That is the lesson a free economy teaches one, the message from the forces of the marketplace. And that is what the marketing intelligence knows, understands. It is the milieu within which it can operate smoothly and efficiently.

Competition leads to a healthy and balanced economy regardless of the units of exchange. The latter can be money, love, status, knowledge, information, perquisites, or any other tradable physical, emotional, or intellectual value. Competition, which by definition entails negotiation, bartering, trading, and so forth, relates to the full spectrum of human problems and not only to the economic arena. Life is a universal stock exchange, a universal bond market, and a universal futures trading, a commodities economy. Negotiation applies equally to the intellectual arena, to the philosophical arena, to the marketplace of ideas. In epistemology, for instance, we find different ideas of science, different concepts of truth, different notions of evidence, varying needs for certainty, and in metaphysics and anthropology we find different visions of reality and different theories of human nature, of values, and of aspirations. As long as there are ego cathexes at stake—ego involvements or identity issues—and as long as the differences are perceived as serious, all professional and social relations become "negotiations."

Understanding the symptoms of our own visceral resistances to these changing perceptions and world-views helps us meet these problems and challenges with realistic solutions—solutions that work, are effective, pragmatic, i.e., market-sensitive.

What are the implications for companies? Customers want quality. And they will demand it, relentlessly, unless they are successfully brainwashed. Brainwashing of customers happens not infrequently, and worse than that, it is sometimes successful. Customers never really expect to compromise on quality. They will always demand good service and top products. No one can tolerate having a new radio crackle with static, no matter how cheap it was, or a car stranded on the freeway, no matter how inexpensive it was, nor a house where the roof leaks during the first rainstorm, no matter how good a deal it was. We will always demand quality; merchants can never avoid confrontations with irate customers. Thus a good company insists on quality without compromise.

The word "value" is often misused in this connection. Value is supposed to represent a compromise between price and quality. That makes sense to the manufacturer. But it does not make sense to the consumer. The consumer wants quality and low price, not a balance of the two. An excellent company gives the consumer that high quality, without compromise, but still at a low cost.

And that is where the smart business person enters into a partnership with the consumer. Business must find new and imaginative ways to make quality and personal contact less expensive. In fact quality includes not only a first-rate product, but also includes first-rate service. This often includes education and training—both before and after the purchase. Quality also includes low price. The two are not in competition. Low price is part of the quality transaction that includes both product and service. And that ranges over a very long time, in some cases even over a lifetime. This is a fundamental concept in philosophy in business. There are only two solutions—and both must be implemented: (1) Create a company culture which understands this need and its value, and (2) automate. It is apparent to virtually every customer that department-store clerks spend 95 percent of their time on record keeping and on bookkeeping details, and only 5 percent on really helping and serving the customer, i.e., on actually making a sale.

Two basic business rules: to be customer driven and to innovate. The latter is the secret of "presence." One does not know that a phenomenon or perception is real unless the quality of the contact changes. You touch someone, and the feeling vanishes unless you rub or caress. Driving, you stare at the road which extends before you and you stop seeing it unless, like a pendulum, you oscillate your eyes and scan both sides of the road. To be customer-oriented is to know the importance of *contact*, that your reality is to be outside of yourself, to transcend yourself. These two powerful principles are not just of commercial value but happen to be universal human truths.

Automation can make products and services better and cheaper. The business, to continue using the moving industry example, needs one operator (driver) who is in charge of the entire transaction and who therefore deals directly with the customer. And that includes the sale. Time is spent with the customer, not with manufacturing, product development, or service. In the moving industry, virtually every step along the way can be improved by automation. Entirely too much work is still performed on the back of the workers; and it is literally back-breaking work. By automating the move, the driver spends time with the customer instead of lifting heavy boxes.

The moving industry is dismally behind the times, caught up in an economic crunch, solving it by overcharging customers, by underpaying drivers, by overworking employees, and by depending on the protection of outdated government regulations. Why? Because this industry is not yet adequately automated. What solution have they adopted? Be tougher with the rules! Enforce them blindly! Punish those who use discretion—rather than building better client relations, understanding that generosity is contagious, and realizing that the keener the competition the more important become customer relations! Toughness is a bureaucratic answer, not a visionary one. Yet the same CEO will pay high fees for speakers at his sales meetings to eulogize risk and creativity. And of all the drivers—and drivers are the core of the business and they must be exposed to the realities of the marketplace—the only one invited to their annual sales meeting was the solitary "Driver of the Year"!

It always amazes me how unskilled in the basics of human relations are the people who work in American industry and meet the public. It is close to scandalous what little knowledge they have of the realities of the marketplace, the importance of the company–customer relationship, the necessity for an all-around good customer–company experience.

The separation of service from sales operations may fit the needs of the company's organization chart, but it does not contribute to the mutlifaceted quality company-customer contact experience. The company which first solves this problem, perhaps through decentralization, has the potential of sweeping the marketplace.

The heart of a business—if its people and customer orientation are to mean anything at all—is a deepened understanding of human nature, the rational part, of course, but the irrational aspect above all.

In general, the public perceives every member of an organization as responsible for the entire organization. Each employee represents the whole company. Each employee in a well-run company understands and accepts that, and knows how to handle any situation to which this fact may give rise. And each executive in a well-run company knows how to craft the company into a body where employees are proud to work.

Finally, marketing intelligence must also and importantly use therapeutic skills, in the sense that the marketer must understand (a) how he or his product are perceived by the market—which invariably is opposite to what he may think of himself—and (b) the immense irrational component in that perception. Popular demand substitutes for reason; packaging replaces substance; claims supersede judgment; cultural consensus is evidence for truth; material benefits and cynical egoism pass for fulfillment and self-respect.

The marketing intelligence seeks the full coincidence, a total conformity, of the internal state of consciousness with the demands of external reality. That has also been called the trance state, or flow state, according to the University of Chicago psychologist Mihaly Csikszentmihalyi. The flow state

> exists when the task at hand and individual skill are evenly matched. Any other combination induces either anxiety or boredom. "When you encounter challenges that are greater than your skills, that's anxiety," says Csikszentmihalyi. "When your skills exceed the challenges, that's boredom."
>
> Put so simply—that people will be most productive when skills match challenge—flow theory sounds hardly profound. But this simplicity conceals the theory's elegance, for it rethinks the question of what motivates people. Most psychology studies behavior that can be modeled experimentally, not the unseen workings of the mind. Therefore it focuses on exterior motivating factors—the candy a child earns for solving a puzzle, the seeds a pigeon gets for finding its way home. But Csikszentmihalyi believes that people often act as they do not for reward, or because of subconscious drives, or even because a behavior has survival value, as sociobiologists argue. Rather, he believes, the pleasure deriving from the flow state has "an autonomous reality that has to be understood on its own terms."
>
> *Newsweek*, 2 June, 1986

This is another aspect of the marketing intelligence, for its motivation is totally internal.

When I started in business, I thought marketing was either shipping or advertising or both. Now I realize that marketing is everything, because marketing is no more and no less than what Freud called reality testing and what biologists call adaptation.

We can call that the subjective or invisible economy in human relationships. Human relationships are fundamentally affected by the relative "phenomenological size or mass"—the apparent, perceived, emotional, or affective size—of the subject and the object, or of the subjective and the objective zones of experience respectively.

That may be generally and mostly true, but it is of special significance if the latter, the object, is either a person or a major life task, such as achieving status, creating value, or whether it is the perceived importance of something, its level of challenge, the opportunity for learning, the need to teach, and so forth.

Equality between the subjective and objective zones of experience leads to synchronicity, relaxation, and to an almost trance-like, natural rather than reflexive, state of mind. Inequality leads to either challenge or boredom. By the way, the distinction between natural and reflexive lies in that the latter is an examination, a perception, a study, an objectification of the former. So that to have a headache, and to suffer from it, is to be in the natural attitude. But to study the headache and to study how one responds to this headache or to pain in general is to be in the reflexive attitude.

A person focused on subjectivity is either self-centered, in which case he or she exploits others, or bored for lack of contact with and stimulation from the external world. A person focused on the objective side of existence feels blessed or insecure, for the source of value and identity is a gift from the outside and not an achievement from the inside.

Maturity apparently comes from a kind of balance, where the gift of existence is moderated by the power over one's own destiny, and where withdrawal into the shell of one's subjectivity is balanced by the challenge offered by the demands of external world.

Subject and object are like two vessels. There is instability if one is more full than the other. Instability is not bad, but it must be understood and evaluated. It is disclosed internally in feelings and externally in behavior.

Marketing is about reaching the buying public, recognizing their wants, understanding how they make decisions, and developing, designing, or refashioning products and services to meet these demands and needs.

Marketing also concerns a reexamination of what the business of the company really is, who the customer is, what the product is, and so forth—under the assumption that fresh thinking in these areas will always benefit the health of the company.

Finally, before any of this thinking is undertaken, the marketing mind must be expanded, stimulated, made more alert and more brilliant. It must also be filled with facts.

In all these areas philosophy can help.

We must begin by developing a list of what the marketing person already knows and understands. Once the knowledge or the database is as complete as circumstances permit, creative thinking begins.

Once creative and innovative thinking begins, it is likely that the first question will be, How can we get more information?

Then we proceed to use the philosophic view of human nature for both mind expansion and the facilitation of brainstorming. This is the most difficult, challenging, exciting, and rewarding part of the marketing exercise. We ask how the human concerns over death, anxiety, pure consciousness, freedom, evil, courage, and so forth, are related to a company's marketing dilemmas. (This topic cannot be developed here fully.)

Then we must consolidate what we have and decide on action plans—or decide creatively how intelligent action plans can be developed. For it is here where the creative mind stops and the engaged mind—the mind that has to place itself on the line through the allocation of resources—takes over. The engaged mind requires philosophy to understand how committed and courageous choices are made. And it asks itself, what are the obstacles to action?

Negotiation

The price of oil fell from $26 per barrel in December 1985 to $9.95 in April 1986. The effect of that drop was that the industrialized nations stood to save $100 billion in costs; but this drop in prices, combined with the concurrent drop of the dollar, led also to ruinous conditions for oil companies.

Let us study some generic approaches to a solution.

The problem is insoluble in the system in which it is presented, whether that be the system which I am as an individual employee or the system which the company is—or beyond. If the problem cannot be resolved within the unit in which it occurs—or in which it appears to occur or in which its symptoms are evident—then the next highest unit (next highest generalization or next highest category) must be invoked and investigated.

One must therefore transcend the system, get out of the system. We must, at another time, develop techniques to facilitate this transcendence of the system. This process is called self-transcendence, because it is the self, or the unit, which is transcended.

The issue then moves (expands, transcends, self-transcends) from the individual employee to

- the company, to
- the industry, to
- U.S. politics, to
- politics with allies, to
- politics with neutrals, to
- politics with adversaries.

But we are not passive in our relation to the next larger system. The larger system also needs us. If the U.S. oil industry collapses, then the U.S. economy collapses—and reliance on foreign oil, mercifully past by 1986, begins anew. If the hospital industry collapses, then not only will many be out of work and the economy be disrupted, but medical care for all Americans will suffer severely. If the automobile industry collapses, then the U.S. economy will experience a massive disruption, and the United States will import where it should export—and risk becoming a poorer, even a beggar, nation. The larger system, the nation, therefore is dependent on the company as well. The relationship is interdependent.

The U.S. government depends in the same fashion on other nations, and that dependency is also reciprocal.

The reciprocity must be clearly articulated, for it gives dignity and power to those who are dependent and humility and realism to those who are powerful.

Various examples can help to illustrate a serious and enduring point.

The oil price crisis (low prices as opposed to the earlier high-prices crisis) was met with Vice President Bush's traveling to Saudi Arabia to help "stabilize" prices, and then Israel's suggestion (in all probability orchestrated) that the industrial nations use some of their windfall savings to support the economies of Egypt, Lebanon, Syria, and Jordan. The help could be tied to the price of oil. That would politically stabilize the Middle East. These were imaginative steps.

There is no room for vindictiveness in this issue, although Western nations may enjoy the suffering of the OPEC cartel, for the latter certainly has created vicious problems in its day.

In general, genius power level thinking means to transcend the narrow range of one's feelings. Then we can cope successfully with evil or with adversaries.

- Do not submit or surrender or adapt to your enemy or adversary.
- Do not destroy or kill or eliminate your enemy or adversary.
- Dialogue with your enemy or adversary; integrate, synthesize, elevate the relationship, search for a win-win end to negotiations.
- The ultimate dialogue with your adversary leads to a joint venture—as should be the case with the United States and Japan. The latter possess extraordinary skills; and their culture expects them to display exceptional group consciousness and unflinching company loyalty. Furthermore, when and where we send technicians, they send engineers. Where we provide expensive back-up contracts, they assume as a matter of honor that a vendor will support its clients. In U.S. suburbia, if a husband returns from work much after five, the neighbors may gossip about philandering. In Japan, if a neighbor's husband comes home from work at five rather than at eight or at ten in the evening, the neighbors will gossip that he is disloyal to his company. Japan's success is a culture issue; it is here to stay. And it is precisely those cultural elements behind their successes that contradict our definition of leadership—which is vision, independence, iconoclasm, freedom, and anti-communalism.

What would be a joint venture? Western ethics and Japanese skills? Western philosophy and Japanese teamwork? Western visionariness and Japanese implementation? Western political theory and Japanese family cohesion? Whatever the answers, this is the true internationalism.

In early 1986, the Walker Museum in Minneapolis displayed an exhibit integrating traditional with modern Japan. It was called "Tokyo: Form and Spirit." It was an inspired attempt to integrate technology with mystical art, Japanese history with contemporary international politics and economics. The true joint venture with Japan would be to synthesize *their* synthesis of East and West with *our* synthesis of East and West. That seems like an interesting and promising prospect.

Marketing is a line function, not a staff function. When revenues are down, human resources might be cut back, but not marketing. It is therefore more interesting—and important—to connect philosophy with marketing, where the connection is less obvious, than with human resources, where one would at least expect it to lie.

Marketing is the relation between a company and its primary reality, i.e., the marketplace. Money is an even more central issue in understanding business, for money represents the "results" and provides the measure of the success of marketing.

Money has different meanings, realities, and values to different people. In fact, the difference is not in the people as much as it is in the function of the money they handle: personal money, company money, cash, checks, printouts, P & L statements, bank loans and invested money—from individuals to Third World nations. But in general, for the economy, money is the lubricant that makes the engine go and it is the measure of the degree of its success. Money is the index of how well marketing succeeds. Money tells us how well subject and object, company and market, mind and reality interact.

And the interaction between one event and another, where one initiates (and is thus the subject) and the other responds (and thus becomes the object) is a fundamental human, existential, and ontological structure. It is described by philosophy under a variety of headings, titles, concepts, ideas, or terms.

In philosophy and in philosophical psychology, this contact is the *sine qua non* of health, of authenticity, of normalcy, and of aliveness. It has many names, all of them good: engagement, intentionality, contact, presence, I-Thou relationship, encounter, the establishment of a single unified subject-object or intersubjective field, playing, wrestling, love-making, communication, validation, acknowledgment, confrontation, etc.

They all mean the same: subject-object interconnection. And they are all sound, desirable, and represent the pinnacle of what is good in human existence.

The opposites, alienation and schizophrenia, cut the subject off from reality.

Notice the difference between the quality of interpersonal encounter in acting, such as in a film, and in real life. The key to good acting is to give the appearance of engaged contact between the actors themselves, leading eventually to engaged contact between actors and audience. Such contact is achieved, at least in part, through body language —especially the eyes. The next time you see a film, observe how good acting consists of body language which conveys full, direct, and close contact.

In real life this is not so. Full contact is observed only rarely. It may be felt, but it is not seen as clearly as it is on the stage or on the screen. Acting has one goal: to demonstrate encounter. Professional acting shows good encounter. What makes poor acting unsatisfying is precisely this lack in the sensation of encounter felt by the audience. It then becomes dull and amateurish.

Herein lies also the secret of marketing and its relation to money. Marketing, measured by money, is the business symbol for the fundamental fact of existence, which is subject-object interpenetration, the dance of life, the dialogue of existence. A subject, that is, an ego, reaches out to the world and seeks an object. That describes the fundamental and the universal condition of the person.

We find the clearest business metaphor for this fundamental, authentic human truth in marketing intelligence. In the marketing intelligence the mind works out its basic healthy relation with the world. The company loves the market just as a man loves a woman or the sun loves the earth—so much in fact that it warms it through radiation and attracts it through gravity.

That is what customer-contact employees must understand and learn—to give the customer a good experience. Sales of luxury items, such as cars, depend for their sales success almost exclusively on the company's ability to give the customer such an all-around good experience. To bring about that experience requires an understanding of the phenomenon of encounter, of meeting, of dialogue. Such is the essence of any connection with reality; in business it is called marketing, but in private life it is called bonding, loving, or attachment. Marketing, an ordinary business activity, has a deeper root, theological and philosophic—the nobility of encounter.

Thus, the study of marketing and of the meaning of money must go to its roots, i.e., revert to the study of the pervasive human phenomenon of encounter. Good salespeople must be familiar with therapeutic skills—and that is also part of the intelligence of wisdom. Although quantitative and analytic studies are always of help in marketing, many aspects of encounter are holistic and systemic and can be uncovered and described only through intuition, which of course is more an art than a science.

Customer satisfaction is the prime productivity symbol for the market. It can be developed and implemented best by the person with an intuitive understanding of the irreducible human phenomenon of encounter—the establishment of an intersubjective field, a conscious unit which, like a cell, encompasses two nuclei in one embrace.

Salesmanship is the skill of a subject-object encounter.
I once met a Swedish salesman in a Stockholm taxi.

"What do you sell?" I asked him.
"Ball bearings," he replied.
"To whom?" I asked.
"To the Russians," he answered.
"How are they as customers?" I was curious.
"Tough, but correct."
"What is your sales secret?" I wanted to know.
He answered simply, "I must earn their trust."

The moral? In order to sell to the Russians, a Swede must have established a subject-object encounter between them. In the vernacular it is called trust. That is a fundamental human need and the ultimate secret of marketing success.

There is a difference between masculine and feminine marketing. Many of the concepts here discussed are masculine, in that they are aggressive, thrusting, forward-moving. This is especially true of the dimension of survival. Systems thinking and wonder are more feminine. But the true feminine marketing intelligence understands the importance of teamwork, of loyalty, of customer cultivation, of pride in quality, and of the self-fulfillment found in performing a service. For leadership in marketing means also to gain pleasure from serving the customer well.

CHAPTER 23

Transformation of Logical, Aesthetic, and Somatic Intelligences

We can arouse enthusiasm for logical intelligence. Let us get into the spirit of logical intelligence! Much of our academic culture is organized to create a society which values and rewards logical intelligence. The academic world, especially at our more prestigious universities, endeavors mightily to mobilize great enthusiasm to create for oneself a logical intelligence and to foster admiringly its products. And logical intelligence indeed is a beautiful thing. There can be great pleasure in the act of thinking logically; there is deep satisfaction in attaining a clear logical mind. Logical clarity for its own sake can give meaning to life. And when applied to monumental problems, such a commitment can make giants out of pygmies, gods out of a vulnerable and empty nothingness. There is magic in the fruits of superior intellectual clarity. In fact, these goals and their pleasures, and the visions of their significance, are some of the reasons why students choose philosophy.

Without attempting to summarize the scholarship on logical intelligence, we nevertheless can think ourselves into the logical frame of mind. We can fantasize what such a mind would do, how it would function, what it would see, how it would feel to be logically intelligent. And through this process of speculation and meditation we will motivate ourselves to more ambitious standards for our logical intelligence. These ambitions will be held constantly before our inner eyes, so we will benefit, for we will increase in intelligence as we proceed with alacrity on our journey towards the goal of mind expansion.

How can we enhance, for example, our powers of abstract reasoning? We must think of theoretical physics. We must study theoretical physics, or at least attempt to move in that direction. That will give us a good glimpse of this kind of intelligence, for theoretical physics is the queen of the sciences of logical intelligence.

We must study logic, Aristotelian syllogistic logic, informal fallacies, and symbolic logic. We must understand the meaning of truth tables, of truth functions, of implication (that is, the "if . . . then" function), of the difference between truth (which refers to a fact) and validity (which refers to an argument or an inference). We must be able to determine if arguments, especially highly complex ones, are valid.

Good examples of complex arguments are those attempting to prove the existence of God. The best-known have been proposed by Aristotle and refined by St. Thomas Aquinas.

The ontological argument states that God is a perfect being, and that a perfect being must necessarily exist, for if it did not it would not be perfect. The cosmological argument states that everything has a cause, which must then also be at least as perfect as itself. The universe therefore must also have a cause. And only God is perfect enough to be that cause.

To analyze the pro's and con's, and to examine the subtleties of these arguments, considering how much is at stake, will enhance greatly our competence with logical intelligence.

We must understand the syllogism. ("All men are mortal, Socrates is a man, therefore Socrates is mortal.") And we must know why such syllogistic conclusions are true and why such arguments are valid. And we must be able to ferret out as well invalid syllogisms.

Also, we must understand why, from the statement, "If my name is Bartholomew, then I am a man," it does *not* follow that "If I am a man, then my name is Bartholomew." The statement "This criminal is a man from ethnic background X" (which may well be true) does not imply "Any man from ethnic background X is a criminal." We must be able to explain why this is so.

There is the fascinating reasoning about probabilities. A large statistical sample does not *prove* with certainty that the rest of reality is like it. And how do we know that the probability of throwing a six in any large number of dice throws is one in six?

We must study epistemology, which philosophers call the theory of knowledge. How do we know that the shortest distance between two points is a straight line? By intuition, by visualization? Or by definition? By postulation? What is intuition? What is a definition? And on what grounds do we accept definitions? Why is an axiom true? Was Descartes right when he insisted that the statement "I think, therefore I am" is indubitable, is beyond doubt, cannot be questioned without self-contradiction? How do we answer questions like these?

How do we know that our senses are veridical, i.e., that what we see is real? Does reality mean we postulate an omniscient observer, one who can compare the contents of our minds with objective (i.e., unperceived) external reality, and then tell us the degrees of correspondence (or the absence thereof) between the two worlds, the realms of matter and of ideas? Or are there other criteria for truth, such as what works, or is practical, or has survival value? Is there then no meaning to objectivity?

What about people who have a predilection for mathematics, for algebra, for geometry and trigonometry, for calculus? What about people who are intrigued by the worlds opened up by mathematical reasoning? Can we be like them? Plato demanded that all his students have that capability, for mathematics was thought to be excellent training for the mind.

Who could think up the brilliant hypothesis that space and time are flexible and that it is the speed of light that is constant—after there was no measure known that could detect any change in the speed of light, regardless of the relative velocities of observers?

What about those who study the nature and functions of language? What about those who make distinctions between language that describes ("the tree is green") and language that does things with words ("I promise I will repay you what I borrowed"; "I sentence you to prison")? Can we manufacture the clarity, the trenchant precision, the compass of mind required to think clearly about these matters? Of course we can!

What about the genius Descartes who figured out how to translate a geometric figure, like a circle, a parabola, an ellipse, or even a straight line, by inventing a system of coordinates and describing in algebraic terms the trajectory of a point? Thus he reached the obvious conclusion that a circle with radius r and with its center at the origin or intersection of two perpendicular lines, called respectively the X and the Y axis, describes the trajectory of a point (another abstraction) which is unequivocally and specifically described by the equation $x^2 + y^2 = r^2$. The new dimensions of calculating power released by this insight still stun and stagger today the imaginations of logical thinkers.

What about the minds of people who continually invent computers, new computer languages, new programs? who work on artificial intelligence, who argue whether artificial intelligence is possible in the first place? All of these minds are necessarily highly developed in logical intelligence. Can you emulate them? Can you try? Will you? Of course!

What about economists, economics, and economic models? How clever and intriguing it is to translate economic realities, which are amorphous and abstract in themselves, into models that predict the behavior of vast segments of the economy!

Or can we think ourselves into the mind that develops computer models for recombining DNA molecules, and then puts into practice the conclusions derived from these dry runs?

On a more practical business level, what about financiers and their ways of creative financing? of refinancing debts? of using endless subtle instruments of the money market to improve a company's financial position? of clever investing? Can you develop your mind to do that? Yes, indeed!

When it comes to visualization, there are people who love riddles, or games of chess, or of bridge—anything to stretch the logical mind, to hone the powers of visual reasoning. The powers of visualization can be enhanced with practice in transcendental intelligence, for that touches upon the vastness and the clarity of our inner space and time. What we call metaphysics in philosophy, theories of reality to be precise, trains us to enter the visualization dimension of logical intelligence. The great visions of being—God, matter, eternity, destiny, the life force, the World Reason, evolution, infinity, the beginning of things--force us to visualize internally what no external eye can see.

Logical analysis, the last topic, is prominent in most forms of strategic thinking and in planning. These typical business activities require great skills of analysis—dividing problems sharply into their component parts. Dealing with financial statements, P & L statements, tax matters, requires the most highly developed powers of analysis. And we are all in a position to work on these issues and gain not only commercially but also intellectually. Our logical intelligence of analysis will be sharpened whenever we engage in these practices, if we at the same time understand what it is that we are doing and comprehend precisely how we are using our minds.

The competent legal mind is an excellent example of both abstract relational reasoning and of logical analysis. A good lawyer can always think a of a new and logical way to approach an old situation. The solution is obvious, except that it takes a logical, i.e. a legal, genius to discover it.

The philosophic analysis of language and of the meaning of words—such as mind, force, matter, God, soul, time, space, energy, peace—also trains us magnificently in enhancing our powers of analysis.

We can improve all aspects of logical intelligence by practicing it whenever we have the opportunity, by constructing incentives, either for ourselves or for our employees. And by ourselves modeling this behavior, and by looking for models in others, we can enhance, through imitation, our performance in logical intelligence.

In order to support logical intelligence we need to have access to transcendental, somatic, aesthetic, and motivational intelligences. Transcendental intelligence provides the inner spaciousness we need to jump the mind from concept to concept and from idea to idea. Motivational intelligence keeps us going when we are discouraged and frustrated by the sluggishness, the rustiness, and the clumsiness of our logical intelligence.

PART FOUR

LEADERSHIP

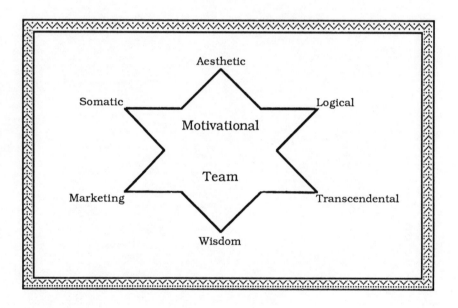

CHAPTER 24

Leadership Criteria

Mentoring

What do we look for as qualities of the ideal executive? What are the correct answers to the questions, What is a true leader? and What are, in my experience, the personality characteristics of the successful director? In identifying leadership traits, rather than asking repeatedly which is the right combination of characteristics, or what is the correct list of personality structures, we must recognize instead that there exist myriads of possible answers and combinations to the question of authentic leadership. All of these answers are based on an underlying metaphysics of the person. These latter are always chosen, and to an extent freely, perhaps by taste, perhaps by fiat, perhaps on the basis of what has shown itself to work, perhaps on some sort of evidence.

We must therefore view any answer to the questions of authentic this or authentic that as merely a possible model which illustrates an underlying theory of what it is to be human. And we must then choose from among these derivative and purely pragmatic models of leadership that very one which appears to us to be most suitable to the occasion, most appropriate to the situation, or most fitting to the person inquiring.

The key is the theory of the model. There are many different and equally interesting and even valid models of leadership. Each model makes its own sense because it derives from a particular life perception or view of the world. This approach to the question of what are the real or the authentic leadership traits should once and for all settle the controversy over executive self-actualization. It is one more application of the underlying principle of polarity, so happily encapsulated in the yin-yang symbol.

The answer has two dimensions: theory and action. The theory we find below. The action is the living commitment by one actual person or several actual people, over an extended period of time and with support from the higher levels of management, up to board and stockholder, to implement a leadership program. Support from above is the secret of leadership effectiveness. Leadership programs fail for one reason, inadequate support from top management.

Persistence is one trait of a leader. To recognize who is the ultimate boss is another. The boss is not always the one with the title or the six or seven figure salary. Nor is the boss the unannointed high priest of the social network or of the informal organization. The ultimate boss is always the market. But the market is not always external. It can be, likely as not, internal to the organization itself.

The measure of the market is the price of the stock. Wall Street analysts will inspect leadership programs instituted at a company and express opinions: Are the programs promising? Can leadership be developed? Is it being done? Will the consequences become visible? When? Is the company promising? Is the company likely to make short-range profits? Long-range profits? Is the management stable? Will there be a new management team? Analysts predict the response of the market. They and the market are, by one definition, the ultimate boss. Any paper boss will listen to the subordinate to whom the true market listens.

Every executive must evaluate his or her own performance and that of the organization, and that means to raise two fundamental questions: *What will you ask from the organization?* and *What will you do for the organization?* (It is good to end virtually every business meeting by asking each participant to respond to these two questions.)

In the final analysis, leadership can be taught in only one way: through personal experience and through mentoring. A mentor is a model who cares. It is a person whose model inspires, but it is also an individual with whom one has a personal relationship. It is the presence of and the contact with the modeling mentor which produces the learning. Mentoring revives the best in the medieval guild practice of apprenticeships. It is the conservative academic practice of tutor and tutoring.

Aspiring leaders must find and cultivate their own mentors, and every manager and supervisor, as leader, must fulfill the role of mentor for their subordinates. Abraham Zaleznik (*Harvard Business Review*, May–June 1977) writes:

> Dwight Eisenhower's early career in the Army foreshadowed very little about his future development. During World War I, while some of his West Point classmates were already

experiencing the war firsthand in France, Eisenhower felt "embedded in the monotony and unsought safety of the Zone of the Interior . . . that was intol-erable punishment."

Shortly after World War I, Eisenhower, then a young officer somewhat pessimistic about his career chances, asked for a transfer to Panama to work under General Fox Connor, a senior officer whom Eisenhower admired. The army turned down Eisenhower's request. This setback was very much on Eisenhower's mind when Ikey, his first-born son, succumbed to influenza. By some sense of responsibility for its own, the army transferred Eisenhower to Panama, where he took up his duties under General Connor with the shadow of his lost son very much upon him . . . .

As Eisenhower wrote later about Connor, "Life with General Connor was a sort of graduate school in military affairs and the humanities, leavened by a man who was experienced in his knowledge of men and their conduct. I can never adequately express my gratitude to this one gentleman . . . In a lifetime of association with great and good men, he is the one more or less invisible figure to whom I owe an incalculable debt."

Some time after his tour of duty with General Connor, Eisenhower's breakthrough occurred. He received orders to attend the Command and General Staff School at Fort Leavenworth, one of the most competitive schools in the army. It was a coveted appointment, and Eisenhower took advantage of the opportunity. Unlike his performance in high school and West Point, his work at the Command School was excellent; he was graduated first in his class.

The role of the mentor is simple: exemplify at all times exactly what you teach.

Following are models shown as criteria lists. They were created in response to questions like these: What are the traits of a successful executive? and What actions are appropriate to bring about an environment that fosters an ideal executive?

Leadership Criteria: List 1

- Motivation and enthusiasm. Subspecies of this trait are
  - Δ the ability to harness a person's freedom and capacity for choice; this means the capacity for the self-generation of energy, the answer to depression;

Δ the necessity to be in an accepting, receptive, and reinforcing world; to be surrounded with acceptance, encouragement, and validation. If that environment does not exist then it is the responsibility of the leader to work towards creating it (through his or her ability to be self-energized, self-authenticating, and self-actualizing);

Δ the capacity to always kindle hope.

- Organizational design or redesign. The ability to translate energy, enthusiasm, and vision into the organization chart and job design or redesign.

- Experience, which requires years of commitment, and which is the ultimate source of intuition. This is what the expert systems in artificial intelligence try to tap.

- Self-discipline; good and long-standing work habits.

- Ability to evoke respect. To be respected as a leader is the key element in being followed and in being perceived as a model or mentor. It requires

Δ a sense of purpose, translated into a vision;

Δ personal maturity and authenticity; centeredness (so that the person lives from the inside out—which we call genuine—rather than from the outside in—which we call artificial); this leads to a sense of personal worth;

Δ ideas, ideals, ethics, and visions which are of such high quality and worth that they invite respect;

Δ the constructive use of failure;

Δ assigning true responsibility;

Δ developing people; empowering them;

Δ realism, which includes an adequate perspective on oneself and one's organization, including a solid sense of one's limitations and the limitations of the environment;

Δ capacity for strategic thinking. This means the ability to think in ever larger time frames or systems;

Δ a highly developed capacity for creativity, imagination, and innovative or "lateral" thinking and problem-solving. Thinking big and visionary thinking are also part of this leadership ability;

- Action orientation. The penchant for action and the impatience with theory is one of the most important leadership traits. This is also the idea central to existential philosophy, as well as to existential psychotherapy.

Existentialism is the philosophy which grew out of what may well go down in history as the most horrible of all the wars ever fought, or ever to be fought, in the entire history of humanity, from the beginning of war with the Neanderthal people to its bitter end when, ten billion years hence, the expanding sun will engulf the earth. Existentalism, like the world of business, defines existence as action. Inaction is non-existence.

Reality, for this philosophy, and especially when it comes down to understanding the nature of the person, exists or comes into being at the precise point where mind meets matter, where interiority meets exteriority, and where the world of ideas intersects with the world of palpable objects.

Action-orientation as the key to reality is as much a part of business as it is of the most influential philosophy of the post-World War II period.

But this situation leads to a paradox. How can one write about action without lies? How can one lecture about action-orientation as central to business without belying the very point one wishes to make? How can one theorize with the mind alone about the finality of the mind-body interface and not contradict oneself in direct proportion to one's clarity and convincingness?

This point cannot be stressed too much, for it lies at the core of the action orientation of business. To talk about action is nothing short of pornography, for talk is seen as a substitute for action. The only compensatory factor, if there can be one, is that words are actions too; for speech is a form of action. And the more sophisticated we get in business, the more speech does indeed matter.

Executives may view me as a refreshing pause from the action demands of their environment. However, I have come to believe that, as a philosopher, I am more concerned with action, with results, with productivity, and with bottom line consequences than are the executives I deal with.

We must not push actions too far. Sometimes action grows out of the body like an oak tree out of an acorn: slowly and naturally. And pushing action may lead to precipitous behavior and premature commitment, where what appears rational preempts and overrules what comes from a more centered place in the person . . . the unconscious source of quasi-automatic action.

What actions can we take to arrive at the correct action?

Leadership traits can be clarified, enhanced, and firmed-up through a fundamental understanding of the intelligences and the deep structures.

Leadership Criteria: List 2

The key to success in American business is (1) authentic leadership and (2) an authentic culture.

We need to define both terms.

Assumptions. The general assumptions are (1) that people, i.e., employees, want to do good work and (2) that the primary function of both managers (that is, leaders) and organizations is to facilitate and not obstruct the efforts of employees to want to do good work.

These assumptions must be taken seriously. They are the foundation of any well run organization and the basis of any meaningful culture.

Characteristics of an authentic and well-led organization:
The secrets of success in an organization lie in its culture. Culture must be understood in primitive, that is, anthropological terms. Rituals, war stories, high priests, ceremonies, heroes, myths, legends, traditions, sacrifices, loyalties, initiations, transitions, transformations, metamorphoses, losses—i.e., elements of culture derived from our study of primitive societies—provide us richly with both understanding and suggestions on how to manage effectively the cultures of our corporations.

A caveat is in order. Culture is important, but there are individualists who wish—demand would be a better word—to operate autonomously and do so just as effectively outside of any strong group feeling or culture connection. It would be difficult to think of Henry David Thoreau, of Ludwig van Beethoven, of Albert Einstein, or of St. Francis of Assisi as concerned about company culture or as interested in teamwork when making their significant contribution to humanity.

1. An authentic organization has a sense of purpose. It is "going someplace" and everyone knows and feels it and willingly participates in it.

   The goals, although often and understandably materialistic, are worthy, so that men and women of good will can subscribe to them not only because of economic necessity, but because these goals conform to the demands of their consciences, because they kindle their enthusiasm. This, according to business professor Peter Senge, is the most important element or component in an authentic organization.

   These worthy goals include such values as money, security, fun, advancement, meaning.

   Purposefulness includes goals—which are intellectual articulations of missions, values, and philosophies—and visions—which are images, visualizations, ideograms that capture the company goals in an artistic, aesthetic, mythical, and powerful and effective picture, phrase, or sound.

   Purposefulness also includes alignment, as in sports, which is the true spirit of teamwork, without loss of individuality. Every member of the organization participates in a single-minded effort to support the goals of the team—not slavishly, like a school of fish, but cooperatively, like mature, creative, and free men and women.

   This effort can be maintained if it is of finite or limited duration, as in a wartime campaign or a technical crash program. It is more difficult to make it a style of life, although it is still the key to an effective organization.

   Attunement, a concept expanded by Roger Harrison, has two meanings. First, it refers to the integration of the individual's private and personal needs with the requirements and the demands of the organization. Second, attunement is like love, where teamwork is based on attending to and caring for the other teammates.

   Alignment is found in the well trained symphony orchestra, or in the professional football team, where every musician member or player willingly conforms to the directives of a respected conductor or coach for the sake of great sound and an inspired performance or a resounding victory following from a game played excellently.

Attunement, on the other hand, is found in the string quartet or the jazz combo, where every player listens not to himself or herself but to the others, so that any playing he or she does is consonant with and in response to that of the other musicians.

2. Quoting Peter Senge again, we must say that an authentic organization provides for its members a sense of personal mastery. The people in such an organization feel powerful and are effective by virtue of being members of that organization. We say that such an organization must be empowering. It is a condition which leads to effective action. It yields results. It develops people. There is a certain magic to an organization which makes people feel better and more effective—even with regard to their own personal goals—by being part of it. For we must remember that nothing succeeds like success and that nothing is more practical than survival.

3. Another characteristic of the authentic organization is, following Senge's terminology, the integrity of structure. This means that the design of the organization must be consistent with its purpose. That is easier said than done. Benefits are a help. Human resource people are key.

It is here where two factors come in and must be considered. One is the quality and strength of the personalities in charge of the organization. We must remember Warren Bennis's point that the stock value of a company is proportional to the perceived competence and esteem of its top leadership. The other point is design. Skill in designing an organization—and workshops, seminars, and training programs as well— is often at the core of its success. Here is where good consultants and good human resources and organization development specialists can help.

4. An authentic organization is receptive to creativity. Receptivity to people, to creativity, and to innovation can be achieved in many ways. One way is through flexibility; rigid modes of operation are abandoned. That can be accomplished by forward-looking and secure personalities in the leadership of the organization as much as it can be by the judicious selection of creative employees. Receptivity also includes honesty. To be honest means both to accept innovation, that is, recognize and acknowledge it when it occurs, and to challenge it, that is, to

have the fortitude to fearlessly arouse it into being because one knows that the truth will spring forth from it.

5. Authenticity in organizations means a culture of high standards, which has the courage and the integrity to discriminate between good and bad work—and acknowledge and reward accordingly. Because of the understandably delicate feelings involved, many managers fear to be fully truthful in discriminating between good and bad work. After all, supervision and friendship, evaluation and compassion, judgment and love, fairness and forgiveness, are difficult to integrate. Other managers, hopefully in the minority, avoid these difficulties and protect themselves by being defensively crude and insensitive.

6. A final trait of the authentic organization is the creative use of failure. Failure—mistakes, errors—must be perceived as a basic source of energy. To the authentic leader nothing is more energizing than the sight of failure: it redoubles his or her resolution and it strengthens his or her determination. A popular story about Thomas Watson at IBM goes something like this: A high-level executive tendered his resignation after having committed a ten-million-dollar error. Watson replied, "I am not going to let you go, now that I paid ten million dollars for your education!"

Now let us talk about the leaders of the organization.

1. A leader engenders motivation and enthusiasm. A leader is self-energizing, self-starting.

2. A leader is experienced and intuitive, recognizing that intuition is born of experience. And experience here refers to experience in time, that is, age, and experience in space, that is, travel.

3. A leader is self-disciplined and has good work habits. The leader exhibits a sound adaptation to his or her social reality, which is the work environment. That includes a realistic assessment of the economy.

4. A leader elicits respect, in at least four ways:
   a. With a sense of purpose (which is a concept only), that is then translated into a vision (which is an image, something that is more effective than a mere anemic concept). Both the purpose and the vision are seen as worthy. What is your vision? Can you describe it?

b. As a person, the leader is mature and centered, which makes him or her worthy as a human being.

c. The leader knows that his or her subordinates are worthy human beings. And the leader shows that in his or her actions.

d. The leader elicits respect by trusting and by assigning responsibility, and thus assuming that subordinates are capable of successfully completing their challenges.

e. The leader cares for people and finds personal pleasure and meaning in developing people. The leader finds satisfaction and fulfillment in making others powerful. Their successes are also his or her successes. The leader knows that caring is a worthy thing to do.

5. The leader of an authentic organization is creative, imaginative, innovative, flexible, open, and "lateral" in his or her thinking.

6. The leader, in his or her personality traits and communication, is realistic, honest, and direct—first about himself or herself and second about others. The leader knows the worth of truth.

7. The leader or leadership has a courage-action-risk orientation. This exists within rational constraints and credible experience. A leader understands the value as well as the inevitability of courage.

Leadership Criteria: List 3

Leadership can be authentic or inauthentic.*

Inauthentic leadership is mechanical and scientific. It develops people for the sake of the work.

Vision and ethics are subordinate to and follow from productivity and profits.

Business is perceived as a crisis response to the anxiety of poverty and loss.

There exist two subtypes of inauthentic leadership:

• The autocratic type, which is monarchic, arbitrary, insensitive, and militaristic.

------

*In the workplace, "authentic" and "inauthentic" are expressions to be avoided, for in evaluating they erode effectiveness.

- The bureaucratic type, which is oligarchic, rule bound, mainte-nance-oriented, naïve, and legislative.

Authentic leadership fulfills or meets the human potential. It is visionary and humane. It develops work for the sake of people.

Productivity and profits follow from the full utilization of the person.

Business is a meaning, a lifestyle, and even a sport or an important game.

There exist two subtypes of authentic leadership:

- The masculine type has charisma and is heroic.
- The feminine type has harmony and is loving.

Leadership Criteria: List 4

The meaning of leadership can also be explored through the following five themes:

1. The source and the uses of power. This theme entails under-standing first the transfer of power from the god-kings (such as the pyramid-building pharaohs of Egypt and the Minoan kings of Knossos) to the state, especially during the reigns of mon-archs subscribing to the divine right of kings, and then its surrender (if our paradigm is, politically, the American and the French Revolutions, or religiously, the Reformation) or return (if we see Socrates as the first individual and consider his resurrection during the Renaissance) to the individual, reflecting the democratic aspirations of a free people.

   Leadership entails understanding power, the need for power, the legitimacy of power, the abuse of power, the pathology of power, the empowering of power, the justification for benign power, power as the province of the father among the arche-types of the soul and as the source of the superego and of conscience, the ignorance of power, the concepts of the death of God and of the death of the father, and so forth.

2. Vision. This is the ability to idealize and to think in the grand manner. It means to inspire people and to invest mundane events with superordinate significance. To be a visionary lead-er is to help others discover their meaning in life.

3. Effectiveness. This is the ability to translate thoughts into

action, ideas into reality. This element of leadership depends on experience, on the knowledge of the business, on professional skills, on good common sense, on alertness, on attention to detail, on persistence, and on dedication.

4. Wisdom and therapeutic skills. This element of leadership refers to the need for personal maturity. It is unquestionably reminiscent of the Socratic notion, developed in Plato's *Republic*, that only the true lovers of wisdom (Greek, *philosophoi*) should be kings.

But we are here also referring to the ability to be understanding, that is to say, to be genuinely compassionate, to be able to see the world through the eyes of another—"to walk a mile in my neighbor's moccasins," as the American Indians used to say.

We are also talking about the skill to establish alliances with people, a term borrowed from psychotherapy. This skill consists in the ability to raise difficult issues and say what normally would hurt but which, because of special sensitivity, can be heard instead as helpful and even as loving.

5. Finally, morality is a key ingredient in leadership. The capacity to be ethical may well be the most distinctive human trait. And if we are to do anything that is important, anything that warrants respect, then it must also be something of the highest moral probity. Anyone who acts in selfishness or with disregard to his or her highest principles will blush in shame and regret the day he or she was born when confronted with even a modest self-sacrificing ethical performance (although there always are be some people who worry only that they might get caught). This requirement of leadership eliminates the charismatic demagogue and the spellbinding tyrant.

CHAPTER 25

Leadership in Action:
Eight Examples

1. Set the Tone

A business professor friend of mine talked to me about the Bimono Corporation, a major manufacturer and exporter of appliances. Their problem is not uncommon. In order to deal with it real leadership was required.

Bimono is one of the Fortune 500 companies, with a strong company philosophy, credo, mission, statement, and a strong caring for people, a commitment to protect them, to provide them with security—all of which is clearly stated in their philosophy. How is that congruent, executives ask, with the fact that economically, i.e., financially, the company must go through an intense cost-cutting program, and lay off 30 percent of its white collar work force? The CEO says he is wracked inside with guilt and anxiety over his need to cause pain and violate the very principles he so adamantly espouses in the company philosophy.

The interpretation of this situation by the workforce is that it is fine to have a company philosophy but then no one lives up to it. "When the going gets tough, the philosophy is shelved," they say.

The CEO said that need not be. The philosophy does not say, he maintained—it never does—that the company will make a specified profit every year and that it will therefore be able always to meet its payroll. The philosophy promises respect and caring for people, openness, fairness, considerateness, compassion, but it also acknowledges that maturity means autonomy and realism. The company promises care, the employee promises maturity.

How now can mature downsizing be translated into practice? It requires both imagination (that is, creativity) and courage: that is all. Bimono's CEO displayed both.

There is no problem: apply your philosophy. It does not say, "This company encourages dependency." It does not say, "You are here to be taken care of, period." The credo should say, although often regrettably it does not make it explicit, that it values and supports autonomy, adulthood, as well as creativity and innovation in its workforce, and that freedom also means responsibility, for both the company and for the employees.

After these problems, this company, and several others, added "maturity and autonomy clauses" to their philosophy and mission statements.

Realism is the solution. Reality is not the decision of one man or of one woman—it is a characteristic of nature and of the world beyond. Individuals need not take responsibility for the structure of reality—only for their response to it. *Autonomy* is realism with respect to human subjectivity. The need for *cutbacks*—not in the National economy but in selected industries—is realism with respect to objectivity.

The missing link is the CEO's duty to face the subjective facts: the need for *courage*, for personal courage in one's own life, and for courage which is difficult, unpleasant, and anxiety-producing. *Cutbacks* are faced by the employees; *autonomy* is demanded of the employees; and *courage* is the sine qua non for the CEO. Here are schematic and hypothetical suggestions, as these were discussed by Bimono:

Place the problem and its only solution before the employees: cutbacks, lower salaries, or both. Specifically, the CEO sets the prime example: cut his pay to one dollar a year. In this way he shows his loyalty. The savings to the company were in this case calculated as follows.

CEO's salary, $2,000,000.

Several members of the management team offered voluntary reductions, worth $1,000,000.

Moderately paid employees, $30,000.

Jobs saved by CEO's and VP's cut in salary: 100.

Additionally, cut by 20 percent the salary expenditures of those whose jobs have been saved, through a combination of attrition and salary reductions.

The total yearly savings were $3,600,000.

And no jobs were lost.

This was leverage for employee morale worth many more millions of dollars.

The CEO set the tone, provided the leadership.

To think in those terms is not yet a regular part of the American business culture. But the time for such loyalty as shown in the Bimono Corporation has arrived.

Working for such a mature and courageous company is worth a lot more in personal growth, learning, character-building, maturation, and increased marketability of the employee than the $6,000 in lost salary. Paying in intangibles is part of a bartering system that is not only more and more in vogue but that is also realistic.

The problem lies not in the presumed conflict between economic reality and the values statement. The problem lies in the fact that top management seems too anxious to be able to live comfortably by the values statement, too frightened to apply it to itself first and foremost—because the values statement says not only love, which is easy, but also autonomy, which hurts but strengthens.

The CEO often does not understand the full meaning of his very own statement. These are the harsh facts and the uncompromising realities. But the ability to face them is the new dawn of a clear day.

The mission statement should be based, as all else, on the two ethical principles of Philosophy in Business:

The facts of human existence (i.e., the ultimate realism) make it necessary to understand and to confront the deep structures. Many business issues, especially the personal ones, are the surface appearance, the visible unfolding, of underlying universal human issues. And it is at this level of depth that they must be managed. Only when we understand their roots can we cope with difficult issues.

The second principle is the faith that attention to real human authenticity (that is, authenticity with depth, not uncomprehending clichés) is good for productivity—and the faith that it is precisely this faith that will make it true.

This next situation is also not uncommon.

The overriding complaint of this organization is inadequate communication with top management. It is a matter of workers' not being heard. Real hearing is more a psychological skill than a matter of memo-writing, memo-answering, arguing, or even taking action. Hearing, listening, an important skill in top management, is not a function of time spent or words exchanged—or even actions taken. It is a psychological sensitivity, a real caring, and the establishment of real contact with people.

People need to be understood and validated. Reasons for approval and disapproval need to be given. People affected by decisions must be consulted and integrated into the decision-making process. The complaints are that top management is contradictory, that it embarrasses the people in the field by giving mixed messages: we have money, we are doing well, but when it comes to funding new projects of importance to the community, the funds are not forthcoming. Field people plan, on the faith that the company will support them, and the support does not come. Top management is seen as obstructing, interfering. It would be bad enough if they were indifferent; then they are unneeded. But to interfere, or be perceived as such, is outright damaging. Field management thinks it knows how to run its business. Top management second-guesses them—based on less experience. And that hurts.

The answer is to confront in both directions—up and down: top management that they need to let people know that they are being heard, and middle or field management that they must succeed, i.e., be effective in spite of their superior's best efforts to sabotage them. A middle person is needed who assists top management in understanding the importance of listening and in facilitating listening skills. And a middle person is needed to challenge subordinates to be direct and honest with their clients about the difficulties they are getting from the home office.

My analysis of the situation follows.

1. The top executives under consideration exhibit either undeveloped or timid autonomy and creativity. They are a group of select people, obviously competent. But when together in a seminar, they do not appear to be people whose potential is released. They seem more concerned with saving their jobs and not making waves than with being innovative, energetic, exciting, inspiring, models for others, or members of a team. They seem not nearly as "big" in their thinking, their presence, in their charisma, and in their leadership capabilities as one would expect them to be.

   When they heard that their CEO's order was, "Spend 80 percent of your time out of the office—and only 20 percent on paperwork," they did not understand that to mean to find the business, to be imaginative, and to solve problems for which corporate had no solutions, but appeared puzzled and seemed to panic instead.

2. There is an absence of a shared vision. One does not get the feeling that these high executives are members of a single organization with a unitary goal. It does not matter if top management has insisted there is such a goal, has made it clear in writing and orally. Nor is it important to decide whether such unity is desirable. The fact remains that such unity of mission does not seem manifest to an outsider, and that should be noted. In fact, when top management was asked, What is your vision for the Company, the response—regardless of later justification—was audible silence. By going in three directions— quality, profit, and people—extra pressure, stress, or tension produces no movement, only vectors which are more taut but not resolved. It is the job of top management to orchestrate into one these three divergent directions.

3. There is a conspicuous absence of therapeutic skills. Business executives do not get to their positions of high resonsibility by being good therapists or loving saints. Nevertheless, they typically get rewarded for competence in hard areas, which they know, with promotions to soft areas, which they do not know. A simple way of stating the well-known resulting difficulties is, They need therapeutic skills.

   That means more understanding of how it feels to be another person, to see the world through the eyes of another. An employee's job is his or her identity. The lack of sensitivity often displayed by executives to this obvious fact is based more upon ignorance of how to handle delicate issues than on any planned malice. But the need for therapeutic sensitivity, how to know of vulnerabilities without being told and how to say difficult things, remains.

4. These executives appear to have a limited marketing orientation. Business is marketing. And what one wants to hear in a business seminar, in addition to whatever else may be going on—positive politics, team building, personal grievances, depression, burnout, or what have you—are new ideas on how to market. When that is not the case, when the major awareness of the executives is not on how to make the business more profitable, then one is tempted to think that the company is too

large. It is so large, in fact, that the staff has lost contact with what feeds the business, its *raison d'être*, with its roots, with its tentacles to the outside world. He or she who has lost touch this way is in danger of becoming ballast, soon to be discarded as excess weight or as obsolete.

5. A final observation is that the executives display ignorance of and insensitivity to what it is like to be the top person in the company. Such an attitude, or such lack of knowledge, is a sign of dependency. The child has little understanding of how difficult it is to be a parent. The young child does little to willingly and freely cooperate with the parent and thus help the parent to be a better parent. Perhaps subordinates feel—and in that they may be justified—that the higher salaries of the top people compensate for their additional responsibilities. Be that as it may, subordinates often expect things from the boss which not only cannot be delivered but which it is irrational to expect.

Subordinates must be taught, also, how to talk to the top person. It is not helpful to say, "You must be a more creative leader!" "You must be more visionary!" "You must be a stronger and a more courageous commander!" That is about as helpful, and it comes across no lighter, as when the seminar participant (let us say a man) returns home after a week to his wife, only to hear her say, "You must become a more inventive and creative lover, like the man across the street!" It is of little value to be ordered to be more aggressive, to be instructed to be more of a leader, or to be accused of not being sufficiently visionary. These are the crazy-making ingredients of what the psychologist Gregory Bateson defined as the classical doublebind.

Subordinates must recognize that leaders are rewarded for doing well within the very culture over whose demise, or at least transformation, they are now supposed to preside. The adult subordinate has prudent compassion and is pragmatically helpful in assisting the leader to bring about what must be done. It is only the greedy stockholder who mercilessly fires the executive who does not produce. Developing the person, helping the individual, is not what one talks about on Wall Street or in the stock exchange.

What is to be done?

In some cases, the answer is to set up a company university or a corporate college, a place where these issues are aired, are discussed intelligently. This creates an atmosphere where decisions can be made, and change can be undertaken in an environment that is experimental, supportive, inventive, and highly professional all at the same time. What characterizes such an institution or such a branch of a corporation is that it is a staff function which has been given line opportunities, if not exactly line responsibilities. Executives and faculty who can make judicious use of such an opportunity will serve well the organizations which engage them and trust them.

Let us look at an example of an industry stridently crying for leadership. The newspaper industry is in the midst of serious change. It is moving from the local paper to a metropolitan behemoth competing with the most modern high-technology information services. It is moving from old-fashioned idealism to a pragmatic focus on profits. To accomplish this transition requires extraordinary leadership, including both vision and a commitment to high ethics. The newspaper industry is moving from its old image of the blustering and arrogant autocracy of the newsroom to the new reality of making a profit, automating, and competing with the information services of the world. An illustration of the change is the typesetter, a pro, who has been on the job for fifty years, who can hardly be retired or be dismissed, and yet is himself obsolete and slows down the modernization of the presses.

Union relations are still a big issue, in part because unions are losing their territorial rights and the newspaper industry has been heavily unionized for as long as there have been unions. Profits are the big problem of the day; and, as in the arts, editors are writers first and managers of profit-centers last.

The image and credibility of the press is low, in part because of these very problems, which are of course highly resistant to solution. The large newspapers of this country suffer, as do many other industries, from intra-organizational communications problems—except that these problems are among the most severe in newspapers, for a newspaper has on its staff the full spectrum of humanity, from people who are close to illiterate to people who are some of the best and most influential writers in the nation. Equal opportunity for women and minorities has come slowly to the nation's newspapers, for they are in fact conservative although in image liberal. These are some of the pains with which the newspaper industry struggles.

The solution lies in leadership; and for the press, the essence of leadership has a relatively simple yet vastly important meaning. Leadership requires vision, and vision realized requires courage. All that can be expressed in a simple formula.

The press means America, for America is the First Amendment to the Constitution, and the press is the primary organ to make that declaration a reality—a reality of dignity and respect for the affirmation and the liberty of the mind. The public press is always the Fourth Estate. But freedom, at least in America and maybe inherently, means economic freedom as well. It means non-interference in people's endeavors to become merchants and to cope in their own ways with the economy. It means also that people are expected to pay attention to the other side of the coin of liberty, which is to take responsibility for themselves, i.e., to be autonomous. Indeed there are problems with that, and exceptions, which we all know and which we all understand.

The press is thus charged with the curious paradox, or conjunction, to be both free, to be the bastion of our freedoms, to defend our ideals—by representing them and manifesting them—and to make a profit at the same time, i.e., to be run professionally, to be a business as well. For no non-profit press can survive. To bring that off, a challenge we all watch and the results of which will affect us all, is to demonstrate to ourselves, to the world, and especially to the totalitarian regimes and to the Third World, that human beings are born to be free, that freedom is in the nature of things, and that freedom pays for itself.

It is time other governments take another good look at the value, both moral and practical, human and economic, of freedom.

And to top it off, we must understand that such an exercise of true leadership is to be carried out by continuing to bring automation to the American press. And automation means not only new reporting and printing methods, but new concepts of what information is, what newspapers are, and what the press is, and what kind of information the population needs, deserves, avoids, ought morally to have, and in the end will pay for.

The world is changing and the readers are changing. Do we know how? Can we adapt? Help? The press is an old product. We must now give it a new form, which will give it new meaning. That is the function of true leadership. To find answers and to inspire followers, that is needed and that is leadership.

The press has always stood for freedom. Economic freedom is only the material expression of the freedom which is the core of human nature. One and a half centuries ago, Daniel Bliss saw the epitaph of a John Jack: "A Native of Africa, who died March 1773, aged about 60 years. Tho' born in a land of slavery he was born free." It prompted Bliss to write these lines,

God wills us free, man wills us slaves,
I will as God wills, God's will be done.

2. Creative Thinking in the Automobile Industry

The auto industry appears headed for some permanent plant closings that could eclipse the well-publicized shutdowns of the early 1980s, even though Detroit's Big Three have just had the two most profitable years in their history . . . .

Six to 10 of the 50 car-assembly plants in the U.S. and Canada could shut down for good between next year and the early 1990s, auto analysts say . . . , a disappearing act that could cost thousands of people their jobs.

The Wall Street Journal, Friday, February 14, 1986.

Following is one way in which a visionary, expanded, developed mind from within the auto industry *might* respond to these dismal predictions, many of which have since become news. The actual recommendations must come from within the industry itself. Here is illustrated only a principle.

We are here dealing with the forces of social and economic evolution. These cannot be resisted for long, any more than gravity, the weather, or an oncoming ice age. We must surrender and follow the direction of these evolutionary forces, be they economic or biological, just as a pregnant woman must follow the contractions of her uterus which will lead to giving birth.

Often the only response in the mindsets of the decision-makers is defensive and desperate rear-guard actions. They are natural reflexes. They include such types of measures as slow and staggered plant closings, slightly greater efficiency, gradually slicing away at the work force, intensified pressure on the remaining workers for increased productivity. In general, these measures amount to a series of small and essentially small-minded panaceas. For a while they work. Anything major would understandably be too risky. But here we try the visionary approach. We use the clichés of "getting back to square one" or of "going back to the drawing board."

Executives in the auto industry should no longer talk of competition, of market share, of the Japanese, or the Koreans, but of the nature of their authentic business. When they discover that, competition ends, market share becomes irrelevant, the Japanese are welcome, and profits, but especially survival, should not again be an issue.

This is not to say that a "finely tuned," analytic, and rational, detailed and hard working response is not appropriate. But it is not enough; it is but a temporary anodyne. And it lacks the excitement of the new adventures that are possible.

We must ask ourselves, What is the business of the auto industry? Ken Orr, president of Ken Orr & Associates, Inc., a major software company, said (in Phoenix, 11 February 1986) that the software industry is not in the information technology business but in the manufacturing business. The problems faced are of flawless manufacture, of quantity, and not of logic. This conceptual shift, once the implications were understood and acted on, also saved the business. Stretching the mind to apply a similar methodology to the automobile industry could lead to many interesting and tantalizing conclusions, including the following.

Put the automobile industry minds to work describing this industry—better yet, describing the world—as it might be (or as one might wish it to be) in the year 2000, 2025, or even 2050. And then consider the implications for the present. They are various. What are the likely trends—perhaps set up seven or so possible scenarios. What decisions are relevant today with regard to these trends? Can we make decisions today to influence these trends? Are some trends more desirable than others? How much influence do we have? What trends appear to be inevitable? What decisions can be made now to participate in these trends, to take advantage of them, to exploit them, rather than to be overwhelmed, crushed, or overrun by them? Strategic planners need to invest all the powers of their profession to examine these issues, continually revising their conclusions, in the most meticulous detail.

The automobile industry is not in the car or truck business: it is not even in the transportation business, for the very meaning of transportation is likely to be changed. For example, the concept of transportation makes assumptions about what is permanent and what is not, what is stationary and what moves. It assumes that A must go to B, when in fact it may be possible for B to go to A, or for A and B to be connected without moving either, or for A and B to no longer need a connection at all. A could be an assembler and B could be the plant. Today, the assembler goes (drives or is driven) to the plant. Tomorrow, the plant could drive to him—parts delivered to the home and assembled there (like cottage industries). Or the assembler could operate the plant from home using automation—robotics and communications technology. Or the product itself has become obsolete, in which case no transportation is required and some even more fundamental restructuring is indicated—and a new way of making a living must be invented. And to make a living means to fulfill survival needs—food, shelter—and also meaning needs (what Abraham Maslow calls being needs).

The automobile industry is at minimum in the contact or the connecting business. We know that by *generalizing* and by assuming that the industry is trying to become *more* than it is, it is trying to find its essence and to express it. What does one really do when one purchases an automobile? What does the customer want? What *should* the customer want? That is to say, what are the irreducible basics, once the psychological and anthropological superimpositions which are invested in automobiles have been stripped away? What is the deeper function of the automobile in our society? And we can define "deeper" in psychological terms or in economic ways. If the automobile is a means, then what are the ends? What problems arise in achieving these particular ends through the automobile? Are there other, and better, ways of achieving these same ends?

How about stretching the minds of the consumers—as occurred with computers. People did not "know" they needed computers—until computers were invented and made generally available.

The automobile is a central feature in the economies of the industrialized nations. What is an economy? What is the meaning of economy? Economics is the study of the relation of human beings to the earth. The economy is that relation of people—in every one of its multifarious ways. It is first the survival and then the adjustment of human beings to Mother Earth. The economy is a contact phenomenon in the widest sense possible, for it includes not only physical survival, but also social and spiritual survival. So is the automobile (trucks of course also) a contact phenomenon. The automobile industry is in the connecting business, in the sense that it is in the heart of the economy, which, in turn, is a connecting activity.

Specifically, the automobile industry is the business of connecting people with work, jobs, careers. It connects people with goods, commodities, such as food, clothes, furniture, and so forth. It brings people together with services—from medical help to education. It connects them with other people, such as relatives and friends. It connects human beings with their political institutions: matters that have to do with the state, from legal and tax issues to voting and serving in public office. It connects people with their deeper emotional and spiritual needs, such as church and sports and concerts. And the automobile industry connects people with nature, such as allowing them to experience the wonder that is the Grand Canyon.

This connection can be established with the electronic cottage as readily, or even more so, as it can be with the automobile.

These connections must be established while observing certain important guidelines: the connections must be international; they must be pollution-free; they must avoid resource depletion; and they must avoid congestion. The latter is an accepted part of modern life. But the waste in work and in recreation hours, the alienation produced, the shattered nerves, and the general "zombification" of the commuter subculture (to which workers are adapted by reading, listening to the radio, staring, or, by the ultimate in alienation, the Walkman isolation instrument) is one of the disgracefully embarrassing side effects of the fact that the automobile (and truck and bus) industry is in the wrong business.

Beyond that, connections must be carried out in terms of a full commitment to automation, that is, with the proper appreciation for the role of high technology in the future of society. Statistical analyses and predictions seem to show, reassuringly, that whereas many jobs will be lost, many others will be created. Job change, lateral displacement, seem to be what is destined to happen.

And, furthermore, these connections must conform to the meaning needs of human nature; they must coincide with the values of civilization. For connection does not mean only worker with work but also person with worth, person with value, person with meaning, person with a response to the eternal questions. No assumption is made here that any one person knows what the values are. A moral person is one concerned with values and struggling with ethical issues. It is not a person who knows and then tyrannizes others. Only mindless dictators and arrogant autocrats are always certain about other people's morals.

There are many other industries which are in the same business. Therefore, both courageous mergers and determined segmentations among airlines, aircraft manufacturers, bullet trains, hotels and plants, space shuttles, and on and on, with the automobile must be considered.

The final contact is between people and the earth and people with their meanings. It is in this context that strategic planning for the future must be undertaken. We will always change. There is no end point. There are only stages. We must think about what stage is next, and when it will come, and what our decisions ought to be with respect to it. This is the kind of visionary thinking required of today's executives with minds that are expanded and that are deepened.

The full measure of this connection cannot yet be fathomed. We can only resolve to concentrate on the problem, cooperate with one another through our thoughts, and contribute our experiences. Above all, we share the contagious exhilaration of the adventure.

What actions can the automobile industry undertake today to deal with such a vision of the future?

- Explore it, define it, refine it, study it for feasibility, and assess the likelihood of its coming about.
- Draw up one or several models, perhaps through computer simulation, of the ways in which such a contact-rich or connection-authentic social and economic world might be structured.
- Then raise the question of what decisions today would be relevant for such a future society. What are some of the things which are possible today—and would make a profit today—which also help position an automobile company for this type of a future?
- One fundamental company strategy is to train larger segments of its personnel to deal with this reconceptualized future. One

aspect is to understand it; another is to help formulate it. This type of analysis requires continuous research and constant revision. The new training is to expand the minds of employees with new skills; it is to make them marketable, at least within their own newly reconceptualized corporation. The corporation was invented in the first place as a novel economic tool, as was the assembly line.

- A prestige section of every company must be devoted to long-range planning—something which of course most successful companies have already established, so that any further modernization should not be difficult. Every company needs a think tank concerned with the future and an idea bank in which the resulting treasures are organized and preserved.

At the risk of being naive, we may try to describe the suggested future—the date may well be 2025.

We envision a decentralized society, with complete villages throughout the landscape, a continuation of the developments of the suburbs. Commuting to cities, as well as living within them in any kind of civilized mode, is becoming increasingly difficult. The new contact or connecting business must invent new ways to shop, to set up schools, to bank, to connect people electronically and by computer with their work, their physicians, their schools, and so forth. And it must do all that in an integrated fashion. To the extent that it makes a profit, it also serves society, for in many cases the profit is a sign of utility to society. Much of this modernization is incipient already. There already exist mechanisms for it in our technology, from electronic shopping and computer-programmed education to office computer terminals in the home. And many who feel abused by the impersonality of automation are experiencing the growing pains of this new society.

Physically and geographically people will be farther apart, but socially they will be closer together and cluster in much larger numbers. What has not yet been studied adequately is the effect of the combination of inevitable decentralization and increased centralization on the minds of human beings. Their human relations, their sense of self, their feelings about their society and their country have not been reasonably studied—and for obvious reasons. Where are the data? Where can the data for the future be found? In past futures?

How will society change? Will nations disappear? Will people define community in a gerrymandered way, to include a little bit of this town and some of that city, and part of some distant country?

The small-town atmosphere that such a future society might foster may create anxieties and produce incestuous limitations on developing the human potential, a situation different from the greater excitement and the more copious opportunities of the large cities. But cities like Mexico City, Cairo, Tokyo, Los Angeles, and New York, essentially do not work anymore, although people in them have blinded themselves to many of the subhuman conditions with which they are forced to deal daily.

Another requirement, as suggested above, is to keep people's values straight, by discouraging them from adapting to subhuman circumstances and keeping their sights on what human dignity demands. The proclivity of human beings to adapt and lose the vision of their possibilities is one of the great obstacles to the creation of a better society and a better future. People too often accept the view that life is cheap. Keeping values straight will encourage companies and their employees to think through the total connection package in human terms.

Given the tasks of connecting, some of the new breed of employees are charged with the responsibility of working for solutions to the problem of connections. They must do so within the parameters indicated, and as they invent long-range solutions they also prescribe short-range ways in which products can gradually be adapted to future uses and needs.

What is or might be a legitimate vision for an automobile company? And how does one determine what that vision is? One way *not* to do it is to have top management congregate and legislate or mandate a mission or a values statement or a vision. A better way is to gain a consensus from the employees. In that case the missions and values statement would at least reflect the actual or the hoped-for corporate culture.

But we must consider the vision as a fact, as a social fact, as an independent phenomenon, as a fact commensurate with the existence of the organization as an entity separate from the members who constitute it. The United States, for example, or any nation for that matter, is more than just the aggregate of the people who happen to be living there at any one time. It exists in some non-material form all on its own. The vision or the mission of a company is determined first and foremost by the actual historical and social function which the company fulfills, the role it plays, in its current reality. The actual position of a company in society—especially of a well-established organization—its true role in the economic order, is determined by circumstances external to the decision-making process itself of that company.

In analyzing the actual, as opposed to the arbitrary or invented, mission of an automobile company, we are also asking about the nature of its business. Thus, to ask about the mission of a company is to ask also what business it is in. The following are relevant considerations—as examples only, of course. And they must be understood in conjunction with earlier comments about the new nature of the automobile business.

We must examine the mission of an automobile company in three phases. One is based on its product. The second follows from the perception the public has of it. And the third depends on the internal operations, or the culture, of the company. (See the diagram.)

The product is not the automobile—or truck or tractor—but contact of people with their world.

It is also identity and home. The automobile industry produces entities—we may call them vehicles, or, better, spatial containers or spatial receptacles—which are designed to give a sense of identity to the owner. They are personal statements, touching memories and the unconscious. Their product expresses archetypes. That is part of the American culture.

The vehicle or container or space is also the place, the "here," for Americans. It is their home. It is where they spend time in isolation or in intimacy, or in thought, in discussion, in planning, and in problem-solving. It is the place around which their world turns. They themselves are stationary; it is their environing world which moves. In the future there will not be, for example, a Toyota car, but a Toyota house or home, or a Toyota electronic cottage. The same theory of place applies to the airplane.

The company as perceived externally represents the economy, which means economic security for the nation and/or for the world. It also represents freedom, in the free enterprise sense.

Finally, internally, the mission of the company as perceived by the public or as seen from the perspective of history is that it must be a good place for people to fulfill themselves as individuals and for them to experience a sense of camaraderie and belonging. It responds to both the individual and to the social instinctual needs of its employees. The company therefore fulfills, up to a point, the functions of school, home, and church.

These missions are ineluctable, for they are socially determined. A company can choose whether or not to actualize these expectations. It cannot readily change them.

That is their true mission.

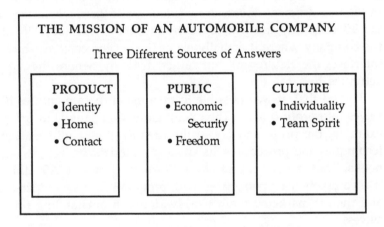

THE MISSION OF AN AUTOMOBILE COMPANY

Three Different Sources of Answers

PRODUCT	PUBLIC	CULTURE
• Identity	• Economic	• Individuality
• Home	Security	• Team Spirit
• Contact	• Freedom	

To this foundation, the company can now add its own unique and distinctive values and mission statement.

3. A Case Study in Leadership

The following is an example of ethical leadership in downsizing.

A large and prestigious chain of private schools—from preschools to college preparatory institutes—was quickly losing money.

The organization consisted of individual schools, assembled in regions, and a rather large central corporate organization, headquartered in New York. Their stock plummeted from 38 to 22 in two weeks. The obvious reason was that a projected 25 percent growth had actually been reduced to less than 5 percent. How was the chancellor to respond? Here is an outline. The reaction was swift, positive, rational, survival-oriented, and affirmative.

The budget process was changed. The principles invoked were to cut expenses not at the schools, which had been the practice for a long time, but at the corporate and regional level.

The underlying question was what to view as fixed. Rather than consider corporate expenses as fixed—for corporate is not a profit center and can therefore not itself compensate for losses—and rather than see the schools as having flexible expenses, the new look considered the school expenses as fixed, for it is there that quality resides. And quality is not negotiable, that is, it is fixed.

The basic elements were (1) the inverted organization chart and (2) the meaning of quality. The company exists in the classroom, not in the boardrooms. If cuts are needed, make them where they will not affect quality, and where, in the end, they will not really affect the company where it actually exists (i.e., at the customer-business interface, the classroom), but rather distantly, where the support activities lie.

Beyond that, it was possible to turn the corporate entities themselves into profit centers. Their prestigious Company University, for example, the pride and joy of the organization, could market its techniques and procedures, its kits and materials, its lectures and its books. That is what Scandinavian Airlines System (SAS) did: first that company used personal-growth programs for its own personnel, and then it marketed them worldwide, with outstanding financial success.

"We must prune now for a later harvest." That was the motto for the school chain. The decision was made not to prune in development programs for school principals. They, it was argued, were the heart of the company. And their training consisted in greater measure of developing their minds, expanding the creative potential, than in providing them with additional techniques and procedures. Stimulation for greatness and for courage in their education was more important than the latest teaching and school administration techniques. The rationale is that new construction they can figure out by themselves, but courage and greatness they cannot.

All decisions were made in light of this question: What is central to our mission? And following from that, What is central to the personal development of the school principals?

The manner in which J.J., the provost in charge of dismissals from his division, helped his company to face its financial crisis can probably serve as a case study of ethics in leadership. Each position was scrutinized meticulously on the following criteria: Is it necessary for the primary mission of the company? What is the performance record of the person occupying this position at the present time? And these sensitive discussions were held jointly among all the managers, so that everyone participated in them. The resultant conclusions were not only better, but also reasonably democratic. It was a town-hall-meeting type of decision-making process—about itself, and not about others. People devised ways of making choices about themselves. The final names were selected. Everyone was apprised of the problem, the situation, and the method of resolution. A generous severance program was developed, including a professional seminar to deal with emotional issues,sponsored by the company and taught on its grounds.

The process was slow, deliberate, careful, rational, participative, and humane. And those who administered it were informed, affectively as well as cognitively, about greatness, courage, risk, change, and the overwhelming importance of adequately understanding anxiety.

The chancellor did not lose his nerve, but calmly maintained his vision and optimistically supported this radical process of reorganizing the company around its central mission.

The critical ingredients, criteria for success, were these:

- The fundamental attitude was one that viewed survival measures not as matters of desperation and panic but opportunities to be healthy and positive. The premise was a biological one: anything one does in the direction of survival is healthy. Evolution is right, and the economy, if followed, since it is part of nature, will produce health. Survival is like strenuous exercise. It is what the body needs; and although it may hurt at first it feels wonderful and healthy (for it is healthy, it is right for the body) in the end. The economic crisis is right for the spirit. Responding to it positively is right for the economy in general and right for our individual economies in particular. This is an example of turning anxiety into strength, pain into meaning, obstacle into stepping-stone. Also, coping so is not a mere technique but a response to what is real, not only in the world, but also in the heart and soul of man and woman.
- The intensive and democratic discussion, or the dialogic and dialectic process, by which—slowly, deliberately, and meticulously—all decisions were made by the staff.

- The compassionate, generous, intelligent, and rather imaginative way in which severance was arranged.
- The vision of the provost's superiors. They had a clear sense of what the company needed or needs, which is the training of the minds of its top executives. The cost-effectiveness brought about by expanding the principals' minds outstrips any equivalent work done with the teachers. That was the responsibility of the principals.
- Patience pays off, not panic. Cool reflection, not precipitous action, brings results. One does not change basic values in mid-course, or in response to a crisis. One does not allow more primitive instincts to govern one's actions when stresses reach high levels. That is true leadership.
- A recognition that economizing must occur at the corporate and regional level—the very people who make the decision for cuts in the first place—and not in the school and the classroom, that is, in the field. This is the meaning both of the inverted organization chart, a reference to Jan Carlzon, the legendary president of SAS, and of the unremitting commitment to quality. Quality means clear vision regarding the nature of the organization's primary values and obligations.
- All decisions were made with vision in mind. That vision has two elements. The goal of the company is to provide the best possible education to its students. Education is the task of the individual schools. And the prime movers in making that happen are the principals of these schools, together with their staffs and teachers. But it is their minds that need cultivation. Once the vision was clear, decisions were as simple as they were radical.
- Decisions were made in the spirit of both courage and with a sense of ethical greatness.
- The commitment to the task exhibited by the provost making these difficult decisions was crystal-clear and total. The energy and the attention he devoted to the solution of this problem was undistracted and unswerving. Like the writing of a novel or symphony, managerial tasks are not eight-to-five responsibilities. They are total and passionate. There is no alternative.
- The ability to excite and stimulate the staff, even when under severe stress. And the excitement is a very personal matter.

First of all, it means recognizing the true worth and potential of subordinates; it means to appreciate what they can do best and what they strive to offer. In philosophy we would say that a person is given room into which to grow, consciousness is permitted to transcend itself, and the ego can reach out because it is understood and it is wanted. This attitude gives hope and support to the mind that wishes to grow. The key to effective management is to find minds that wish to grow and then make it possible for them to make the contributions which will give their lives meaning.

Second, the task has to be worthy in itself; it must have meaning on the human level, and it helps if it also has superordinate cultural and political significance.

Third, the person in charge must be a high-quality person who has and (fourth) demonstrates a high level of commitment.

A person whom one respects can be followed; but the respect must be built on genuinely valuable human qualities.

- There is a willingness to make hard and difficult choices, and to carry them out personally. This is the secret of gaining strength through adversity. A person's spirits are lifted high on a beam of anxiety and on a wave of pain.

- The task of responding to financial stress in a company must have all the credible signs of ethical greatness. This means that the company is not merely after profits but after the protection of all its assets: stockholders' investments, employees' job security, students' education, and the well-being of those members of the communities they serve who are affected by the financial stress.

- The activity—the struggle against the financial crisis—must have higher meaning. An educational institution is not dedicated only to educating its students. It is in the education business in general; and the ultimate student today is the globe. The globe is a single organism; and it is uneducated. Educating in a particular instance is a guide to educating in a general way. How we deal with the student is training for how to educate the Globe. "Global education" is the task for our generation.

- A free economy is at stake. The private chain must prove to the world that freedom in enterprise is as important and as productive as freedom in one's personal life and freedom in the political life. A free people are not just a productive people but also a moral people. That is the Jeffersonian faith in the common man.

• Furthermore, nothing affirms the self more vigorously than to meet successfully an overwhelming challenge. It builds character, maturity, and moral fiber. Such a feeling of achievement in constructing a personal identity is one of the great exhilarations of being alive; and it is a sui generis sensation. In completing successfully a task such as this response to the financial crisis one also builds the substance of a personality. Only a religious experience surpasses the emotional charge afforded by such an accomplishment. It is the experience of God creating Man and Woman, for in this act of vision and of courage a person is created.

• The significance of self-worth and self-respect cannot be overestimated. People ultimately work for respect, not for money. Ralph Kramden, Jackie Gleason's notable character, was boastful and pursued ridiculous schemes for one reason only: to gain self-respect and a sense of worth. He was a loved and funny character because all Americans felt a sigh of relief when they could laugh at their own failures to gain self-respect, and thus they were able to forgive themselves for their inadequacies.

• Self-respect and self-worth are immortality projects. They are means to feel the solidity of the ego. The ego becomes large and tough, massive like the granite mountain that is El Capitan in Yosemite. Is that real or pseudo immortality? Intellectually it may mean little, but emotionally, affectively, experientially, it is proof positive that through one's own efforts no less, one has achieved eternity, permanence, immortality. God is not only deathless, eternal. He is more than that: God is self-created, *Causa Sui,* His own Cause. And that ultimate symbol is also the deeper meaning of self-respect.

   You give a man the chance to earn his self-respect and you will have given him the closest chance yet to live in the imitation of God. And that is the deepest meaning behind the manner in which the financial crisis was met.

4. The Frustrated Executive

To be an executive is to be frustrated. A large portion of the often high salary must go to compensate for the moral and emotional pain that results from constant and intense frustration. These are then the parameters within which the executive operates.

The financial squeeze is always on—as a matter of policy. It becomes therefore the mode in which everyone thinks. Pervasive and permanent insistence on cost containment *does* help the bottom line. But, in order to be effective, it must be perceived, not as technique but as a real emergency.

What are the debits of such an attitude? It can be perceived by employees as arbitrary, as harassment, as producing distractions, as violating agreements, and as indifference to persons. What is the resulting cost in lessened productivity, diminished creativity, and weakened loyalty? These ramifications need to be explored.

Beyond cost cutting, here are some further typical complaints of a high executive, such as a vice president.

- Too much work, stress, chaos, confusion.

- Frustration with personal effectiveness. Business is an endless series of frustrations. As long as executives can call them challenges they feel good. But the frustrations can get excessive and calling them challenges then becomes vacuous; it becomes a rationalization and denial and leads to depression. The intensity of frustration is related to increased competition, which in turn is related to the fact that most companies are getting better in all aspects of their operations. It becomes necessary to excel merely to keep up. Efforts and competencies which in earlier times would have led to sterling performances are required today merely to keep pace with the competitors.

- The lateral view—towards peers. The executives are not listening to the message. For example, the executives in a management training program, is designed to elevate the culture of the company and thus make the company more competitive and create stability for its future, are not responding as expected. And the reason appears to be not the program's quality, which is approaching its maximum, but the sluggishness and indifference, the alienation and the narrowness, of the executives themselves. And yet any manager knows that once such cynicism takes over he or she has really been defeated.

  This is the situation from the point of view of the leader responsible for the program designed to change the culture, the so-called change agent. The message, which is the product, to the executives in the training program, who are the clients, is good, even superior. But the clients—students, participants, employees, subordinates, managers, executives—do not respond, do not buy, do not, as it were, pay their bills.

- The view to the top, to superiors, to the bosses. The CEO and his or her immediate associates, the executive or management committee, always appear to interfere. The CEO, whose endorsement is critical for the success of any culture-change program, does not support the program adequately, does not understand the situation clearly enough, does not show enough interest, does not validate the work, does not understand the importance and the value of the project, does not appreciate the benefit of the program to the organization, and in general does not do what is needed.

- The view below, to subordinates. The staff is not sufficiently efficient; nor do they display enough imagination. They are not helpful enough, not interested enough. There is insufficient automation, and what exists is not fully utilized.

- The presence of the irrational, of politics, of evil, of the neurotic, of the schizoid, of sabotage, of destruction, of turfdom, of alienation, of the inauthenticity that uses rather than meets people.

  Those feelings can be avoided by deliberate rationality. Some executives are very thoughtful in what they do, are able to explain their actions, and the explanations do not function to rationalize unconscious impulses or irrational habits or personality traits. It seems clear that the thoughtful executive thinks through what needs to be done and then does it on the strength of the reasons. To be governed by reason is an engineering and scientific trait. It is also a stoic virtue. It is also a jurisprudential necessity. It is also the core of the Kantian ethics, known as deontology: It is when a rational rule motivates the will and governs one's actions.

  The threat of irrationality can also be ameliorated by contact. People need to feel heard, and listening is a psychological more than a logical function. The feeling of being heard is the sense that another person has contacted one's core, understands, cares,

and considers how to deal with it. This is a validating experience—an experience which confirms one's existence and one's
value. It is the social environment's contribution to one's sense of
self. Some people have this extraverted and expansive connecting trait, and others find it difficult to be close in this form to
another person.

Reason and contact are thus two ways to establish trust and
loyalty, which lead to the alliance between boss and subordinate that make for meaningful and productive work.

- To the organization as a whole. The executive needs to show
profit, and that, assuming the vice-president is in a staff function, can be done in two ways.

   The culture-change program is profitable to the organization.
That may be difficult to show; it may involve faith. But demonstrations of contributing to profitability—if fairly and rationally assessed—should be welcome. In actual fact, interestingly enough, most CEO's view culture-change intuitively and
pay little heed to statistical evaluations. That may be wisdom. Culture-change programs are endorsed or opposed, it appears, mostly on intuitive grounds.

   The culture-change program can be its own profit center. That
is not an easy problem to solve; but with sufficient imagination
it constitutes a breakthrough in management: staff functions
pay for themselves, calculated not in terms of utility to the
company but in absolute terms. Inviting outside participants and
sponsoring lectures must then be designed to be profitable and to
benefit the marketing needs of the company. To move from staff
function to profit center is to find ethical ways to charge the
customer for advertising.

How do we cope with this outline of a situation, generic and
typical of many a top executive's headaches? We need to make up
our minds to the following realities:

1. This is an exercise in adaptation and survival.
2. It is a game; and it is the only game.
3. We must not only evolve in order to deal with it—and evolution
   is an intrinsic value—but we also must accelerate the progress
   of evolution itself, so that also the rate of growth increases.

4. We measure the results of our game in profits. The benefits are economic; they are also emotional and spiritual. But we keep score with the numbers, the profits. By viewing business as a game, we learn to play the game better.

5. How can we accelerate our personal evolution, the kind of evolution we require in order to cope effectively with the frustrations described above? By understanding the concepts of multiple intelligences and of accelerated evolution. To cultivate the multiple intelligences is to also accelerate evolution. We can do that best by analyzing the resistances to both, for resistances exist in our customers as well as in ourselves. We can achieve results by studying the obstacles which keep us from achieving results.

- One must cultivate one's multiple intelligences daily. The resulting increased intelligence will also increase, enhance, and accelerate the effectiveness of the intelligence training itself. This becomes a self-accelerating system. One's intelligence can be expected to increase at an accelerating pace.

  The effect is spiraling progress: Accelerated effectiveness will become accelerated evolution, and it will show itself in terms of one's self-chosen and self-selected measurements—which can be profits, promotions, recognition, self-satisfaction, knowledge, meaning, and so forth.

- The message to the participants in a culture-change program must be: *Take personal responsibility to uplift your spirits and to be loyal to the company* in spite of insensitivities and injustices at the top.

  And the corresponding message to the CEO of such a company is: Listen, support, teach—do not intimidate, and *be sensitive to the emotional needs of the employees.*

  (More of this practical discussion can be found in Chapter 10.)

5. Self-Esteem and the Burdens of Leadership

Who understands the burdens of leadership? Who is not pained by being misunderstood?

I go to a restaurant to meet a company president for breakfast, and announce to the manager, "I am here early for an important meeting. May we have a quiet place?"

"Yes, we try to please," she answers.

She takes me to a booth and then says, in jest, "If you sit here, then I can overhear your conversation."

"Why would you want to do that?" I ask.

"To make a lot of money," she answers innocently.

"If you listen in to us you will not make a lot of money but you will get a lot of headaches!" I correct her.

"Then I'm not interested," she replies.

Little does she understand the problems and the anxieties, the questions and the sleepless nights, the sense of frustration and the feelings of self-sacrifice that go with the quest for authentic leadership!

The accepted *business* order of priorities is

- strategic issues;
- team-building issues; and
- personal, psychological, and philosophical issues.

The *real*, workable, meaningful order or priorities is the exact reversal of that presumption:

- personal, psychological, and philosophical issues;
- team-building issues; and
- strategic issues.

Strategic issues are business plans. We have a problem, how do we solve it? What are the strategies, tactics, business decisions that need to be made? The steel industry is concerned with foreign competition. What strategy will help? Persuade the government to pass tariff legislation? Diversify? Invest heavily in research and development? Automate?

Telecommunications companies are facing new problems of competition, both because of the AT&T breakup and because of the arrival of newly organized long-distance carriers. High-technology firms find it difficult to compete with IBM. How is that to be accomplished? By entering into areas where IBM is not interested? By being IBM compatible? By taking advantage of being small, adaptable, and flexible?

The solution to these issues requires good teams. A team works for the benefit of the whole organization. Fragmentations, turfdom, being rule-bound, saying "no" mindlessly, exercising control for psychological and not for business reasons, creating needless stresses, all result from lack of teamwork.

To work as a team empowers. And the words used today to express the success of teams are "alignment" and "attunement." To be empowered means that people can accomplish things working together which amount to more than the sum of their individual contributions. People then feel that they are powerful and successful not only because of their own capabilities and diligence, but because they are privileged to be members of this particular team. The realistic satisfaction of the gregarious instinct yields a deep and primitive sense of fulfillment.

But a team is successful only if it has authentic managers, leaders— formal or informal. And the most common issues discussed, in my experience, and the most effective ones once they have been discussed, are the more personal issues. These are issues that are usually relegated to the field of psychology and its many cognates. These issues have today been deepened through philosophy, which is not a new approach but merely updating what has been the case throughout the entire history of civilization. For the insight that the unexamined life is not worth living was not the vision of Freud but of Socrates, and the realization that human beings must be free was not the insight of Sartre but of Moses leading the Israelites out of their captivity in Egypt.

Solving small problems and making small progress takes some of the power out of emotional issues. We can solve emotional conflicts more readily if the external pressures which intensify them are removed.

What are these issues? It is the human qualities that matter. Needed are

- unstinting loyalty and cooperation,
- total commitment and dedication,
- full utilization of creative possibilities,
- stark realism and maturity,
- the wise acceptance of limits, and
- the unqualified ownership of personal responsibility.

Every leader needs self-respect. How is that to be attained? By people's supporting, challenging, and encouraging the leader. That is what a good friend does and a loyal spouse. But such is not enough. Depth exploration discloses more.

First, the need for self-esteem is not one person's problem but a universal human condition. There may be here degrees of intensity, of repression, and of manageability. But the lack of self-esteem comes from the fragility of the human situation, from our free will, and from our capacity for guilt—the latter two being intimately connected. This is true of every human being. Sometimes we need to turn to theology to understand our more limited psychology. The "impostor syndrome" is no different from the universal fear of being a fraud, from the concept of Original Sin, and from its Calvinistic amplification—transmitted historically to Puritanism in England and then to Presbyterianism in America.

Lack of self-esteem, which is universal, can be better understood by linking it to the "repetition compulsion." Let us say your father was a consistent business failure. You, if you are a man and if you have patterned yourself after your father—which is only natural— will repeat that syndrome in your own life. But you will not know it. The unconscious part of you will do it. And the unconscious is truly unconscious. You know nothing about that part of you. You see only its effects. All your energy is spent, over a lifetime, to counteract the power of the repetition compulsion.

You work hard not to fail. You succeed at what you do. But the restlessness persists. As you climb higher on the organizational ladder, failures are easier, more visible, and more spectacular. And being more dramatic they are also more severe. Thus, as you succeed over a lifetime in averting repeating your father's proclivity for failure, you really set yourself up for an even greater failure, by assuming that ambition is natural and by never really stopping to think whether or not that ambition is authentic.

An interpretation referring to the unconscious may also release the unconscious. The sudden fear, the moment of scariness, the quick opening to an icy darkness—these are moments of truth. They contain wisdom. They must be explored, not denied; for in them lie answers.

It is important to have friends and lovers who prop one up, who support, and who encourage one, who give pep talks and stimulate one to action. But such support, loving as it is and helpful as it may be, may nevertheless spring from the anxiety aroused in the friend who has witnessed another's unconscious. The anxiety of experiencing the unconscious is contagious.

What is needed in addition, at a deeper level, is not to respond with the equivalent anxiety, the anxiety of denial, but with deep understanding, accurate witness, and genuine compassion. And that means to love in one's friend the lack of self-esteem, the anxiety, the emptiness, the nothingness, the vacuum, the fear, the fragility, the vulnerability, the weakness. For that is ultimate love. That helps all of us to forgive ourselves our nothingness.

The simple truth is that man must forgive himself that he is not God. For we are responsible for our trespasses, which include not having willed perfection sufficiently. We must aspire to imitate God, to be like God, even to be God. Even the mere aspiration to be God is sinful, but so is our lack of infinite determination to be like God also sinful. And we know that our will for perfection is insufficient, for the simple reason that we have not attained our goal. This failure makes us inherently guilty. For that we must forgive others—and ultimately ourselves.

This is an inherent structure in the soul or the psyche. It emerges in mythology as original sin and it is institutionalized by the predestination theology of reformers such as Calvin, who insisted that most children were born sinful and deserve to be punished for that.

Thus, the lack of self-esteem is not a minor nor a psychological problem, nor does it have a cure. It is part of the human condition. It has been described better by mythology and theology than by psychology and by the behavioral sciences. The lack of self-esteem must be understood and it must be loved. It must be appreciated. The wisdom in it must be extracted.

These insights can lead to changes. They mean mature and courageous decisions on becoming someone else or at least on being different. The changes have to do with the realism of growing up—a process that never ends. The self—or ego, psyche, or soul—has a natural tendency to grow up. Which means a natural tendency to become independent, strong, self-sufficient, and to give up dependency modes of existence.

But the internal urge to grow up alone is insufficient to overcome the massive inertia of the child. Only with the addition of powerful external forces—reality, the real world, the market, survival, peer pressure, or what have you—will the psyche be forced to adapt itself to the exigencies of maturity. Such necessary growth occurs often best under emergency conditions and at precipitous speeds. In executives, this situation arises when decisions need to be made, and quickly, for which the mind of the executive is ill prepared emotionally.

There comes a time for the *beau geste* , the grand gesture. The chief must show that he or she is not greedy but loyal, not self-seeking but committed, not self-centered but self-sacrificing. A sense of integrity, duty, responsibility, ethicalness, justice, fairness, love, devotion, dedication—which transcends the usual utilitarian, pragmatic, and prudential business considerations—is not only appropriate, but at high levels of management, it is also expected. For what is being managed is not money nor property but people. And the true reward is not good business or a high reputation— although these may be side products—but self-respect, pride, self-esteem, and a feeling of deep satisfaction for being that kind of a person!

In too many companies across the nation and the world one hears complaints like these, fair or unfair: "These top people hate one other, when what this organization needs is their cooperation." "There is no real team running this company." "The leadership of this company is nothing but crassly and crudely competitive." "The leaders think only of themselves." "The leadership is greedy and looking out for themselves; they don't give a damn about this company." "All the leadership wants is golden parachutes; they don't care what happens to their subordinates." "The best thing that could happen to this company is an unfriendly takeover."

What would be a "grand gesture"? Only the executive knows. But examples have been

- resigning because one is not the right person for the job, or cause the job cannot be performed with integrity;
- cutting one's salary to help meet a fiscal crisis;
- closing the office and spending all of one's time in the field;
- setting up for top management an ongoing bona fide therapy group, where undiscussable issues are made discussable, so as to create a realistic team;
- challenging, under stressful circumstances, one's closest friends to behave with adult and mature integrity;
- making an exceptionally difficult but clearly courageous decision, then explaining it and taking full responsibility for it.

Let us consider for example a company, of which there are not a few, in which the employee population, especially its management—including those who work in the corporate area—is exceptionally intelligent. Many companies are staffed by young, well-educated, and surprisingly well-experienced executives. A primary task for the top leadership of such a company is to harness, tap, utilize this extraordinary reservoir of talent. This can be done by creating an environment, a culture, in which people are empowered. This means that employees are given the opportunity to develop their talents and that the principal rule of human interaction is, "We are here to make our colleagues and buddies successful."

Such an attitude requires the insight that we must prosper as a team. And to do that, we must understand the need for teamwork, we must activate the will for teamwork, and we must tolerate the frustrations of teamwork.

And how is all of that to be done? We must recognize that the "one choice for the executive" is the decision between being an isolated and alone individual and being an intimate member of a team, a family. The solution, if there is one, would look perhaps as follows.

How does one establish a team, which is a family, in a business, which is not a family? First, by understanding the paradox between being an individual—free, entrepreneurial, independent, isolated—and being a team—intimate, close, connected, bonded, supporting. We need both—profoundly. And second, by making an individual and risky decision to choose and will a commitment to the company, to oneself, to each other, i.e., to peers, to subordinates, and to superiors. Each commitment is unique and different. That is integrity; that is ethics. That is maturity.

6. Letter to a Friend

As we parted, you seemed strong and determined. I trust it will endure.

First, your principal, underlying, and overarching concerns are to exhibit and to express

- a strong *will*,
- steely *determination*, and
- a full-bodied *commitment*, to the company and to yourself.

Herein lies the difference between (1) being youthful in spirit, having reached the peak of your existence, being better equipped and more thoroughly prepared to live life to its fullest and in its richest possible way than ever before and (2) aging, having given up, depression, involution.

The manner in which this renewed vigor will express itself is through the recognition of the mission of your company, which is to redress old abuses and thus help solve the health problem in the United States, and which is to maintain freedom by demonstrating the success of the free enterprise system in an uncommon area.

This in turn is to be achieved by improving your skills to persuade, motivate, and stimulate those who depend on your leadership for their own success. For you know what to do and you know how to do it. You must charge up your people like a Napoleon and motivate them to more effective action.

Second, here is a triangle of values that may make sense as the firmament within which the constellation of your life can be encompassed.

1. Your philosophy—world-view or mindset—might be that life is a game, "the only game in town." You enjoy it, you are engaged in it, you play it exceptionally well, but you are also totally realistic. The company is part of the market, and is thus independent of you. You have helped give it birth, but, like a child who has grown up, it will go on its own way. And it is right that it be that way. Your commitment to its success and to your contribution to it is total. So is your realism total regarding the independent life of the company.

   Two metaphors invite themselves: the nun and the psychoanalyst. Both, in their ideal forms, are fully committed to their work and to their patients. Neither is seduced by the gratitude, the love, the fawning, the sycophancy, the projection, the efforts at controlling, or the manipulations of those who appreciate their work and their contribution.

   The nun's ultimate oneness is with God. She does God's work in her school or hospital. There she is loving and committed. But she knows she is not doing her social work to be loved and esteemed by others, but because her relation to God demands it. She knows that if she is successful her pupils and her patients will cease to need her, will leave her, will enter other relationships , and will eventually forget her.

   And so it is with the psychoanalyst. His ultimate oneness is with himself—in lonely, perhaps atheistic isolation. There he is committed to his profession and must be loyal to his system of ethics. His obligation to the well-being—the maturity and independence—of his patient is absolute. He may be tempted, by his own countertransference, to be seduced by the love of his patient, but he must reject even the most alluring offers of loyalty and affection, for his obligation is to the unswerving authenticity of the person who pays him to be assisted in growing up.

These are models for one's relation to a company. It implies total commitment, total loyalty, placing the welfare of the organization above all personal considerations—but doing it with full realism, with no illusions, with the knowledge that our own existence is but a transitory phenomenon in the life of the company. But we also know that the company needs us—as we need it.

Your ultimate security, however, lies at your center—either with your own isolated ego, or with God, or with some final earthly love or friendship. And it must be a love or a friendship which will survive even death.

2. Your second major project in life is the old ideal of perfection. You must do what you are doing better than anyone else, anywhere. Why? Because the soul strives for perfection, the ego wants to realize its potential, it seeks to fulfill its possibilities. The ideal of self-realization, developing your capacities to the fullest, represents also one of the most beautiful and noblest feelings of fulfillment known to the human condition.

But as you become the best you can be, you also achieve your career, your professional, and your financial goals.

One of the things you need now is that you must become the most effective executive possible, and as soon as possible. And you will do it by sharpening your communication and motivational skills, which you can do through education. Instead of a private physical fitness coach, which is common, you, as you think for yourself, will have English-language, logic, and singing coaches.

3. The third component in your plan for life is integrity. You have cast your fate with the position that compromising your deepest values is not practical but sick, is not utilitarian but diseased. You live by the faith that honesty with others, but mostly with yourself, is the healthiest way to live. You know

that the world is made for people with integrity, for people who speak with their full bodies and not just with their heads. For the truth is as physical as health is physical.

Best wishes,

Peter

7. Staff Functions as Profit Centers

How can one solve the financial problems facing staff functions? Staff functions can be defined as the part of a company which does not earn any money and which is therefore supported by the earnings of the money-making or line functions of the rest of the organization.

This poses problems in two areas. One is financial. Human resources programs and personnel, to use one example of a line function, are the first to be cut when a recession sets in for the company.

The second problem is one of the self-respect, the self-esteem, and in particular the sense of independence of the managers of these staff functions. Financial dependence becomes a problem of image or self-image; it becomes a question of identity. People do not like to feel beholden to others. Managers like to feel that they earn their positions. And since costs and profits are the sine qua non of any business, executives need to feel that their positions are secured by their own efforts.

The most obvious way for the managers of staff functions to feel their self-worth and to demonstrate their contributions to the organization is to create profit centers themselves—unorthodox as that solution might be. Staff personnel must have their right to exist, their place under the sun, guaranteed, so as not to be at the mercy and the whims of the "higher-status" line function managers.

The solution to this pervasive controversy must be created not for one company alone but must become a bellwether for all of American industry. This "universalizing" approach to an issue illustrates the philosophy-in-business principle that company problems have both deeper and higher (universal) aspects. And it is only when these issues are addressed at higher or deeper levels that meaningful solutions can be expected.

The specific philosophy-in-business principle alluded to here is this: problems need to be addressed at their real, i.e., philosophic, level, rather than at their apparent, surface, and purely business level. And there are two such levels: depth and height. The level of depth refers to the underlying human issues, the unconscious, the eternal questions, such as the inevitability of human freedom, the fear of abandonment, and the guilt of an alliance with evil. To the degree that we can trace a major business decision not only through its convoluted logical and analytic labyrinths, but to the anxiety of free will and to the corresponding need for courage, and to the degree that we can unravel the inner structures of courage and the exact configuration of the love, commitment, compassion, and witness needed to support it, to that extent we touch the deeper regions of an otherwise ordinary business choice. *The level of height is the principle of universalization. It means that we do not choose for our organization alone but for all mankind.* We establish a universal rule, a general principle, a comprehensive solution, an international policy, a model for others. Our problem is but a single manifestation of an industrywide or even worldwide need. And in thinking through what may appear a puny issue in the cosmic context, we are contributing to the larger welfare of the globe.

The possible solutions are three. One is that top management assumes full and personal responsibility to certify that the staff function (human resources is always a good example) is valid and of benefit to the company. And that is that. No more discussion required; no more comment from staff functions. Respect is granted by edict.

The second solution is to devise measurements on the profit advantage to the full company of the human resource or other staff programs. Such measurements require thorough exploration and analysis. Although the cause and effect nexus is distant and certainly loaded heavily with subjectivity, a relentless effort is to be mounted to establish criteria to satisfy even the keenest critics. Establishing such measurements will in itself influence the attitudes and the programs of the human-resource or management development or employee-relations functions. It will tend to make them more profit and cost conscious in their design of programs. It will call to their attention, for example, that one of the most cost-effective devices is follow-up. It may be uncertain and expensive to set programs in motion. But to continue what has been started is economical. Follow-up programs are in themselves profit-oriented, for money is made through perseverance, continuity, and consistency, and not through occasional passionate impulses.

The third solution to the staff-profit center controversy is for the latter to generate profit themselves. Scandinavian Airlines System is a good example. Their training functions—which are a joint venture—have been profitably marketing packaged training programs. Some of them originated within SAS, but many have been bought from outside sources. At the beginning, the only customer was SAS. Today, the joint-venture company markets its training programs all over Europe. This program started simply by expanding what was designed for in-house use. The key issue in transforming a staff function into a profit center is to make certain that the profit activities do not conflict with the legitimate staff functions but, beyond that, actually enhance them.

To solve that problem for one company is to perform a much-needed service for all of American industry.

Here are practical rules:

1. Making a staff function into a profit center requires the full cooperation of every member of the organization.
2. This project gives all managers and employees the opportunity to provide for themselves an environment in which each member's talents are tapped and used. Each person is responsible for himself or herself, as well as for every other member of the organization, to uncover talent and to find ways to make use of those talents—because it is through helping people *discover* their talents, through assisting people in *developing* them, and by giving them the opportunity to *use* their talents that they can be validated, recognized, and can make a contribution.
3. A staff-function-turned-profit-center is not an entity separate from the rest of the company. Every project must be thought through to enhance specific missions, strategies, and tactics of the larger organization. If, for example, the staff function produces teaching materials or audio-visual aids, then these must not only do honor to the company due to their high quality, but they must support, let us say, the basic sales and marketing efforts of the parent company as well.
4. The staff function needs to keep records of their financial contribution to the parent company. These consist of three entries:

actual cash received, profit contributions made to the rest of the organization, and personal growth facilitated in staff and line functions in the total organization. The profit contributions to the rest of the organization are estimates only—of course. And they must be reported in terms of a probable range. The criterion of assessment is, How much more would the company be spending and how much less would it be earning if our function did not exist? But the figures should be fair, that is, not inflated, so that if all staff functions pooled their figures, they would produce a rational total.

5. The participants in the extra work and thought required to make a staff function into a profit center should receive rewards for the successful completion of their efforts. The profits that they make from external sources they should share.

There are two types of profit—first there is money and then there is personal growth and increase in marketability. First, regarding money, they could, for example, set up a stock company, of which the parent company would own 50 percent. They would then share the rest. And second, regarding growth, value measure must be devised, agreed upon, and publicized. And that must happen for two reasons in turn: to teach people to think in terms of growth and consequently to value these personal gains, and to urge people to follow up on the values of growth and marketability that they have received. For visible value is realized only through follow up.

Each company can find their own solutions.

A Corporate College or a Company University

Following are some strategic considerations.

The function of a corporate college is to be the *consulting arm* of or to the company. A corporate college will

- send out pairs of speakers, from its staff and faculty,
- include outsiders—i.e., visitors from other companies, from schools, or from the public service sector—in corporate college sessions,
- encourage its staff and faculty to make public speeches, nation-wide,
- establish open information seminars, and then
- bill the companies or agencies for services rendered.

The rest of the company must feel that the outside corporate college activities add value to the corporate college service function by adding value to the company itself. Thus, making money—which contributes to the self-respect and independence of a corporate college—must also increase and enhance the sophistication, effectiveness, and usefulness of that same corporate college for the entire company of which it is a part, of which it is a staff function.

But in redefining itself as the national consulting arm of its parent company, it exhibits imagination and leadership in furthering and in forwarding the necessary reconceptualization of the meaning of its product and of its service in the United States and in the world.

8. Integrity: the Key to Leadership

As leaders assume more and greater responsibilities, the question of their integrity becomes increasingly severe.

The claim to integrity is brought about by two forces. As the soul approaches middle age, it becomes more satisfied with its inwardness and with its own roots than it was before. It becomes more secure in the foundations which exist within itself. As death comes closer, as death seems now a reality and not just an idea, there appears to also come a greater security from the inside, a feeling of centeredness, a belief in a ground that truly exists in the seat of the self. These were feelings that were quite absent in one's anxious and shaky youth. The soul demands integrity from within. At a time when executives may be reaching the peak of their careers, the concept of self-validation begins to make experiential and not just intellectual sense.

Furthermore, as the executive increases his power over the destinies of other men and women, it becomes obvious to that leader that the lives of people cannot for long tolerate the absence of integrity. Employees, like humanity at large, will simply suffocate in an atmosphere that stifles them with injustice, with insensitivity, with unethicalness, with lies, with devious promises, with indignity, with cowardice, and with shoddy models. Integrity has survival value; integrity is part of evolution. Integrity is adaptation, not to the immediate exigencies of turf and of personal ambitions, but to the enduring values of the soul, to the health of the spirit, to the needs of consciousness, and to the survival of what is human.

And there can be no self-validation other than through integrity, because integrity means that one's life conforms accurately to the intrinsic needs of the self. A soul that egotistically believes in the legitimacy of Machiavellian mercilessness and actually accepts the brutalization of self-serving manipulation is an undeveloped soul. It is a soul that has not reached the fulfillment of its own potential. It is a soul that has deprived itself of receiving the richness that life offers to it. Such a soul may die before it has savored what might have been!

One must have compassion for the executive who is impaled on the horns of the dilemma of integrity. The observer has it easy: to be ethical is a simple categorical imperative, an unconditional command. But to be oneself in the midst of the agony of leadership conflicts, to be oneself the very one who must choose between career and what is moral, that is often a Hobson's choice.

The test is in the question, why me? If that is what you feel, then you are stuck in existential isolation. You are the one who is nailed to the cross of your predicament. The problem is hooked into your flesh, it is not wafting above the conceptual elegance of airy calculations. The price exacted can be immense. For people in high office have invested most of their years in the position which is now threatened by the urgings of their consciences.

There are light years of difference between the actor and the spectator, between the victim and the observer, between being on the inside and watching from the outside, between looking out and looking in. And the secret of coping with the damnation of being condemned to be oneself lies in one's openness to anxiety. The only way to own oneself is to plunge into the chilled and paralyzing waters of anxiety.

A common experience is to be betrayed—by one's superiors, for whom one worked; by one's peers, whom one trusted; or by one's subordinates, for whom one sacrificed. You must remember that the greatest of our ancestors were betrayed—and responded to it with depth and nobility. Don't be surprised but rather expect betrayal as inevitable, as normal, as in the nature of things. Think only of Socrates, of Jesus, and of Gandhi.

One responds to betrayal with bitterness, with cynicism, and with willing and stoic isolation. One builds a fortress and lives in it. One creates a moat and remains contained inside. One becomes armored like a turtle, protected like a cactus, and defended like a porcupine.

Well, it is not good. It is bad. It is abnormal to the child that still dwells within us, for we find our authenticity in contact. We may have no choice but to live in a citadel and under siege. But our eyes moisten with gratitude when we hear that it need not be that way.

Words of meaningful solace must be the contribution of philosophy.

- Face your death. Your age and your responsibilities make it right that you gain the strength which only the knowledge of certain death can impart.

- The reality of self-validation, the security of inwardness, the confidence in integrity come in the middle of life, because then begins your reconciliation with death. "Death," in the words of Rollo May, "is a young man's worry."

- Do not give up on people. Know that everyone, even the worst, is solving in his or her own way the inextricable and the inexplicable problem of existence.

- Know that integrity will win out because nature and reality respond in the end to integrity. This fact does not suggest you should be blind to your own limitations, nor that you should overlook, painful as that may be, the potential authenticity of your adversaries.

- Evil is as real as good. You can live with that. It gives your life a destiny and your existence a meaning. It makes free choice and courage into virtues. And as a human being you are given the opportunity to be virtuous: take it.

- In Europe alone forty million human beings died in World War II. But even the unspeakable evil and the horrendous chaos of that war were in the end overcome.

- People who use others and who are narrowly concerned only with their own material welfare are in fact incomplete human beings. But it may only be in middle age that this truth transcends thought to become an actual perception. Do not give up on them. On the contrary, show them with your life and with your behavior that you want to teach them the value of love, of contact, and of acknowledgment. These treasures are, in fact and in truth, more real and more important than money and promotions.

- A safe rule to always remember is that "What I hate I also envy."

- Your commitment to integrity must express itself in the body. "The body speaks its mind," said Stanley Keleman, the bioenergetic therapist. Others can then feel that commitment without an exchange of words. *We often confuse the genetic body with the body transformed through our life's decisions. The biological body does not give a message. But the conscious choices we have made will be sculpted into our body and will speak fortissimo.*

- Genuine fulfillment is that orphic revelation which occurs when cynics finally understand that with their own actions they have reconciled themselves with their enemies.

CHAPTER 26

Creativity in Health Care

I have developed opinions about the health-care industry in the United States, and below is an outline of some of them.

The higher purpose of a private or proprietary hospital chain can be expressed in two models: a triangle of values and a series of concentric economic circles.

A Triangle of Values. The industry stands for the values of love, freedom, and survival--not by choice but by the fact of its actual history. It must own its historical and its social (that is, present) reality. It must take possession of its past, present, and future, that is, of its past reality, of its current reality, and of its future reality. The proprietary, hospital chains are in the healing, caring, mercy— i.e., love—business. Beyond love there is death management as a task for the hospitals. When we are faced with a life threatening situation, with evil, with pain, and with despair, with the anxiety of death, we turn to a hospital for succor.

It is also a free enterprise business, and therefore it is committed to freedom. It expresses this freedom in the economic arena.

Finally, it is a business, and must therefore make a profit. Without a profit the values of love and freedom are unrealizable. Without a profit the stock goes down, and the company becomes an attractive target for an unfriendly takeover. Profit is the *that* to the *what* of love and freedom; it is the matter to the form of love and freedom. Profit therefore means survival, life, respect for life, the will to live—any and all of those.

Individuals committed to fulfilling the potential of these companies—as long as they see to it that these goals are honestly entertained and honestly pursued (and they have a role in making that happen)—can then also feel that they participate in something worthy, something greater than human greed, and that they share in a constellation of high-minded human values.

I do not say this is what these companies are. I do say this is what they can become, should become, are destined to become. One knows that by extrapolating from what it objectively is in potency, from what it objectively is able to become. The industry will become the embodiment of the values of love, liberty, and life to the exact degree that men and women of good will make a commitment that it be such! It is not necessary to argue that in addition such a commitment is good for business, because the value of life inherent in this constellation already means that it is good for business.

Concentric Economic Circles. The second higher purpose of this industry is that it must solve three problems, and must solve them for the entire country and not just for themselves.

The three problems are: The problem of staying in business in general, health care in United States, and the human use of human beings.

The solution lies always above and beyond the central problem itself, health care in the United States. In so doing they must also solve the problem of business in the United States: how to stay in a high-investment business, a business with a high capital base—the kind of capital-intensive business this country, but even more so a developing country, needs—in the midst of fluctuations, uncertainties, increasing competition, and intensified government intervention correlated with decreasing government support.

The health care industry needs to make a quantum leap in efficiency, and that more often than not entails the use of automation, which in turn means changing the culture. And this—to create a culture which "thinks automation"—is not an easy task! But it is a high priority— and still mostly unmet—task for modern business.

In short, a company must solve for the nation and for the world the problem of running a business in an inescapably increasing internationally competitive environment.

It is the function of health care business to solve for the government—which means for the people, for the nation—the problem of how to provide quality health care under increasingly difficult (emotionally and financially expensive) circumstances. Social Security and Medicare will run out of funds in five years, and the nation, with ever-increasing deficits, will be in no mood to raise taxes to the level needed to provide adequate care.

The solution will need imagination. Examples are accelerated healing, home care, more trained personnel distributed throughout the nation, a new status for healers, radically greater cost effectiveness, a new sense of responsibility and morality—for both healers and patients—a revolution in the area of liability, new perceptions of anxiety and its relation to illness and to health, and new theories—of the order of paradigm shifts—of being healthy, staying healthy, and how to get there. In the long run, we will need a new definition of what a totally integrated health program really means.

The hospital functions then also, and perhaps preeminently, in a consulting capacity to the nation. Health consultants think through the meaning of health-care delivery in our democratic and capitalistic society, against a background of religious healing, of religion-supported hospitals, of teaching and of university hospitals, and of the archetypal demands traditionally—but no longer—satisfied by the medical profession.

Finally, a company must solve the people problem, and do so not only for itself and for its industry, but for business per se, worldwide: how to use human resources, how to guarantee self-respect, how to preserve human values, how to link authenticity in regard to the human condition with survival. It must solve the problem of how to view quality as a human responsibility first and as a source of profits second.

In this model, love is the product, liberty the social, cultural, and value context, and life is the constraints, the limits and parameters.

The health-care problem in the United States is essentially that of the aristocracy of medicine. The knowledge and the technology exist for the most superb care in the world—which includes wellness, from exercise and recreation, to nutrition and the gratification of instincts. The situation can be compared to the transportation and communications facilities available to the president of the United States: private jet, private helicopter, latest in communications gear. Anyone could accomplish a great deal with that kind of help. However, the expense of first-class medicine, like the expense of first-class communications and transportation, makes that help not available to everyone in the population. And "expense" is a misnomer. There is not enough equipment and there are not enough technicians to accommodate all of those who need help—even if the money were there.

Granting these premises, how does one then solve the health-care problem in the United States? Perhaps we are here concerned with the number-one symptom of the number-one value crisis in this nation in this decade. There are essentially only four classes of solutions:

- Prioritize health care. As in war, those with no chance to survive get passed over and those in whom there is hope get the scarce treatment. This means, roughly speaking, that health care will be directed more toward the relatively young people than to the old, because with the former it would make a greater difference over a lifetime than with the latter.
- Instantly risk ending the Cold War unilaterally and reorganize our society so as to use the saved dollars for making health care available to all Americans.

It is clear that such drastic solutions require radical changes in our most basic values. Or to state it differently, incredibly difficult and vastly unpopular choices must be made—choices about what it means to be a human being and choices about what is ultimately right and wrong. We need to revise the meaning of freedom, of responsibility, of life, of obligation to our fellow human beings, of the function of politics, of love, of compassion, of priorities, of capitalism versus socialism, and on and on and on.

In order to avoid such Draconian measures, we must think of compromises. Therefore we strive to

- increase, that is, improve productivity, and
- develop new concepts of health, of delivery, and of prevention— such as HMO's or PPO's.

Here, two contributions may be of very special significance. Contemporary philosophy, theology, and literature—and they have influenced psychology—have developed the significance of the I-am experience. The latter may be viewed as the subjective equivalent of what Freud, objectively, called the instincts. For to satisfy the instincts is also to feel centered, grounded. Health is intimately connected with the I-am experience. The immune system seems to respond to the gratification of instinctual drives.

The I-am experience is an important part of this book. It is connected with the concepts of greatness, of courage, and with the deep structures of human existence.

The presence of the I-am experience cannot be detected by psychological tests. But it appears to be precisely the much sought-after effective agent in the psychological stimulation of health. It is the key attitude for bringing about optimum health. The I-am experience, eloquently described in contemporary philosophy, may be the secret and elusive psychological health factor. It may be the answer to the mystery of psychosomatic medicine. From a financial point of view, that insight prepares the way for lower-cost health care, and for better health for all.

Furthermore, the I-am experience can be taught—not just taught, but taught specifically, efficiently, effectively, and economically through information technology. It can then be applied in didactic seminars or in group therapy settings. This is a controversial curriculum, but one that shows promise.

Traditionally, the I-am experience is thought to have its origins in a happy childhood. A loving mother and a secure environment, an accepting family and good models, all these can contribute to the feelings of being grounded, of being acceptable, and of being centered. But hopefully it can be taught through a liberal arts education or through psychotherapy. The former means to join the great minds of history. The latter is to have a loyal and wise friend with whom the student can recapture lost memories and relive them in a new light.

But what teaching and therapy have in common and what high technology lacks is the ingredient missing in information systems: the human touch, the personal encounter, the love, the care, and the commitment. Computer-aided health care (CAHC) includes computer-aided instruction in philosophy (and kindred humanistic topics) and computer-aided therapy. It compresses instruction, personal, applied, and interactive, to leave extra room for the human interventions of love, care, and commitment.

Herein lie the seeds to the solutions of the health care problem of the United States. All health efforts are then of the human-contact variety. All else is done through automation.

What remains, and is urgently needed, is a technological genius who can make it all work! The true benefactors are the effective business executive and the inventive whiz in applied technology, for they get done the critical business of humanity.

We can legitimately call such an approach a true and courageous business contribution, for it promises to protect us from unpalatable and even impossible ethical decisions. And it is right that we make a commitment to such business endeavor.

The final solution to the health problem in the United States requires the inversion of some of our most fundamental emotional attitudes and cultural biases. For example, the ancient role of the physician is threatened. The physician is being replaced by an HMO, PPO, or GHS plan! For the concrete healer is substituted an actuarial abstraction. We therewith are poisoning the root structure of the soul. We are assaulting the pillars of our civilized world-view. We are fooling with an archetype. And the healer or the physician (remember that Jesus was one) is being eliminated and in his stead is placed a cost-efficient health provider delivery system. Violence to the archetypes is violence to the architectural integrity of the self. And it is not the physician alone who feels assaulted, but society at large. For the physician is not the invention of the medical profession but is a social and even an anthropological phenomenon, invented and demanded by all members of the social order.

The physician is special—magical and mystical—because he or she has the power of access to the body: invasive access, through examinations, through injections, and through surgery, through radiation and through dangerous drugs. Our attitudes towards physicians are not unlike our attitudes towards lawyers, for the latter have access to the power of the state. If we need magic exerted on the power of the body, we consult a physician. And if we need that magic exercised on the power of the state, we consult a lawyer. These strong needs and emotions refer to elements innate to the soul, and to change the method of health delivery is also to violate these a priori yearnings.

Hospitals not run by physicians may be eminently practical fiscally, but emotionally they mobilize mountainous resistances against healing itself.

Of course, the American health-care problem includes the problems of the elderly. People are required to be bankrupt before they qualify for government aid. At $2000 or even $3000 a month, nursing homes quickly deplete whatever savings or assets people accumulated during their working years. Harvard Medical School researchers, in a study completed in 1985, found that a 13-week stay in a nursing home would bankrupt one half of the nation's 75-year olds, and that a one-year stay would mean that 75 percent of that age population would have nothing left.

The health care industry is in a good position to understand these problems and to know what kind of proposed solutions make sense. If the free enterprise system is to survive, then such questions must be answered.

Here then are some of the thoughts that a true health care marketer must entertain, and around which a truly revolutionary business can be and must be created.

To achieve this type of rethinking of the meaning of the corporation requires double-barreled newness: new minds and a new commitment to these new minds.

The next point then is to challenge executives to higher achievements and to higher standards for themselves personally. But this challenge, again, is double-barreled: it is a matter of imagining the genius-power level of human performance, achievement, insight, intuition, vision, clarity, originality on the one hand, and of assuming full personal responsibility for working towards reaching it on the other. One is the concept, the image, the idea, the form; the other is the existential choice, the determination, the decision, the courage, the persistence, and the will power to bring it into reality, to make it happen.

And although on the one hand to aspire to genius-power level achievement is forever bound to fail, it is equally true to affirm that everyone has just this capacity. We need to develop it, fulfill it.

High executives can be expected to be self-educated, articulate, well read, and demanding on themselves, especially in the development of the creative potential of their consciousnesses. We must expect of them that they be good listeners and that they be flexible with their biases. The key point is that we have a right to challenge and to demand that they have high expectations of themselves, and that these expectations be of a mature kind. When people and their jobs, and when customers and some of their significant needs and even their very lives, depend on the person of the ethically developed executive, then we have not only the privilege but also the obligation to expect that these executives have high standards for their own being and for their own performance—just as we would of politicians and generals in wartime.

To achieve genius power level performance must become a way of life, a style of existence. It must be so for the executives personally and for the company as a whole as well. A new culture must be imbued with both values.

We must avoid the illusion of enlightenment. We must avoid the mistaken belief that just because we have once a good or deep experience, we know how to apply it and how to make it work throughout the organization and throughout our life. A single good experience can be more harmful than none at all. The result could be not zero but less than zero.

Unless the experience is followed up—virtually indefinitely, and with continuing and self-reinforcing supports, with lifestyle changes—it can be of considerable apparent meaning but it is of no real enduring value. And the follow-up has to be both an individual and a group decision and commitment.

The company—primarily in the area of its intractable problems—is the product, extension, manifestation, or influence of two sets of systems. One is the world external to the company—the market, international economics, and world politics. The problem lies in the structure and not with any issue inside the organization itself or any decision that an incompetent executive may have made.

The other system consists of problems or conditions internal to the top executives themselves. And by "internal" here is meant their individual or collective unconscious. The individual unconscious consists of unfinished childhood business: jealousies, depressions, invalidation, anger, repetition compulsions, envy.

Their collective unconscious consists of whatever infantilism, immaturity, neuroticism, hidden agendas, manipulation, or puerility exists in their relationships, how they are among themselves, and the manner in which they resist such understanding. The unconscious of top management, individual and collective, is reflected in the organization. The organization is the unconscious of top management made visible. But it is also the external structure made visible.

The problems we refer to are those which do not respond to rational analysis or strategic planning. We can argue that their sources come from two directions. Problems are thus conceptualized as projections. When we view them in this fashion we may also have access or a key to their solution. Then we do not work on the problem itself but on the source of its projection.

One of these sources is the larger, the external context. Most theories and techniques of creative thinking emphasize getting out of a groove or out of a rut in one's thinking. These techniques look for ways to go beyond, to transcend, the system in which the problem is experienced and formulated. Once this (or one) larger system has been found, new possibilities for solutions emerge. In a company this may mean asking anew the question of what kind of a business it is, what effect radical rethinking of its mission has on product lines and services, looking for historical currents and forces that control it or at least affect it, and searching for political and international solutions rather than for narrow and localized ones.

The other source of projection is the unconscious. And it is just as difficult to find it as it is to unravel the larger external system. But again here, once we reach the resistances to deeper thinking, we can affect and control our world-view, our actions, our attitudes, and our spontaneous and unthinking reactions, to the rational benefit of the positive contributions we can make to our company.

By knowing this, at least we understand where the problem lies and what steps, if any, could be carried forward to deal with it.

The most important and the most difficult corporate problems must be viewed as resulting from invisible forces. The mark of genius is to make these forces visible. There are internal and external forces. The internal forces are the unconscious of management, both the individual unconscious, the intrapersonal, and the interpersonal, collective, or group unconscious. The external forces are systems effects, economic, political, historical, and others more difficult to identify. To the degree that these forces can be made visible they become open to discussion and available for management. We then know what it is we are up against. The company is then the sum of the projections from the external and the internal invisible, from the external and the internal unconscious.

Hospital patients—before, upon, and after admission and upon release—would benefit from a direct commitment by the hospital to helping them cope with the eternal questions. It is within the context of a hospital stay, more than at any other time, that these Question cascade into awareness.

The best hospital—which is what hospitals, hospital chains, and integrated health service promise continually to create—is one that has made its principal commitment to attend to all the relevant fundamental needs of its patients.

The hospital's mission statement could read, "Our mission is to provide our patients with the ultimate comfort." The proof rests on the personal experience of the patients. The hospital, or the larger company, promises to make them feel it. And the only marketing of the truth of this motto is through networking; it is satisfied patients talking to their friends and their physicians. It is the community leaders—in business as much as in politics, in education as much as in the professions—who hear about quality through the waves of reputation that emerge continuously from the hospital.

Virtually any hospital stay is the result of some kind of physical, emotional, or moral pain. The patient is not "in discomfort," is not undergoing a "minor procedure" which, upon "admission on a Friday afternoon, will allow return to work on Monday morning and thus, through the miracle of modern medicine, avert a threat to the family's income." The truth is that the patient is confronted with ultimate dread, with a threat to being itself.

And the patient comes to the hospital with few or no tools with which to meet this ontological emergency; nor is it traditional that the patient is given the basic tools by the staff. And not infrequently, the patient is led by his physician to feel foolish for his or her inability or unwillingness to repress the deepest issues of human existence which now invade the consciousness ("flood the awareness," as Jung used to say).

Does it not seem reasonable that the hospital which addresses itself to these issues helps provide the experience of ultimate comfort to the ailing and needy patient? The eternal questions thrust themselves with all their might on the patient's body, heart, and soul. Society—including the medical profession—provides decreasing meaningful understanding or coping organisms to help manage, with authenticity, this crisis. The patient is told to minimize the emotional meanings. Repression is what is expected. But authenticity demands of us that we validate and explore the plethora of actual and potential feelings mobilized by what is in effect a situation *in extremis*, seemingly minor or not. To meet the emotional needs of the patient, and to do so fully equipped with the powers of religion, theology, philosophy, the arts, in short with the wisdom of the ages, the compendium of the applied humane studies—systematized, studied, integrated, utilized, institutionalized—that is quality care.

A hospital stay is for many not merely the best, but also the only exposure that the patient will ever have to true philosophy and theology. The exposure to the confrontation with death, real or imagined, is not a classroom exercise; it is real. So it is with doubt and with self-deception. The hospital teaches the patient, not through poetry or drama but through the reality of anxiety and of pain, the vulnerability of the body and the weakness of the soul. It demonstrates the unfathomable importance of other people and of their care, their love, their understanding, and the self-evident beauty of their unconditional commitment to them. It illustrates the holiness of grace—the giving without expectation of reward. It places us face to face with our deepest ethical dilemmas. It shows us the truths buried in anxiety, the depths hidden in guilt, the inevitability of disorientation, confusion, ambiguity, and uncertainty. And in a hospital experience all of these lessons must be learned, not squandered.

Are we equipping our hospitals to minister to these emotional (really, philosophical and theological) needs of our patients? Does not their ultimate comfort demand attention to these matters? Does not our simple obligation as moral human beings hold us duty bound to be sensitive to these matters and to ask how we can attend to them? Should they not be institutionalized? How far along on this path are we?

The ultimate source of pain still rests, as it always has, on the eternal questions, which Paul Tillich, Martin Buber, and Rollo May have termed our ultimate concerns.

There are, many believe, answers to the eternal questions. And that does not mean narrow sectarian and dogmatic ones. There are answers which fit our democratic institutions, traditions, and commitments. These answers can be expressed literally, as they would be in philosophy (and for some in religion), or they can be manifested symbolically, as they are for many in mythology or in the institutional and practicing religions. The staff needs to have a feeling of what these answers can be, and not only must they know these things for the sake of the hospital bottom line! Nor even for the benefit of the patients alone! In the end, the answers to the eternal questions matter because they are burning issues for each one of us. Most of our busyness is not truly productive but an escape—"killing time"—from the anxiety of facing the inevitable and understandably difficult eternal questions. Many of us live as if we strive to die before we must face these questions.

Much of this work is already done. Many hospitals are of the highest quality. But the effort must continue and it must be expanded.

Armed now with this information, everyone connected with the hospital enterprise shares in the responsibility to answer these eternal questions in minute and practical detail. And these are questions which can be answered only by the practicing staff—managers, employees, patients, and physicians—not by outsiders and not by books.

Here is a generalized, formal, and systematized articulation of the question we must ask of the hospital ambience: what behavior and design changes are required in order that we may demonstrate a deepened understanding of the eternal questions and meet the demands which they make upon our patients? Some religious hospitals have attempted that, with success for their congregations. How can a secular hospital do that, with success for everyone? Everyone is duty-bound to discover answers. Some answers will be small and insignificant; others will be massive and inspired. All will be important. Gandhi said, "Everything you do will be insignificant; but it is very important that you do it."

That is the challenge to the philosophic hospital administrator. There are no right answers. But every thought about this, every discussion concerning this theme, and every action taken on its behalf is in fact already a final solution to the eternal questions.

Psychologists have for a long time searched for the character trait that is associated with good health. Candidates include a positive mental attitude, a good mother, and self-esteem. Endless tests have been used trying to find correlations between good health and personality. (Cf. Kenneth Pelletier, *Holistic Health*, and *Mind as Slayer, Mind as Healer*.) Since it is believed that most modern illnesses are stress related or stress induced, it has become important to identify the one personality trait or attitudinal phenomenon which can be viewed as cause.

No psychological test, evidently, has been able to identify this factor. It was necessary for philosophy to come along with the existential notion of the I-am experience. This includes the concepts of greatness and of courage, the notion of centeredness, of authenticity, of choosing to be oneself, of willing to be one's freedom, of choosing to claim one's power. The I-am experience also includes the centrality of the individual human, localized-in-space-and-time existential act in determining the nature of truth, reality, and knowledge. Here it is called the vertical dimension of leadership consciousness. The I-am experience is the center of being, the fulcrum of the universe.

This I-am concept is the key to health. Signposts in the concept of health are auto-immune diseases (failures of the immune system to ward off external enemies) and accidents, for we contribute to each of them. A reassessment of stress is part of what is required. A reconceptualization of anxiety is at the heart of this matter. Diseases and accidents are anxiety related. Related not as much to *having* anxiety as they are to *avoiding* anxiety. For anxiety is the call of the center to itself. Those who are their anxiety are also themselves. To live inside one's anxiety is therefore to also be in superlative health. These are the assumptions.

Accelerated healing is accelerated philosophy. Behavioral scientists have sought to identify and isolate the psychological factor that makes the difference between health and illness. The contention here is that the differentiating factor is the I-am experience. It is the will to be oneself. Technical knowledge and skills— like nutrition, exercise, all branches of medicine, pharmacology— are not enough; they are the necessary but not the sufficient conditions for health. What is also needed is the I-am factor.

This is not only the secret of health but also the essence of accelerated healing. The secret of accelerated healing is to find expeditious ways to rekindle the spark of authenticity in the human breast: to take advantage of the lesson of the illness; to help take responsibility for the illness; and to experience the speed of the cure and the healing.

These are not new ideas. What is new is the organization of philosophical material referred to here as philosophy in business or as the three-dimensional development of the consciousness of decision-makers.

The hypothesis deserves to be examined and tested. Testing is difficult, because there is no easy way to define or describe authenticity—the I-am experience— much less to teach it. And, as usual, teaching the I-am experience implies, beyond teaching, analyzing the resistance to it.

This is the next stage of work and of growth.

The master table can function as a workable map of the mind, and with sufficient technological ingenuity and psychotherapeutic expertise, one can use this material as a central component of, among other things, an accelerated-healing package. The secret lies in computerizing the philosophic material. The program needs to be didactic, but also interactive. A television monitor will help. Relationship with a person, perhaps a teacher or a facilitator, must be included. We need to combine philosophy (i.e., theory), high technology (i.e., application), and a human being (a personal encounter).

Needed are ways to connect clients with the appropriate philosophic ideas about human existence—which lead to insight about the structure of their problems—and then to demonstrate how these ideas can lead to decisions and to actions about their own personal issues.

Part of this computerized package is to understand the proper, and irreplaceable, role of a human being and of a personal human encounter and commitment in the psychotherapeutic process. Another part is to understand that therapy is neither a new technique of healing nor exclusively for persons who have problems. Therapy is help with life's problems, help which has been extended by all forms of wisdom to all types of people from the time of the earliest stirrings of the human consciousness.

In this line of thinking could well lie the future of health care in the Western world. It brings together philosophy and business, philosophy and psychiatry, philosophy and physical health, and ties it all together in the wrappings of high technology. It will make a radical difference, medically and fiscally—and it will be a difference in kind, in quality, not just in quantity. It will put the person at the center and place high technology at the service of the deepest and most authentic human values. Morally and politically, humanly and economically, this seems to be an opening to the revolution in health care required today.

Another way to look at the health-care situation from a philosophic perspective is to say that healing has fallen from the firmament of two hearts in touch to the cellar of a second generation of alienation.

The image of the healer is in conflict with the socioeconomic realities of our day. At the conscious or discursive level, we verbalize and conceptualize healing (as we do so much else) in terms of outcomes—days in a hospital, access to health care delivery, technology and pharmacology required, and costs . . . , mostly costs. At the level of the unconscious we depend on the archetype of the healer. And the healer fulfills two functions: we need the healer for our own salvation and we project on the healer our own unresolved conflicts. That is why so many emotions are tied up with the healing professions.

The need for a healer has its roots in the problem of existence. One formulation of that problem is that we have natural needs, that these needs "must" be satisfied, and yet that they will not and cannot ever be satisfied.

The nature of these needs has been stated in a variety of ways. The key word is "centeredness."

Immanuel Kant classified them as our needs for eternal life, for love, and for justice, and said they were innate to a rational mind. Carl Gustav Jung wrote of archetypes and archetypal needs. These are inherited patterns in the soul, and if they are met with external validation, there follows an indescribable sense of exhilaration and of fulfillment which floods the consciousness. Humanistic and existential psychologies prefer the term authenticity—establishing harmony with one's true self. And Freud, earlier, defined centeredness as meeting the demands of our instinctual drives.

To discover our center is also to know that we are born that way, that we were made, created, with those needs in us. We should not feel guilty for having these needs and impulses, nor should we expect anything less from the world that created us and in which we live than that it will also satisfy them. For the world—so says our primordial myth, the expulsion from the Garden—was originally created specifically for man and woman; and the Garden represents the state of innocence.

But reality is otherwise. It is pain and impotence, it is difficulties and depression. Its pain is constant labor, intense frustrations, and often devastating obstacles. And its depression is invariable impotence, inevitable defeat, and chronic self-contempt.

Human beings need an explanation. But they need more than logic to meet this paradox; they need succor, compassion, and support. Essentially, they need healing. The emotional function of explanation is principally to make them feel better about the bitterness of their fate. That is why myths are good explanations. The truth of a myth is measured by the amount of relief and of peace that it provides.

History's first episode of healing is the story of the Garden of Eden—for there was total health. The end of the story, however, is that this original path to harmony and health is now blocked forever by "the cherubim, and a flaming sword which turned every way, to guard the way to the tree of life." (Genesis 3:24).

Analysis of this story, the one myth by which we all live, shows

that there are two types of healers because there are two paths to
health. And today we find ourselves confronted with the need to
find even a third type of healer.

There is health and healing in the tradition of Jerusalem, which
is contact with the inner God-like self—for God is now sought inside
the isolated and rebellious ego and no longer found as the outside
paternalistic benefactor. That is the path of pride, of arrogance, of
independence, of self-affirmation, of defiance, of courage, and of the
willingness to die. That is the human being who was twice-born
(William James's phrase) in the Garden of Eden, through disobedience to God and by eating from the tree of knowledge. Health is a
function of defiance, of disobedience to God; it is the final act of independence. Today, this is the path of the Shcharanskys and the
Sakharovs. That is the healer who empowers by laying on hands,
who makes direct contact with his or her patients. It is the healing
power of love and bonding, of loyalty and example, of individual
commitment and personal challenge.

The other healer comes from the tradition of Athens. This is the
technocrat, the descendant of Adam called Tubal-cain, who "was the
forger of all instruments of bronze and iron." (Genesis 4:22.) The use
of instruments—of indirect rather than direct, of mediate instead of
immediate means of contact—reflects the hope for magic, for magical solutions. It is a God-substitute.

The second type of healer is already once removed from primordial health. We face today a third generation of healers, and those
are the ones tied up with economic and political contaminations.

In other words, healing is originally a direct-contact phenomenon.
That truth is represented in the Garden of Eden, man and woman's
primordial state. Outside of the Garden of Eden, technology tries to
replace the magic of God. Here we talk of surgery and medication.
That is the first level of alienation.

Today, the state, with its power, and the atomic age, with its
high technology, take over. And the result is that we talk economics. Now money and costs take over. The healer thus reaches a
second level of alienation. For at this point the issue becomes low-
cost technology, efficient diagnosis and treatment, and cost-effective
health maintenance delivery—as if health were a product that
could be mass produced!

The salient feature of the third type of healing is equating health with money. When we think of it, we move past the obvious. Prima facie, the *healing=money* equation makes fiscal sense. It is a kind of economic axiom. How else could we deal with the health problem? Money is a, probably the, symbol for life—for existence itself, even for salvation. Any analysis of banking in philosophy in business must be alert to that possibility.

However, what happens with the third generation of healers is that the symbol transcends the reality. The symbol, which is money, becomes more important than the reality, which is health. As a society, we therefore do not make a commitment to, or guarantee, health for all—and real health, not partial or compromised health—but offer it as a patchwork, sparingly, in a titrated fashion, deeply suffused with compromises, rationalizations, inequities, and so forth. We would not view national defense in that fashion. When, as the enemy strikes, would we as a nation say, "We shall not defend ourselves . . . , because it is not in the budget?"

With that remarkable equation we have made a statement about who we are and what is important to us. Life itself, with its essence of consciousness and awareness, is of less value than the symbol which we have learned to use for bartering our goods and for calculating our successes. We are our objects, our things, our artifacts, and our tools. We are not ourselves. We are removed from ourselves; we are strangers to ourselves. We are estranged from our authentic nature. That is the message of the expulsion from Eden. That is why Pogo's statement, "We have met the enemy and it is us," has found such wide appeal. That is perhaps as clear a statement as we can make of a second generation of alienation.

But healing, as Martin Buber so well understood, is first and foremost a relationship—beginning with the contact a human being has with his or her God and then with his or her genuine nature, and eventually with other and very special human beings. But the inevitable alienation in today's second-generation healing technology and economics destroys the original healer archetype for us all, an archetype which had its birth at the dawn of Western civilization with the story of the Garden of Eden.

That is why health care is inescapably in crisis today. Who has the vision and the courage to return us to the truth about ourselves?

CHAPTER 27

Quality

Reflections on Quality

An executive from a major appliance and electronics firm, in fact, the regional sales manager for their number one prestige line, said to me, as we happened to run into each other on an airliner, "This company must move from being manufacturing and finance driven to being quality and customer driven." And he asked me, with specially punctuated emphasis, not to quote him.

These are useful concepts, diagnostic, well and succinctly stated. Why the silence? The conclusion is not easy to escape: evidently this important company, at least in the perception of one of its top executives, does not wish to harvest the full quality creative potential from its highly paid managers!

In business today, discussions of quality prevail. It is generally accepted that in quality resides the competitive edge. Quality leads to profits. Drop in profits is due to drop in quality.

It is understood also that quality is a function of the commitment of employees. The solution to defects in quality often is to redesign the workplace in order to encourage and reward greater commitment among employees to product and to service. The buzz word is "involvement" or "employee involvement." The redesign of work or of the workplace gives the message to the employees that the company expects from them more autonomy and more cooperation, more teamwork. And there are new rewards offered by the company. Some of them are monetary. But the incentives include as well generators of enthusiasm such as badges, parties, and public recognition.

From the perspective of philosophy, such approaches may be necessary but they are by no means sufficient. They produce the framework at best. At most, they facilitate quality or make it possible. They create an environment, perhaps, which at least does not interfere with the employees' quality-oriented creativity. Redesign helps, but possibly only by ten percent. The empirical evidence appears to confirm such a low figure of relevance.

Companies need loyalty and commitment from their employees.

Employees need meaning for themselves and from the company.

We have but one life to live. From that simple fact follows a searching question: What must you do before you die in order to feel that you have done honor to your life? This is the problem of death, it is the question of your immortality project. If you, as is true of many, fail to get an answer to the question of your destiny, then try fantasy exercises. If that fails, then try a monastery or a convent! But persons of conscience will find buried within their breasts, invariably albeit not always obviously, the answer to the question of the meaning of their lives.

The meaning of quality in a person (a desideratum drawn from the ideal of perfection) is that individual's solution to the problem of existence. Conversely, the answer to the problem of existence is quality, quality in the person. Personal quality, quality as a necessary value, as a survival value, radiates dramatically into the quality of work. Quality is the spiritual survival value. A person who understands the philosophic realities of life--which are embraced in the concept of nihilism or the threat of non-being--knows that quality, or its cognates perfection and excellence, is then also the answer.

Perfection (the medieval, scholastic synonym for quality, excellence) is the answer to death. To do something *really* well is an end in itself, as symbol for a deeper, ontological and existential situation or reality. Thus, quality in both self and in work is exhilarating, fulfilling, and it answers the problem of nihilism, i.e., of death and evil, of our vulnerability and inadequacy, our unacceptability, our guilt, and our nothingness.

Combining all of these considerations, we therefore aver that the problem of existence, which is the issue of nihilism (death and evil), is to be resolved, at least in part, at the level of the employee--company relationship. The needs of the company are such that it must command the full loyalty of its star employees. And in return—since a soul can be bought not with money but only with another soul—the employee deserves the full loyalty and commitment of the organization.

Redesign

We must ask, Can quality be achieved by modifying work? Can redesign change the core, the consciousness, the attitudes, the values, the decisions, the character, the commitments of human beings? A company no longer purchases labor. Today it buys the hearts, the wills, and the minds of its employees. It simply cannot be competitive otherwise.

Quality can be produced only by a loyal, committed, and dedicated workforce. The big question for every manager and CEO is how to bring into existence and then how to maintain such a high class of employees and such an aligned organization.

The magical answer has often been in restructuring, in reorganization, but mostly in redesigning work. But that is risky and difficult. In fact, it is like launching a massive new product or investing in total retooling. The alternatives are ominous: the company will either succeed big . . . , or die!

But what is the truth?

Environmental manipulation is easy. It is visible; it can be installed. But the heart of the matter are the human wills and minds. These are more difficult by far to change. It takes a greater mind to change a mind than to install a new design. Such human aspirations require more effort and a deeper commitment on the part of upper management than structural change. The human dimension makes inordinate demands on those who lead, true. But discharging these demands does indeed fulfill the archetypal needs for quality among those entrusted with top executive responsibilities.

The curious truth and the good news is that in concentrating on human qualities rather than on design nuances, the company is not at risk and the actual cost is low.

Connection

The real issue is the connection between, on the one hand, a human being, the meaning or destiny of a person, the deeper reaches of human nature (as Maslow called it), and on the other, the work that person is expected to perform. Quality springs from the heart of human beings. Quality is the commitment to pride. Quality is an expression of the perfectibility of human nature—and the pleasure one receives from pursuing it. Quality grows out of the Renaissance ideal of self-realization: fuilfillment in life is to experience one's possibilities, it is to realize, to bring into being, the maximum of one's potential.

The will to manage can be activated or actualized if it is possible for you to *connect* your job with a deeper human truth, with the eternal questions, with a spiritual reality, and with a matter of destiny. Only a company which will allow that, or even show you how that is possible within the scope of its business, is a company worthy of a quality employee.

But the company cannot guarantee that it will equate work with the personal values of its employees. The organization can make the realization of these values possible, it can prevent interference. But the actual connection between the work one does and the basic values of one's existence—necessary to make work meaningful and not to waste one's time and life while earning a living—can be accomplished solely and exclusively by the worker, the employed person, the individual, isolated, and responsible member of the organization.

Quality needs no incentives. Quality is self-satisfying. Quality is part of the larger phenomenon of self-validation.

The key is that there can be no ulterior motive or purpose for the production of quality. Quality is its own reward. Pride in quality makes sense because pride in oneself makes sense. It is almost insulting to reward someone for being fulfilled. "If you fulfill yourself as a human being," says the parent to the child, "I will increase your allowance." "If you find meaning in life, I'll buy you a new car." How ludicrous! What incentives do we need for salvation? Is not the exhilaration of living life to the fullest, of making sense of one's existence, of reaching out for one's destiny, of making progress towards meeting our values, so that we will be spared the guilt of having lived in vain, is that not reward enough? Is not the ultimate reward the ultimate reward, period? Why reward us for finding the ultimate by motivating us or even by thinking that we might be subject to seduction by merely the penultimate?

Are these exaggerations? Is the workplace the right place for salvation? Of course not! But to find meaning in life is still our prime task as human beings. We spend our quality hours and quality years of the only life we have to give—to ourselves, to our loved ones, to our ideals, to our values, and to the world—with companies. And companies need loyalty to produce quality. So where does that leave a person of conscience?

The Subjective Side of Quality

In philosophy we concern ourselves with the subjective, the personal, side of quality.

What is quality? Quality internally at work means pride in producing quality products and satisfaction in living within quality relationships among human beings. Quality externally in the marketplace means valuing good customer-company relations and experiences, for their own sakes. A quality company is one where employees grow as they work, where people develop as a result of their responsibilities and their associations. And what is a quality person? It is a person with wisdom—a person with interpersonal skills and with a philosophy of life, a person who has integrity, is sensitive, exudes compassion, and is courageous.

We must *challenge* people into quality (*not just* to leadership, courage, greatness, love, and ethics)—*not just* organize them towards quality. We do not teach the desire for quality, we cannot teach it, for it is already present, even if only latent. This is a Platonic approach, because the truth already resides within. People want naturally to do good work; the answers to the secrets of quality already reside within the soul. We need but remove the obstacles to their expression. In part that is done through releasing the natural proclivity for pride, perfection, in short for quality.

Quality is a survival technique —in one's business life and in one's personal and private life.

Abraham Lincoln said, "A house divided against itself cannot stand." Similarly, quality cannot be divided. For it means that a person is divided against himself or herself. Persons divided against themselves cannot produce quality. Quality work can only come from a quality person, and a quality person can be expected to do only quality work. That is the human principle of quality.

When we speak of needing quality, we mean that we need quality people: quality leaders, quality decision makers, quality inspirers— and foremost, quality workers. For, when it comes to management, 90 percent of problems are people issues and 10 percent are skill issues.

Analysis and Intuition

Repeatedly one is struck by the fact that experienced practitioners in management speak a different language from that of the theoreticians. The professor, even if he or she is a consultant, is measured on a different scale, recognized on different criteria, valued by other norms and standards, and conceptualizes in a different language from that of the business executive.

Analytic approaches, which are academic, often are counterintuitive and even counter-pragmatic, i.e., they often seem not to work. Reality itself is amorphous. Theory often does not appear to have relevance to the actual situation. It does not seem immediately applicable. It seems to complicate the simple intuitions of everyday life. One can of course argue both ways. But experience in business leads one to this conclusion. Why might that be?

Scientific analysis distorts subjective reality—which is the locus of motivation, where the real work is performed, and where the true decisions are made.

In the quest for quality, one rule prevails. *Design* for quality, like self-regulating work teams (SRWT), quality circles, QWL (quality of work life) projects, is far less important than to challenge *people* to quality. The latter is to touch the will, to touch the yearning for perfection, and to educate—and it is to educate in the human dimension, not to manipulate with technology the environment. That is the most difficult education, but it is also the only education. It is the true fountainhead of quality.

The analytic and the intuitive must be integrated. We must create or design a *structure* (which is the analytic and manipulative approach) which then facilitates, encourages, and frees people to permit themselves the *motivation* for quality (which is the intuitive, subjective approach).

The prescription for quality is first to create the *will*, to stimulate the sense of *ownership*—which are intuitive and existential events—and then to design and install the *structure* to support it—which is a formal, a logical, an analytic phenomenon. In philosophy in business we take the position that quality, like all other leadership traits, results from the nature of the individual more than it does from the system. This is not to deny that structure matters! But the knowledge that structure matters and the ability to change structure are individual, personal, insights and decisions.

Furthermore, a quality person can do quality work even within a poorly designed structure. And beyond that, a quality person will help design a correspondingly suitable structure. The converse is false. A low quality person will not function well even in the embrace of a quality design. The ideal is of course a combination, an integration, a synthesis, a marriage, in which the formal quality structure supports the living quality person.

Motivation

The question of quality finally turns into the question of motivation. The question of quality reduces to the question of how to motivate people to quality. We must talk not only of the will to manage but also of the will to quality.

It is always helpful to ask questions about obstacles to motivation. What are the obstacles to the birth of the will, to the emergence of ownership, and to the creation of an appropriate structure? Why don't we have what we need? Where did we go wrong? Where are we going wrong?

The quality of the person, and what is required to improve it, is far more productive and conducive to quality products and services than a mere administrative redesign of the workplace

Moreover, to change the people is cheaper than to change the design. Education is the ultimate change agent, although no one claims that it is easier to change people than to change the design. Quite to the contrary, it is easier to change the design than to change the people. That is why it is more tempting to change the design than to change the people: *for to change the people one must change oneself first.*

The view of philosophy is not that you have to bet the company in redesigning the workplace, because philosophy in business is education and individual decision. Instead, you challenge the individual to will to release his or her proclivity for quality. You teach leadership, to every employee. And leadership means to assume constant and daily responsibility for quality, in yourself and in others. This sense of leadership must be driven down into every nook and cranny of the organization.

What about teamwork?

The Team

Teamwork is part of one's personal responsibility. Each individual is accountable for the satisfactory functioning, the alignment, of the team. And what is the role of the team? No one can impose that, at least not readily. A team decides for itself what it is and what it wants to do. It is the function of each member not to manipulate the team or to dominate it—unless a general and social, or economic, agreement to do so exists, as it would in hierarchical companies—but to ferret out what seems to be its purposes and to help achieve them.

Each member of the team has the obligation of being fully sensitive—as in a jazz ensemble—to every other member. Every team member is responsible in two directions, for answering two questions. First, what is the purpose of the team—which includes its role within the company? And second, what are the realities, the strictures—often economic—of the team?

Gandhi, in a political context, expressed well the individual's responsibility for the full organization:

Politics is more than going to the polls every two years and electing someone else to solve our problems. We must realize that each of us is a politician, for true politics consists of how we treat the person next to us—at home, next door, across town or around the world.

Using philosophy is not to sell a new management style and betting therefore the entire company, but to challenge the individuals, mostly through education, to become individual centers of quality leadership. The rest is easy. The rest follows.

Challenging the will comes first; restructuring the organization comes later. Redesign without philosophy is empty; philosophy without redesign is inefficient.

"At Ford Quality is Job One"

Here is the company philosophy of the Ford Motor Company. It can show how philosophy and business intersect in the marketing intelligence.

MISSION

Ford Motor Company is a worldwide leader in automotive and automotive-related products and services as well as in newer industries such as aerospace, communications, and financial services. Our mission is to improve continually our products and services to meet our customers' needs, allowing us to prosper as a business and to provide a reasonable return for our stockholders, the owners of our business.

VALUES

How we accomplish our mission is as important as the mission itself. Fundamental to success for the Company are these basic values:

People—Our people are the source of our strength. They provide our corporate intelligence and determine our reputation and vitality. Involvement and teamwork are our core human values.

Products—Our products are the end result of our efforts, and they should be the best in serving customers worldwide. As our products are viewed, so are we viewed.

Profits—Profits are the ultimate measure of how efficiently we provide customers with the best products for their needs. Profits are required to survive and grow.

GUIDING PRINCIPLES

Quality comes first—To achieve customer satisfaction, the quality of our products and services must be our number one priority.

Customers are the focus of everything we do—Our work must be done with our customers in mind, providing better products and services than our competition.

Continuous improvement is essential to our success—We must strive for excellence in everything we do: in our products, in their safety and value—and in our services, our human relations, our competitiveness, and our profitability.

Employee involvement is our way of life—We are a team. We must treat each other with trust and respect.

Dealers and suppliers are our partners—The Company must maintain mutually beneficial relationships with dealers, suppliers, and our other business associates.

Integrity is never compromised—The conduct of our Company worldwide must be pursued in a manner that is socially responsible and commands respect for its integrity and for its positive contributions to society. Our doors are open to men and women alike without discrimination and without regard to ethnic origin or personal beliefs.

Following are thoughts on how philosophy can be related to the MV/GP.

Mission

A company must contribute meaning to the society in which it exists. A company is like a person or a nation. Its value lies in the measure of meaning it provides to all those it affects. And meaning goes beyond "a reasonable return to our stockholders," legitimate as that is. Meaning refers to ethical comportment with customers, the economy, and the political life.

In medieval times, the cathedral dominated the environment. Most buildings clustered around it. Today, and in a similar way, the buildings of the big corporations dominate the city, and other structures assemble around them. There are many differences; nevertheless, the corporation today dominates society as did the church in earlier days. This historical reality assigns to the corporation a major moral responsibility.

Thus, the company has a moral obligation to provide a good and a meaningful experience, a quality experience, to all those with whom it comes in contact. That is the normal ethical obligation any person has to other human beings.

But the company, being an institution itself, also has a moral obligation to those other institutions on which it exercises a significant influence. The institution it affects first and foremost is the economy. The effect of the company's operations on the economy involves also a moral obligation on the part of government and society—an attitude expressed by the bail-out of the Chrysler Corporation.

But we must not overlook the political implications. Ford is an international company; and to the degree that it influences and affects the nations in which it operates, it is an agency of America's foreign policy, even though it is not specifically designated to make foreign policy. Ford is an American ambassador, *de facto* if not *de jure*. Ford, by virtue of its mere existence, serves as example and is an agent for international relations.

These are moral issues, and to the degree that we perceive them as such, they invest our lives with higher levels of significance.

Values

The premier value for this company is people, and the people to which it refers are its employees. That is most commendable.

Here philosophy is of significance. For if we are going to be concerned with our people, we must first understand what people are all about. And for that we need more than common sense or popular psychology. We need the knowledge in depth that is provided by an acquaintance with the history of ideas.

So let us discuss, using for as an example, what it means to be a human being and how that can help one be more intelligent and more sensitive, more effective and more compassionate, in dealing with the people issues.

How would you explain to your children what you believe are the basic themes—facts, realities, and values—of human existence? What are they? How do you manage them?

To what extent does this company practice what it preaches: belief in the value of its people?

The second value on Ford's list is the product. A car is one of the most important purchases a person makes. What does a car mean to a customer? How is the automobile related to our basic human needs and values? Consider the following:

A quality automobile should protect us from death; it can give us freedom; through it we may be able to express our love, commitment, and affection. It can also be a vehicle for isolation and for loneliness; it gives people an opportunity to express their aggression; it can be used to make a statement about one's identity; it can be a source of pride; it can be a thing of beauty; to some it is a home—or a home away from home. It is something eminently practical. (One elderly gentleman to another: "I have reached the age at which I want a car that just works!") And, as suggested earlier, a car connects a person with work, with the political process, and with services—such as schools and medicine. A car uses up natural resources and has contributed to pollution—which has raised ethical problems and political controversies in current societies.

We must then ask automobile company executives, Do you believe that a deepened understanding of what a human being is will help you design better cars, market them better, and provide a more ethical product and more ethical services to your customers? If you do, can you give at least one example?

Guiding Principles

Quality is a philosophic concept. It is related to more than good business sense. Quality, the first guiding principle of the Ford Motor Company, is the ancient value of perfection modernized and driven directly down into business and industry. Quality means more than beating the competition. Quality is a matter of personal pride. It is a way to find meaning and significance, satisfaction and joy, in the work to which most of one's life is dedicated. The quality of work that one does is a reflection of the quality person who one is.

Customers want more than just quality cars. Customers want also quality contacts with the company and its representatives. And quality contacts means good communication. The more deeply you understand a human being the more successful will you be in establishing, in the language of the guiding principles, "excellence in...our human relations."

Good human relations are based on one's ability to see the world through the eyes of another—and to find pleasure and value in doing that.

One must confront the executives with questions such as, How good are you in understanding how other people perceive their own world? What can you do to improve yourself? And to help others improve?

The team is important to the success of the organization. A successful team has a common vision, acceptable to all, which aligns and coordinates the actions of all its members. To be a member of a well functioning team can provide one with a sense of exhilaration, fulfillment, and meaning not to speak of support and general happiness.

But there can arise conflicts between our need to be independent and autonomous individuals and our desire to operate successfully as a team. There also are conflicts between what people consciously and rationally say they want and what they unconsciously and irrationally actually desire. These conflicts lead to "politics" and in particular to "turf" issues.

We therefore are confronted here with leadership issues. And leadership is not only a business concern. Leadership is a personal matter, it has a personal dimension.

Leadership requires courage as well as a commitment to greatness. Leadership demands that decision-makers be willing to expose themselves to anxiety, guilt, and loneliness. And leadership is a commitment to service, because it is right and because it is needed— and often without rewards.

Again, in this regard executives must be challenged with such questions as, What kind of a leader are you? What are your strengths? Your weaknesses? What is your opinion of the quality of the leadership of your company? With what characteristics are you satisfied? Where must it improve?

Integrity is the last of the guiding principles Ford lists. It means that this company has made a commitment to stand on a firm ethical base.

The capacity to be ethical is typically and purely human. Animals can feel and perhaps be compassionate, and even forgiving. But they lack a sense of justice, ethics, fairness, equity, and democracy. It follows that the more ethical we are also the more human we are.

Why be ethical? An ethical society and an ethical organization are ethical only because individual human beings have made a personal commitment to establish and preserve a moral order. Ethical behavior exists because free human beings have used their freedom—and often put their lives on the line—to make ethical choices. Nothing ethical will ever occur unless an individual person makes that happen. And ethical behavior springs from within the freedom of the human soul—it is a commitment, it is a decision, it is purely personal, it is a risk, it is a leap of faith. And above all it takes courage.

The ethical person, as was discussed earlier, is ethical not because he or she will be rewarded but because it is right. More often than not, the ethical person is ignored or even maligned: Socrates and Jesus, Gandhi and Martin Luther King, are but a few examples. But what makes us human is the personal choice of being ethical.

Agani, the executives must be asked, What is your opinion? How would you measure your own commitment to being an ethical person? How would you rate your colleagues? Your subordinates? Your superiors? Do you feel that in your company integrity is never compromised? Can you think of instances in which integrity was upheld? Cases in which it was in fact compromised?

Another comment on quality can be built on the Pillsbury Company's mission and values statement:

THE PILLSBURY COMPANY
MISSION AND VALUES

The Pillsbury Company exists by public approval and our function is to serve the public interest. Since 1869, Pillsbury employees have built a tradition of quality. Our people have brought Pillsbury to the successful position we hold in the food industry today. We are proud of our heritage, and we are committed to achieving even greater success.

The Pillsbury Company is a diversified, international, market-oriented organization.

OUR MISSION IS TO BE THE BEST FOOD COMPANY IN THE WORLD.

By the best, we mean a rapidly growing company that supplies premium quality products and outstanding service to our customers and provides a superior return to our stockholders. In addition, we are committed to being an outstanding corporate citizen and creating an environment for our employees that makes Pillsbury an exceptional place to work.

We will conduct our business with the highest ethical standards and believe the following values are fundamental to our success.

PEOPLE MAKE THE DIFFERENCE

It is important that we:

- Attract, motivate and retain the most talented people in our industry.
- Promote mutual trust and respect for each other.
- Encourage promotion from within and provide fully competitive compensation.
- Practice open and timely two-way communication, with the expectation and confidence that well-informed people will do the right thing.
- Keep an open mind to new ideas and encourage innovation and risk-taking with the knowledge that sometimes we will fail.
- Provide opportunity for all employees to develop their potential and make the best use of their abilities.

QUALITY IS ESSENTIAL

It is important that we:

- Attract, motivate and retain the most talented people in our industry.
- Make product quality and product safety the responsibility of every employee.
- Market premium quality, great tasting products at a fair price.
- Take pride in all the products and services we provide.

EXCELLENCE MUST BE A WAY OF LIFE

This demands that we:

- Maintain a dynamic, growth-oriented environment that promotes teamwork and encourages individual initiative.

- Provide leadership and rewards that will motivate employees to practice excellence in every dimension of their job.

- Pursue functional excellence as an integral part of our total business performance.

- Set priorities and execute plans consistent with our strategic objectives.

    We believe that if we live by these values, we will establish Pillsbury as a premier company and achieve our long-range objectives.

Here are questions that inevitably invite themselves.

How can such elevated goals be realized? How is it possible not to feel cheated and disappointed? Is it fair to be touched and tantalized and then let down? Is it worth trying after all?

Is it not the mark of a pervasive yearning for ethics that companies wish to prepare philosophy statements, or at least that their employees and the public demand it? Are these not signs of an overarching ethical horizon, bigger that the company?

What can be done to realize such eloquent and worthy statements in the marketplace? How can they be reconciled with the ever-present storms of economic competition? What must happen in companies so that such pontifications become realities?

And, what is more, how can these philosophic positions be translated into profits? For unless that is done, the company will not survive. It will go under, values and all.

Are managers and employees, the public and the stockholders, worthy of an investment in such high-minded goals? Are they not greedy and self-serving, are they not out to think only of money and of themselves? Is idealism a hoax? Are there just a few members of an organization interested in ethics, while the rest laugh and run away while they can with a profit?

Here real leadership is required. For the leader is the person who has the vision and the character, the faith and the will, to make these virtues become realities. A company philosophy, for good or ill, is part of mankind's eternal attempt to create meaning out of stone and love out of wind.

CHAPTER 28

Leadership Training

The test of the value of philosophy in business or developing leadership intelligence is to find ways to apply it. In this chapter we develop not precise applications, but general guidelines, which can make it possible for any one with the patience, the understanding, and the resources to develop workbooks and programs which teach, apply, and implement the fundamental principles of philosophy in business.

The first teaching or learning component of philosophy in business consists in the development, the presentation, and the explanation of the general theory. This theory is the theory of multiple intelligences, which is then applied to develop the leadership consciousness, through readings and lectures.

But when we move to the second component of teaching or learning, then the focus is not on the subject matter or on the logic of the mind of the presenter as a model of linguistic elegance and organizational form, but on the learning needs of the participants.

The lectures should become programs, designed with sophisticated learning theories in mind. The lectures should therefore be interspersed with experiences, to create an ambience of confluent education. We must recognize that what relates to the outside lives of participants will be retained by them more quickly—and more of it will be requested—than if one were to proceed simply on the basis of what the logical exigencies of the material proper demand. To start with the interests of participants or the practitioners, if that can be done without compromising the integrity of the subject matter, will of course accelerate the learning process.

Since this second component focuses on exercises and on applications, it may fruitfully contain some of the following elements:

- One must be aware of the key importance of the person in charge of presenting the material and the program, whether viewed in the mode of teaching or of learning. The centrality of the teacher, professor, sophist, trainer, facilitator, therapist, group leader, performer, or what have you cannot be overemphasized. In the order of significance, the personality of the leader is what counts first, the extent of his or her knowledge—specific first and general second—comes next, and the skills through which the knowledge is to be transmitted appears third.

What is most difficult to teach, and therefore also difficult to change, is the fundamental personality structure of the presenter. For personality cannot be learned—not readily, at least. To acquire the necessary knowledge to be a teacher in a certain subject requires long and arduous work. The personality structure is only marginally relevant to the acquisition of knowledge. But skills are more easily—at least more quickly—learned. That is the rationale for the hierarchy of teacher proficiencies. But the critical character structure and the personality that make for a good model are mostly beyond the pale of education.

- The student, participant, practitioner, or client must be given a good grasp of the theoretical material. That can be facilitated in traditional didactic ways, with programmed learning, exercises, study questions, test questions, and so forth: the student traditionally is asked to compress, elaborate, amplify, truncate, compare, contrast, or dialogue about the presented didactic material. Any experienced teacher has competence in developing such a program and materials.

- One must think of colorful ways to illustrate principles, to dramatize them, to make them concrete and mnemonic, and to render them real, for example through music and dramatization. One should give the participants something to take home, as reminders. Imaginative gimmicks, like plastic cards on stands with key concepts, would serve this purpose well.

- The participants must be urged to find examples of the theoretical principles. Ask them to find illustrations in their personal lives, in the social world around them, in their professional, career, and occupational pursuits, in the news, in history.

  Analyze newspapers: who is making what decision? What must it have felt like? What occasioned the leap that was the decision? What was the context? What were the causes? What was the history that led to the decision? If you don't know (which is likely) then make it up. Who in the news story is living through an existential crisis? How would you cope with a similar situation? Go through any high-quality newspaper or news magazine and list the existential crises discussed or alluded to there, and examine the actual and the possible modes of coping with them: withdrawal, suicide, denial, deflection, projection, sublimation, confrontation (head-on collisions), submission, negotiation, fantasy, living through the experience, rational analysis, heroism, teamwork, systems analysis, manipulation, control, cheating, and so forth.

- Be scientific about your life: keep a journal, and then monitor it. Draw conclusions and winnow generalizations from your material as might a social scientist or a psychologist.

- Use autogenic training, including imagery, as part of making these views your own, owning them, internalizing them, integrating them, slipping them into your unconscious. The advantage is that using these techniques of suggestion makes your understanding both encompassing and deep.

- Design specific exercises, games, and simulations to practice the experience: the existential crisis, decisions, intersubjectivity. Games will do. So will psychodrama.

- Ask, What is the fallout, the spinoff, the halo effect, the transfer of learning, from the principles of philosophy in business to your ordinary and normal life? Monitor how such a learning program affects the rest of your life.

A concerted effort to bring to life the principles of philosophy in business and to provide programs of specific and clear applications should accelerate learning, accelerate evolution, and bring human beings ever closer to fulfilling their God-given potential.

All eight intelligences need to be developed, like chambers in a multiple balloon, the kind that clowns assemble, each of which will inflate if the air pressure is sufficient. The effect should be lasting. The result should be invigorating. The practitioner of the multiple intelligences should feel light and renewed, refreshed and stimulated, inspired and encouraged. The new mind will feel its greater potential. Life will be easy, not a burden. Work will be joyful, not weighty. Difficult decisions become part of a game. The fun lies more in the playing than in the winning. As you take yourself less and less seriously you feel yourself becoming more and more effective. Nature, society, and the world at large respond favorably to the person with expanded Intelligences. It is as if the world were created for the multi-intelligent individual.

All of these characteristics of leadership intelligence can be readily described, interestingly illustrated, and methodologies can be devised to cultivate, nurture, and expand them. Finally, applications to life in general and to business in particular are not difficult to find, so that the case method can be used to make these eight intelligences efficiently and effectively available to high-level executives.

How a Leadership Seminar Works

Participants will be given a chance at self-diagnosis: they will be helped to understand what kind of intelligence or intelligences dominate their minds and their lives and which one or ones they are most comfortable with. Eight intelligences will be described. Each of them should be easily recognizable by the participants.

The exposition of the intelligences will be amply illustrated. The illustrations can be exciting, although it will take time and work to assemble what is needed to make them interesting and memorable. A film, like those made from Tom Peters and Robert Waterman's *The Search for Excellence* or Alvin Toffler's *The Third Wave*, but created specifically for this program, might accompany the presentation.

The seminar will encourage the participants to experiment with these eight intelligences and to evaluate what they mean to them personally. Furthermore, participants will be challenged to enhance, nurture, develop, expand, amplify, and enrich each one of their eight intelligences. Exercises, games, and dramatizations need to be designed.

Then the insights about the eight intelligences will be applied, specifically but not exclusively to business. (More on this later.) Here the case study method should be invoked; some relevant cases could be purchased or developed.

But the general principle of application is wider than business. The language of business must be understood simply as a convenient language of survival and adaptation. Words such as productivity, company, cash flow, shelf life, control, management, effectiveness, accountability, solvency, capitalization, profitability, marketing and the market, decentralization, the organization chart, strategic planning, benefits, culture, and product advocate, do indeed have their origin or application in the world of commerce and industry. However, they are but useful concepts for managing reality—any reality. They are concepts of value to everyone, for we all are in the business of life. Fields like politics, high technology, the military, psychology of all kinds, from psychoanalysis to organizational psychology, education, banking and finance, physiology, and medicine—cytology is a good example—have their own unique vocabularies, their special way to understand their reality, to conceptualize it, to cut it up, to organize it, to manage it. Each way is a helpful way to distribute the pie of reality for purposes of coping with it. We are here talking about the power of language and the pragmatic value of conceptualization. Specialized languages are transferable, and often have been transferred, to the realm of common sense, for example in such terms as interfacing, fine tuning, defensiveness, reparenting, identity crisis, anemia, acting out, revving up, formatting, and so forth. And all this occurs in spite of the best efforts of English teachers to prevent it.

Team building—using such instruments as the *Singer-Loomis typology test*, the *Johari windows*, and a conflict resolution scale, using the "stops-starts-continues" practice, and making lists of individual strengths and weaknesses, both as we and as others see them—shows how powerful conceptualization can bring about adaptive changes in attitudes and in behavior. Another useful instrument is the *Thomas Killman Conflict Modes*, which, incidentally, are competing (forcing), collaboration (problem solving), compromising (sharing), avoiding (withdrawing), and accommodating (smoothing).

Then the program concerns itself with applications—personal, political, corporate, and professional. The premise is that executives already know about management, organization development, team building, productivity, quality circles, marketing, selling, manufacturing, distribution, information systems, finance, and strategic thinking. They do not come to the seminar for help or learning in this area. The seminar exists solely to cultivate their intelligences, to expand their minds, and to invigorate their spirits, and to make that stretching of the mind a lasting one, and enable them to teach it. The work of being business executives they do themselves, and they do it well. The book and/or seminar is not designed to give them muscles, or robots, or prostheses. But it is meant to strengthen them, to enhance what they bring with them: ample natural endowments and wide experience.

Adjuncts to enrich the program will be group discussions, music and art, case studies, diagnostic psychological tests, diagrams—on overhead transparencies as well as on slides—interesting and inspiring quotations, workbook exercises, home study aids, books and other reading materials, and video taping. And we cannot forget the importance of privacy and silence, of companionship and dialogic interactions, of physical exercise, and of thoughtful diets.

The key to it all is profitability. Profit is the cresting of the wave of developing leadership intelligence. Nothing is more uncertain than business. Nothing is predictable except that each day will bring surprises. Some are disasters and others are opportunities. In many instances the former can be turned into the latter. Perhaps the most significant application of leadership intelligence is to find ways to make the business profitable. In the real world of business no logic is more convincing, no poetry more moving, and no voice more clearly heard than a profitable bottom line.

Application means to translate the eight intelligences into organizational design; to implement them with benefits and advancement; to make the corporate structure consonant with the leadership mind.

The underlying principle here is that profitability is a function of people. In the long run, profitability is directly proportional to the quality of people engaged, to the thoroughness of their development, and to the degree to which the whole person is utilized. Every employee is an executive. The more clear-headed persons are, the more sensitive they are to their environment, and the more expanded their intelligences are, the more their behavior will also be truly effective and helpful for the company. The wider the scope of the executive mind and the sharper its vision for detail, the more trustworthy will be the risks and the more credible will be the strategies. The wiser the mind, the better will be the communication. The ultimate formula is that Intelligence expansion equals productivity and profits. *This is an act of faith. It is the fundamental faith of the executive and it is the power of the faith that will make it into a reality.*

The seminar will be taught first by those who assemble and

produce it. Later it will be taught by those who have been trained and certified for it.

This program is to expand the minds of leaders. But what is a leader, and who is a leader? Leadership is to be taught in a leadership school. And the top leadership school must have the following triad of characteristics.

One: Its method is to attract a superior faculty and a superior student body or superior group of participants in the leadership-enhancing and mind-expansion program. And what will attract this high quality of participants is the quality and the power of the ideas that the leadership program represents. In other words, the power of the ideas of developing leadership intelligence is what should attract leaders to such a program. And the ideas that are expected to be powerful are the ideas of developing executive or leadership Intelligence and what each of these Intelligences represents and contains.

That ideas have their own efficacy, their own worth, their own reality, their own energy, that ideas mobilize social and political movements in the world on the strength of their own integrity, worth, and value, that ideas have an independent reality and existence in themselves, that is strictly a Platonic notion, the single most important thought that has sprung from Western civilization.

Two: Its purpose should be quality without compromise. And that means focus on ethics. Quality is an ethical commitment and an ethical posture. The matrix of a leadership program, the air which it breathes, is ethics without compromise. It is a commitment to benefit mankind, to be of service, to be loyal and dedicated to the most far-reaching needs of humanity. It is to place others before self, but only after the self has been sufficiently developed to make that a worthwhile gift.

Three: The proof of the success of any leadership coaching, training, or development program lies in its alumni. Their accomplishments, their achievements, their influence, and their good works are the proof, if such exist, that leadership-training based on the Theory of Multiple Intelligences is worth the paper on which it is written and the air which carries its soundwaves. The alumni, to the degree that they with their lives do honor to the ideas and the program that fed them perhaps a few of their ideas, are the only proof needed and the only proof possible for the value of such a program and for the truth of its concepts.

We can define a leader as a person with an expanded mind. An expanded mind is highly interested and developed in a maximum number, preferably all, of the eight intelligences.

In addition, a leader has an expanded "body." "Body" refers to that part of reality with which the leader identifies, which gives him or her an identity, with which the leader presents himself or herself to the world, and in terms of which the eternal questions are worked through. The technical term for this "body" is self-transcendence, for the leader is more than this self or ego, the leader is an ego who has gone beyond itself (transcended) into the world, appropriated some major region, event, goal, thing, or institution within the world, and now marches forward through life, enlarged, valued, important, and worthy by virtue of this identification. In psychoanalysis and other forms of psychology, this important emotional investment and attachment of one's self to a major portion of the so-called lifeworld or social reality is called a "cathexis." Examples of these larger "bodies" are education, a company, a business, an organization, a team, a project, an industry, a profession, a political party, a research project, a family, an idea, an ideal, a work of art, a book, an invention, a good deed, in short, anything to which one can be fully dedicated and which will give meaning to one's life. The object of the commitment is the body of the executive.

Another characteristic of the leader to whom these comments are principally addressed is to have major responsibilities. The leader has commitments to many people and these commitments are not minor or unimportant; they are of great moment and of high significance. And on this significance are often dependent the jobs and security of numerous people and their families, and the preservation and growth of vast sums of money for which the executive is accountable.

Finally, the true leader holds certain deep religious and/or ethical convictions, beliefs which are expressed in his or her career and with which he or she will not entertain compromises.

A leader is also a person capable of facing the eternal questions and making them work in an organization. The authentic leader knows therefore that the ultimate reality lies not in the marketplace, nor is it found in money and profits, but in facing the ultimate needs of human existence and human nature. This is a matter of depth. It is discussed in perhaps its most specific detail in chapter 8. For to be comfortable and feel at home with the eternal questions reflects precisely that profundity and that skill which makes the true leader.

In one sense, only those who have enjoyed major responsibilities for an extended period of time can be said to be leaders. They can be said to have proven themselves. On the other hand, everyone is a leader, at least a potential one. In fact, leadership is first and foremost exerted over one's own life and soul. Every employee is a manager, every citizen a president, and every subject a king.

One may be appointed to be a manager, but leadership is always earned. More than once I have heard a major and a successful executive make this comment: Many people reach the top not because of their leadership abilities and character traits but in spite of their deficiencies. They are placed there by their superiors, or are selected by a majority or a consensus. But once they are at the top, they must prove themselves. And henceforth their position is never assured. They earn it daily. Daily their jobs are on the line. The first thing a CEO needs to tell the board is, "I expect every 90 days that I shall be fired." The question we must then ask of leaders is, "Are you willing to confront your own deficiencies and improve on them?" "Are you ready to analyze your resistances to develop the many mansions of executive or leadership intelligence?"

It is the mark of a leader to take personal responsibility to make the best possible use of any potentially helpful material coming out of any coaching program or book or from any employee. A company, by virtue of its employees, is a cornucopia of creative ideas.

Furthermore, the attrition of inspiration and the neglect of decisions made while inspired are always problems with books, courses, or programs. In part, loss of inspiration and resoluteness is normal, good, expected, and should not concern us. But on the other hand, we often experience a profound sense of loss when great ideas slip by us, when certainties vanish, and when resolutions are forgotten. Attrition hurts. Leadership is to seize a peak experience, extract from it its true value, and both create and implement an action plan which promises to give enduring life to that peak experience. And no one but the leader affected can make that commitment, take that decision, and see to it that it is carried out. Anyone can have a peak experience; but to maintain the flame of inspiration lit is the true mark of genius. And for that the leader—not the book or the program—takes full and personal responsibility.

It also seems to be true that leadership coaching, through book or program, works better and is more successful with accomplished persons than with people of ordinary abilities or average achievements.

Following is an outline of seminar planning:

1. Design an advanced seminar in philosophy in business to achieve a strategic advantage through leadership, innovation, and productivity.

   Each seminar has a special focus, based on the unit's unique needs. The ideal length is two and one-half days.

2. Purpose. Show, demonstrate, exemplify, how to diagnose and solve problems—personal, business, political—through the use of the multidimensional (or multiphasic) approach of philosophy in business. Examine problems at all levels: including finding ways to teach the poor, the marginal, the mentally ill, children, the ineffective, and the disaffected.

3. Send out letters to all previous seminar and lecture alumni and ask if they would be interested in brainstorming ideas on how to use philosophy in business for the benefit of the company's bottom line. If so, they would receive a copies of manuscripts and would be contacted for

   a. comments on the contents;

   b. personal and professional applications for themselves;

   c. suggestions about associates who might find personal and professional applications for themselves and for other members of the organizations, singly or collectively.

4. Explore applications of the ideas of philosophy in business to your unit's

   a. quality,

   b. marketing,

   c. prestige.

5. Explore pesenting to staff, clients, boards, or to the community

   a. lectures,

   b. workshops,

   c. seminars.

6. Make available several individual packages of material which can function like a library or a database. The topics could include, for example,
   a. marketing,
   b. anxiety,
   c. will power,
   d. creativity,
   e. ideas,
   f. ethics,
   g. vision,
   h. motivation,
   i. innovation,
   j. courage.
7. A seminar would consist ideally of the following elements of a philosophy-in-business high intensity training program:
   a. pre-testing;
   b. pre-work;
   c. theory—abstract and theoretical presentations;
   d. Illustrations, metaphors, images, teaching aids for clarification of the theory;
   e. applications and examples of the theory. Consider each major item of philosophy in business for solutions to current problems:
      • The eight intelligences;
      • The twelve deep structures or existential ultimate concerns;
      • The nine negative feelings or the existential crisis;
      • Sample coping devices such as
         Δ the crisis of the soul
         Δ courage
         Δ dialogue
         Δ the integration of evil
         Δ the management of ideas
         Δ access to the unconscious
         Δ levels of depth of analysis
   f. diagnostic tests, experiences, exercises—to facilitate confluent education;
   g. bottom-line, return-on-investment, profit, productivity, and quality implications. There would be constant monitoring of this factor, since ROI consciousness, and the exploitation of opportunities, must be a central theme of this work;

  h. take-home mementos, products, and materials;

  i. follow-up work;

  j. follow-up testing.

8. Teaching aids:

  Use films and videotapes.

  Use cinematic clips (from movies, newsreels, and television programs) and dramatizations to illustrate philosophy in business points.

  Decorate room with pictures of great men and women, with quotations of important and eloquently stated ideas, and with fascimiles of great historical documents—e.g., the Magna Carta, the American Declaration of Independence, Lincoln's Gettysburg Address, Martin Luther King's "I have a dream" speech—and with fascimiles of the cover pages of first editions of great books or essays, such as Einstein's papers on relativity, Thoreau's *Walden,* and Darwin,'s *Origin of Species.* Add prints of great works of art, and do not overlook the power of music: popular, classical, musicals, oriental, African, and electronic.

9. The direct and indirect costs to the individual units, centers, or components would be minimal.

10. A training workbook is soon to be published.

CHAPTER 29

Change and Power in Leadership

Plato and the Importance of Ideas in Business

Ideas are the ultimate reality. They are objects and they are tools. This view is in the tradition of Plato; it lies therefore at the heart of Western civilization.

The difference between Ideas and objects is three:

- Generosity. Ideas improve when given away.
- Replacement. An idea cannot be destroyed; it can only be replaced with a better idea.
- Recollection. No one can, strictly speaking, "give" you an idea, since you have ideas to begin with. To give you ideas is but to help you to remember them. To understand something new is essentially to assimilate it to what you already know.

Here is a list of the principal ideas of philosophy in business.

Idea 1. *Ideas.* An idea is worth little without a person who, committed to the idea, fleshes it out, brings it into being, and translates it into reality. It is the embodiment of an idea—"the word made flesh"—that is the answer to the question of the meaning of life.

A leader's tasks are two: develop new ideas and implement the "right" ones. It is relatively easy to have a new idea. It is not difficult to develop hundreds of new ideas. What is not easy is to select an idea for implementation, to risk a commitment to that idea, and then to advocate that idea—in short, it is not easy to actualize an idea. And that, in fact, occurs also only on the most rare of occasions. But precisely because of that rarity, the actualization of an idea is also a noble act. It is noble, because the realization of that idea presupposes an act of courage, the investment of a live person, a loyal commitment by a human being, and taking a chance with one's time and honor.

To choose an idea is to take a stand.

The real world, i.e., authentic existence, consists of eternal ideas translated and made to live in the everyday world of action.

An authentic business is therefore a useful idea made real by an individual commitment. That returns dignity to American business.

Idea 2. *Leadership.* We must define the leadership mind, which then becomes the desideratum of business. Leadership is to develop the intellects, the wills, and the hearts of decision-makers, for we define mind as consisting of intellect, will, and heart. This is a true need of all walks of life, including business and politics. And that is the "greatness response."

How to do it?

Idea 3. *Intelligence.* By developing innovation and creativity through expanding minds horizontally, it prepares the leadership mind for change and it can infuse it with brilliance. This is done through the theory of multiple intelligences. It is practical, extensive, time-consuming, and it summarizes the history of ideas. It is nothing new, but it reminds one of what one already knows. This is another Platonic concept, that of the theory of recollection.

This idea is the *intelligence* dimension of leadership. It is emphasized *frequently* in management training.

Idea 4. *Character.* Developing the height and depth dimensions of the person; the height refers to an immortality project, which every human being needs; the depth refers to courage, greatness, commitment (loyalty), being centered or being grounded, and morality, without which an authentic life does not exist. This is done through deep structure (boundary situations) theory.

This idea is the *character* dimension of leadership. It is emphasized *infrequently* in management training.

Idea 5. *Genius power.* Our foundation diagram is three dimensional. The first two dimensions, creating a plane, are innovation and character. The third dimension is the level of genius and of power. Genius-power is a category-step above innovation and character. The genius-power level is as different from the innovation-character complex or plane as character is different from innovation. Character and innovation form a plane, whereas innovation alone forms only a line. Each step is a dimension leap from the other: The first dimension, the line, is mind-expansion, creativity, or innovation. The second dimension, creating a plane, is mind-deepening, and character-forming, which means the development of greatness and of courage, as well as the commitment to an immortality project. The third dimension is elevation to the genius-power level, which is the ultimate breakthrough of the human mind, occurring perhaps only once in one person every century.

This idea is the *genius-power* level of leadership. It is treated *inadequately* in management seminars.

The Five Essentials of the Leadership Mind

The following characteristics of the leadership mind are based on personal, individual, observations, and not on empirical studies in the behavioral sciences. There is a so-called objective, scientific, an-alytic answer to the question of leadership. There is also a subjec-tive, literary, aesthetic, and experiential answer to leadership. Both are valid. The latter moves into depth and it is vertical, whereas the former moves into breadth and is horizontal.

Warren M. Anderson was president of Union Carbide during the disastrous Bhopal accident.

> Methyl isocyanate poured into the air, killing a thousand seven hundred and fifty-seven people within a few days. More than two hundred thousand people went to the hospi-tal. Some people are still dying from the effects of the gas. Sixty thousand Bhopalis cannot do a full day's work, according to a recent article in Business Week, and nearly a fourth of the women in the first trimester of pregnancy at the time of the accident have miscarried, given birth premature-ly, or borne handicapped children.
>
> *The New Yorker,* 13 January 1986, pp. 17-18.

Anderson said he would devote the rest of his life to ameliorate this situation.

What are the elements of leadership required in such an extreme situation? How does one answer such a question? What is the full measure of the subjective side of leadership? These questions must be dealt with in an inward fashion, from the inner perspective, because it is from within there that the answers must spring. It is from the depth that commitment and resolution arise. Facts will help, but the agony of personal decision is the final truth.

What follows was written while I was in the midst of observing high level executives manage a most difficult strategic issue in their company. They were confronted with the necessity to make exceptionally harsh and intensely painful decisions, decisions requiring above-average levels of both empathic compassion and personal courage.

Here then are some subjective observations.

Exnihilation

The leader seizes an impossible situation, and out of that nothingness creates a situation of value, of life, and of meaning. The leader is always locked into the life force. Nothing can sever the leader from identification with the forces of nature that wish to live. The leader is the manifestation of the eternal life energy, the energy that has sustained this universe in being, and the energy that has propelled evolution forward—from geological history to biological history to the histories of consciousness and of ideas. The leader gives hope because life gives hope, and an authentic leader is a compact representative of life itself.

Exnihilation is the opposite of annihilation. The latter means to destroy, to turn being into nothingness. That is evil. The former means to turn nothingness into being. That is good. Annihilation is depression, exnihilation is euphoria, enthusiasm, and exhilaration.

The Bible begins with the words, "In the beginning God created the heavens and the earth." That is the ancient voice of civilization defining leadership.

For example, a business needs to provide for its employees at least three values: survival, meaning, and camaraderie. Most actual businesses have all they can handle in just surviving. The concern here is and must be with the market and with stockholders, and not with the sentiments and personal emotional needs of the employees.

Most actual businesses have a hard time sustaining their visions, values, and missions—the kinds of things that give employees pride in their organization. The reason is first and foremost their financial problems, and these are ominously and unfailingly raised by the increasingly intense competition. Virtually every business is getting better. Therefore, a business which because of its excellence would have cornered the market only a quarter of a century ago, today barely survives.

Employees need to feel emotionally supported by their corporate culture. They need to feel secure in their jobs and acknowledged in their creativity and loyalty. All too often the crises of survival are too intense to allow for realistic attention to these understandable human needs.

The three values—survival, meaning, and camaraderie—tug in different directions and threaten to split apart any organization. This creates an impossible situation, a situation familiar to most intelligent executives. And only a decision, and it is a decision, for authentic leadership can seize it, manage it, and create value out of it.

Another word for this leadership trait is faith.

Service

Leadership is the last word in service. A leader is obligated by virtue of his or her talent to choose self-sacrifice for the benefit of others. The leader is condemned to live with loneliness, anxiety, and guilt—all three some of the greatest pains known to humanity. That is the nature of the sacrifice. For leadership is to make right but unpopular decisions, decisions of high quality but of low acceptance. Leadership is to make decisions that have consequences no one else wishes to have on his or her conscience. For leadership is to be held responsible, because one *is* responsible, for decisions made or not made. Instead of praise and acknowledgment, the true leader must expect envy and ingratitude. And these curses will not disappear.

Service requires not egocentrism but teamwork.

Courage

Leadership is to know that decisions are merely the start, not the end. Next comes the higher-level decision to sustain and to implement the original decision, and that requires courage.

Courage is the willingness to submerge oneself in the loneliness, the anxiety, and the guilt of a decision-maker. Courage is the decision, and a decision it is, to have faith in the crisis of the soul that comes with every significant decision. The faith is that on the other end one finds in oneself character and the exhilaration of having become a strong, centered, and grounded human being.

The true leader has come to evil, seen evil, dialogued with evil, and conquered evil, through the integration of evil.

Morality

Then there is integrity. For there can be the courage to evil. There can be satanic leadership. The sine qua non of leadership is impeccable integrity and trustworthy honesty. There is little controversy about basic human values: respect for the individual, which means respect for life itself; justice, freedom, and equality of opportunity; love, compassion, and forgiveness; accountability, responsibility, and maturity; truth, wisdom, and knowledge; honesty, openness, directness; sharing, trusting, caring.

Problems arise only when values are in conflict. There the leader takes a stand. But a leader is not evil. A leader knows that evil is real. And a leader—from the pharaohs of Egypt and the Minoan kings of Knossos to Winston Churchill, Konrad Adenauer, and Martin Luther King—knows that his or her primary function is to use power (or to relinquish power, as the case may be) to protect us from evil, to guarantee for all of us a moral order.

Centeredness

There is a fundamental concept in philosophy and psychology— existential philosophy and humanistic psychology in particular— which is properly called being *grounded, centered* or *rooted*. It is the sense of self-worth, of knowing one's true value, it is self-love, self-validation, self-respect, and self-acceptance. It makes others listen to what one has to say, and it produces instant trust.

There is serious danger that business executives confuse humanism with dependency. Humanism means both compassion and accountability. To be human is not only to be dependent, but equally to be independent. There can never be a choice between compassion and accountability: they form an integrated whole.

Many clichés dominate the language of centeredness. A common phrase is "to be in touch with one's feelings," "to trust one's instincts," or "to allow one's intuitions to control one's behavior." Passion, intense anger and intense love, often accompany the centered soul. But so does a sense of security, rightness, fit, and peace of mind. The connectedness with the ground of one's being is transmitted to others and yields for us automatic respect, attention, character, weight, and mass. People respond to the sense of groundedness in others even though they may neither see it nor understand it. Centeredness is what makes some people seem powerful, and its absence is what makes people perceive themselves, and be perceived by others, as ineffective and even impotent.

Centeredness is a great mystery, since it cannot be explained to the uncentered person. Nor can it be achieved through centering techniques. Similarly, when a person does become grounded, it is obvious, it feels right, and feelings of tranquility, lightness, and certainty flood the psyche.

The centered person is grounded in the seat of the self and is rooted, not in thought but in flesh, not in civilization but in biology. The centered person is therefore in touch with the forces of nature, the forces of life, and the forces of evolution. Events in business occur in small measure because leaders make decisions; but they occur in large measure because the forces of the economy and the winds of the market make them so. The centered person has the gift of seizing these forces, like a wild horse, and riding them. An uncentered person merely makes strategic plans and manipulates with tactics, for that person does not understand any of this. And herein lies the difference between a manager and a leader.

For example, personnel changes in the top structure of a company (firings, hirings, reshuffling the organization chart) may be interpreted as the individual acts of the the board, the chairman, or the CEO. But these highly sensitive and personally disruptive changes in top-level personnel are at a deeper level only the surface manifestations of natural forces, in particular of economic forces, that is, forces of the marketplace. Perhaps 20 percent of the change is the deliberated decision of the top executive and 80 percent is due to the forces that buffet us and can no more be withstood than a rowboat can resist the waves of the ocean.

Thus, if one gets fired, one can look upon it as a message, and the message is that one has not been listening to the forces of reality that brought this about. These forces can be heard only by that part of us which is connected to the primeval forces of nature. And that is our unconscious. A person not in touch with the unconscious, that is, an ungrounded person, will also not be able to seize the economic forces and harness them to his or her advantage.

Centeredness is in all probability as well the secret of physical health. If one believes in the truth of psychosomatic medicine, then one can argue that being grounded, saying "I am" from the source of one's being, or living from the inside out—all of which are synonymous expressions—is correlated with physical health, with the natural conquest of disease, and with the normal functioning of the immune system. Centeredness is the source of authentic faith, belief, and realistic self-confidence.

How does one achieve centeredness? Certainly not by pretense, technique, nor even by decision. It arises from below, it ascends from the depths, and therefore it cannot be imposed from above. The decision and the project to be centered spring from an uncentered mind. The center must always be discovered. It announces itself—if one learns to listen and look for it in the right places (i.e., in the places where it can be found). And as a rule it is not a question of whether it exists or not but more one of whether one looks in the right location and whether or not it has been found.

Centeredness is accountability, for it means to be constantly in touch with what is real. (Dreams of brittle or rotting teeth, for example, are unconscious wishes that one need not sink one's teeth into the substance of the actual world.)

Centeredness, then, is the last requirement of leadership, for it makes the leader credible.

CHAPTER 30

Philosophy In Concert

What happens when we assemble the parts, when we winnow from the deep structures and when we gather from the intelligences, when we use them all to try to solve some of the real questions? Can we use philosophy to understand our true restlessness and literally to do something about it? How does philosophy really work in doing something concrete for us? Must we be abstract first in order to be concrete later? Can we change the world merely by understanding it? How much does understanding really help in coping with the world? Are thinking and doing incompatible? Are they discernibly different? Could thinking be a form of doing? Or doing, a form of thinking? Is it true that we must change ourselves before we can change others? That we must be different before the world can be different? Or is that rationalization, an anodyne for our impotence . . . , or even laziness?

If, for instance, we combine marketing and motivational intelligences, the deep structures of death and love, and the transpersonal ultimate concerns with transcendental intelligence, we get a full metaphysics. Let us explore and experiment.

(Here we invoke what we might call an updated version of the philosophy of the German thinker from the early nineteenth century, Arthur Schopenhauer. But if you know him or other thinkers grounded on biology and evolution, you will find these thoughts a bit easier.)

Nature

Nature films are popular. What do they show? Lovable animals, indifferent and cruel animals, but above all, they show a relentless cycle: survive, watch for danger, eat, procreate, compete, fight, kill, eat what you kill, and be killed. Parents care for their young, tend to them, protect them, and teach them. There are feelings of care and affection, and expressions of sorrow and loss, when, for example, upon the return of the mother, she finds that one of her offsprings is missing—perhaps a mouse, which was caught by an owl while the mother mouse was searching for food. Or a baby seal gets crushed to death by a heavy bull while its mother is out in the ocean chasing after fish. She comes back to nurse her baby, gives out the normal howl which identifies her to her pup, only to find that there is no answer, only silence. The seal, in her own way, is stunned.

There is love and indifference, care and cruelty, sacrifice as generosity—a mother for her pup, her life is dedicated to procreation—and sacrifice as wasted life—through needless death, when a human kills for the love of hunting.

The individual tries to survive and so does the species. When a choice needs to be made, the species is of more value than the individual. Is that justice?

We ourselves are part of that animal kingdom. The instincts of struggle for survival, for procreation, for competition, and the horror and the utter inevitability as well as the perverse rightness of death are all part of the ancient marrow of our bones, of our eternal genes. Our social behavior—turf, ambition, love—is the residue of these instincts. They are polished and disguised, but in essence they remain unchanged.

Meaning

How does one make sense of this? The mind of man and woman is a product of biological evolution, and that mind rebels against its ancestry. Consciousness has developed a sense of equity, of justice, and of fairness. The mind adheres to a constellation of values which is independent of the rules of biology, survival, evolution, and cosmic indifference. Philosophy is the name for the yearning towards meaning. Philosophy is what happens when the mind is in unresolved dissonance with reality. Philosophy is the response to the emergency which occurs when two products of evolution, mind and nature, clash and must find their resolving harmony.

In understanding that meaning, a few principles suffice. And they are really metaphors; they are symbols. They are poetic ways, if you will, of organizing the world into significance for us.

There is the life force. It is mindless, wild, evolutionary. It insists on nothing but existing, on being, pure and simple. It has no purpose other than to survive.

But this life force is not unique or isolated. It is not limited to the biological order. It is not restricted to what we call life. Better yet, we are entitled to call life everything that exhibits energy, potential or kinetic, and every other form there is. The life force derives from the geological order. And that derives from the orders of astronomy and cosmology, the science of all there is. The inert bodies of the universe manifest physical energy: the sun, the galaxies, the winds, the heat and the cold, the forces within the atom and the gravitational attraction among the planets, the moving plates under the earth, the hot magnum within, the rains of the sky and the tides of the ocean, the exploding supernovae and the imploding black holes. All these forces, part of one universal force, swirl, move, wave and weave with infinite power.

Life is but an outgrowth of that. We should call these movements, these changes, some ominous and others generous, not the life force but the universal energy. It feels like one thing, one event, one phenomenon, one state of affairs. We have a singular name for the universal energy because it appears to us as a unifying reality. The perception of unity is intuitively right.

What does this universal energy "wish to do"? Where is it going? What is it up to? It is the mind, the product, the crowning glory of that energy itself, which asks this question. It is a natural question, for it springs out of nature itself. Nature asks itself, Why am I?

And what is an answer? What is the only answer? To be, that is all. To be the energy, to express the energy, to manifest it, and no more and no less. This is the meaning of just being. Energy is, wants to be, and must be. And the more it is what it is, the more it is also fulfilled.

We and Immortality

We, human beings, participate in this energy. We are this energy. It is one, but that oneness moves nevertheless in all directions. As we identify with that energy, we also sense our unity with all of nature. And that perception gives us one of our senses of immortality, or better, of eternity. It is the knowledge that we have always been and always will be, although in what may appear—but appear only—to be different forms.

Our sense of being alive, our feelings of living, our experience of being a body alive, that is the cosmic energy, the universal force itself. We are that force. We feel our being that force. We feel that we are that force. It is not diluted nor disguised, nor is it deflected or sublimated. Our feeling alive is the raw life force itself and is the universal energy made nakedly visible. To the degree that we can feel our aliveness, to that precise same extent, we also perceive the universal energy. In other words, to be alive is a feeling, and that feeling is the direct perception of the life force. No further evidence is required or even relevant.

To the degree that we identify ourselves with that energy, surrender ourselves to it, to that extent we are part of nature, we are in harmony with existence. And in this state of harmony we are fully ourselves, we have solved the riddle of existence, and we have found the meaning of life.

True, we are that energy and we are that life force. But we are more. We are also conscious of that energy and of the world which it manifests or into which is has "hardened" or been made visible. We are consciousness. And as such we are self-conscious. We are aware of being conscious. We are more than the world energy, we are also aware of the world energy. And just as the energy is wild, so is the consciousness of it peaceful. And just as the life force is hysterical, so is our consciousness of it tranquil. And our understanding of that consciousness has been developed by the sciences of consciousness, from idealism in the West to mysticism in the East. That consciousness is also eternal. It is the second source of our sense of immortality, our feeling of eternity.

And the singular consciousness, which is you and I, is part of the universal consciousness, the world mind or the world reason. And that is an eternal concept, a concept of eternity. The universal mind—vast as it is, and it is infinitely vast—is nevertheless a singular experience. That is why in all the great visions of being, the world religions, we have had monotheism. And we, in our singularity, replicate that cosmic singularity. All the other singularities within the world, the other centers of life and of consciousness, are like mirrors within mirrors within mirrors, all of them reflecting the same image, the same truth. The one and the many are indistinguishable. During his religious and metaphysical moments, the great seventeenth-century mathematician Leibnitz called these "monads," and his total view the "monadology." He meant that the solitary universal mind is accurately reflected in the plurality of every single individual mind. The world is like a million raindrops, each reflecting the very same landscape.

How do we know this? We are here talking in symbols, images.
But the images represent deep truths; they express insights we can
confirm through sensitive introspection. They fit. They resolve. We
say, "Aha!" And they provide a final answer the problem of
existence.

Extreme experiences, which open for us the eyes of the heart and
divulge a more profound truth, confirm these solutions. These
extreme experiences are anxiety, will, passion, ethics, and grace.
When in their presence, we are willing to revise the science of the
universe to accommodate not only facts, but our intuitions. And that is
how religion and philosophy are born, and that is how the arts are
confirmed. Novalis said poetry is the true science, for these are the
things that matter most.

Praxis

How can all this become practical? If it is true, we must revise
accordingly the way we perceive, think, and value. We must find a
love, a friendship, an intimacy, in which these ideas are visibly
expressed. We need a lifestyle which makes visible our philosophy.
We need a task, a meaning, a commitment, an ideal, a lifelong pursuit which exhibits a unified—i.e., a carnal and a spiritual, a pagan
and a mystical—philosophy of eternity. Philosophy is the next step
after religion.

We must interpret how we earn a living as part of a destiny which
understands these philosophic truths. We must abandon ourselves,
that is, our feelings and our decisions, our thoughts and our hopes, to
a philosophic view of reality in which we believe, which we can
accept as true. We must strive forever to solve the eternal questions.
We must do that through art and through business, through sex and
through politics, through prayer and through jogging, and on and on
and on . . . . To the degree that we feel fulfilled we know that we are
also living a true philosophy.

The ultimately practical is the enhancement of the motivational
and transcendental intelligences. The life within us will become so
potent, so full, so very rich, that all we do will be accomplished at a
much higher level of Intelligence than ever before. We will have
reached the true peak performance. We will be in tune with the
forces of nature and of the cosmos. We will have cleansed ourselves
of the resistances to the active forces within us which wish to

express themselves, the forces which are no mystery because they are the forces which we ourselves are.

We will no longer be able to tell whether we are free because we are now one with the massive forces of nature or whether we are free because we now possess a great clarity of consciousness. We can start, *ab initio, ab ovo, ex nihilo,* any process whatever that we have chosen to value. For nature, the cosmic energy, and the universal life force are in the same universe as the spontaneous freedom of our pure consciousness.

Wagner saw this as the source of his inspiration, his music-making. Nietzsche saw this worldview as making possible his Zarathustra. You, also, can use this worldview, this web of the deep structures and the intelligences, to create a new life for yourself, to make happen the life you want.

The key to success is to want what is healthy, what is consonant with your nature, what follows from authentic values, and what is in harmony with existence—in short, what is within your true potential. These may be vague words, yes; nevertheless, they point towards the truth. For to wish the fulfillment of idle fantasies will not yield satisfaction, only hollowness. It is the dreams that are rooted in your genuine self which, when realized, feel fit and appropriate. And that is the meaning of happiness.

CHAPTER 31

Personal
Conclusion

The Journalist

Jean-Louis Servan-Schreiber, journalist and
president of *l'Expansion*, France's most important business magazine,
asked me three questions:

Why did you go from the university to the business world?
I have always felt obligated to apply philosophy, to make it
work. My first effort was to interest students in philosophy, period.
My second effort was to combine philosophy with psychotherapy, in
the belief that psychological questions are, in their depth, really
philosophic ones. In pursuing that goal, I wrote five books, gave
several papers before the American Psychiatric Association and
other organizations, and participated in the establishment of
several institutes for the clinical teaching of philosophy.

My third effort was to bring the practical applications of philosophy to the business community. In doing that, my goals were four:
First, my aim was to explore, like a scholar, what meaning and what
possibilities there might be to the intersection between philosophy
and business. In other words, I was curious what philosophy could
teach business and what business had to offer to philosophy. Second,
there was the desire to be where the action is, as it were. I felt somewhat unreal in the academic world, petty and ineffective, and the
business world appeared to offer me the opportunity to be truly in
touch with what is real, and what is exciting. Engagement, encounter, contact, these are the words from philosophy that describe for
me the excitement of being in touch with ultimate reality. After all,
has not that been also the nature of the philosophic quest?

Third, in my opinion the power to improve society lies with those
who constitute the economy. As business would become more aware of
its moral obligations, as business recognized more and more that functions of church, school, and home had been transferred by society to

it, business could also be expected to better discharge that responsibility for the general welfare of society. This point may be a bit romanticized, but in its essence I believe it contains substantial truth.

Finally, I believed that there were questions of ethics, of vision, of courage, of greatness, of irrationality, and of plain humanity that philosophy had developed at length which had a critical and essential place within the business community. There were people there, responsible and powerful people, and they, their bosses, their subordinates, and their customers--not to speak of their suppliers, their stockholders, and the general public--needed philosophy every bit as much as students at the university and patients in psychotherapy.

What kind of people have you met?

I cannot claim that the people I have met are representative of the business community. (Nor can I claim that they are not.) I have met people of surprising intelligence and of grave responsibilities. I have met people who work extremely hard, have inexhaustible energy, and are serious about doing an excellent job. I have met people who find deep meaning in the work that they do, and who are fully and completely devoted to doing it well. Although I have seen some executives who practice on-the-job retirement, the monitoring of most corporations is so meticulous that it is not easy for executives to get away with that.

I have met people who, by comparable academic standards, are vastly overpaid. I have met people who are rarely really clear what the right path of action is, but who are willing to take the risk and summon the courage to make the hard and fast choices necessary to continue running a business.

I have seen impatience with concepts, lack of understanding of the value, the respectability, and the power of ideas. I have seen alarming naivete regarding the sensibilities of the soul. I have met people incomprehensibly insensitive to the emotions of others. But I have met people of extraordinary flexibility, people who are willing to listen, and hear opposing and difficult viewpoints, with much greater alacrity than was true, as far as I have been able to determine, in the academic community. I have met people hungry for learning, thirsting for depth, and passionately desirous for ideas.

I have met good people, people concerned with morality, with treating their people well, with worrying how their decisions affect the home lives of their subordinates, with deep concern of how to be of service to their organizations and to their customers.

Probably what has impressed me most is that I have found a better understanding, in both mind and action, thought and behavior, of the meaning of the existential concept of groundedness, centered-ness, authenticity, freedom, in short, of the I-am experience, in the top layers of the business community than I had met anywhere else before. That understanding, the grasping with body and soul of the I-process or the I-am experience, the central concept of existential psychotherapy, is the key to being an effective person. Top leaders in the business community have often exhibited this trait and welcomed a conceptualization and an understanding of it. And they understood what my students and my colleagues all too-often failed to see. That was a surprise to me. And a big one: the toughest philosophic concept—the capacity to create ourselves from nothing, the potential for choice and creativity, the development of something out of nothing, in short, the principle of exnihilation—was also the clearest and the most applicable to the lives of some of the top executives I met and confronted, and with whom I dialogued.

On the other hand, I have seen companies bought and destroyed. I have seen companies that are devoted to two activities exclusively: budget meetings and firing people. I have seen the evil of the irrational concern with turf, the jealousy, the sabotaging, the lack of loyalty, the ignorance, and the pettiness. But not much of that! I feel that in general the survival of the fittest is also the survival of the best.

I have seen far more genuine idealism, both in Europe and in the United States, than I ever expected.

The overall feeling about the people I have met has been joy, health, the richness of human emotions, excitement, meaning, and endless opportunities for those with an entrepreneurial spirit—but also enormous frustration for those who do not understand that a human being is both free and responsible. Dependency is out; autonomy is in.

How have you helped people?

I am not sure I have, but assuming I did, what has that been? I hope I have given them what top executives have had in short supply: understanding, real understanding.

Psychologists call that validation. But validation is not to approve any old thing that a person does. Validation is to demonstrate to a person that one genuinely cares for him or her. Validation also means that one has an in-depth understanding of the real issues, at the most basic possible level of profundity, that concern a mature human being. C. G. Jung said it well, "A psychoneurosis is the suffering of a soul that has not yet found its meaning."

I believe I have upon occasion helped people to see their way out of what at first sight was to them an inescapable maze.

To persons who are concerned about their immortal souls, who worry that there may be an afterlife retribution, I remind them of the story of Luther, and I let them know that they have to live through all over again in the solitude of their own souls the history of the Reformation. To people who struggle with their own creativity and have difficulties in making hard choices, I remind them that the first sentence in the Bible is about creating something out of nothing—and that we are created in that very image. I acknowledge their sense of loneliness, and let them know that loneliness is to be suffered through, is a window to a deeper truth and character. And I let them know that we are meant to understand loneliness and not to repress it. Nature responds to those who open their hearts to their anxieties and to their guilts, not to those who manipulate them away with techniques for presumptive solutions and with denials by means of distortions of what is real in the human soul.

Beyond understanding and validation in depth, there lie also some specific issues with which I believe I have helped. For example, I have supported them in their need for courage. I have tried to be with them in the spirit of true understanding before they had to make momentous decisions or after some major disaster had struck them. I have also acknowledged their inescapable need for meaning. I have tried to be a good listener to their exposition of their visions. I have tried to be there for them when they were concerned about a legacy or a monument for them, an immortality project that would be of true benefit to their organizations. I have tried to explain to them the nature of their freedom and the character of their responsibilities. And I have tried to place all that in a context sensitive to the urgent profitability exigencies of every living business.

I have tried to kindle the enthusiasm and the loyalty of their organizations. And I have tried to impress upon them what is needed from them so that they can become worthy of their organizations. I have tried to give realistic hope, hope that fits the realities of the situation, in times of depression, in the frustrations of anger, and in the face of blatant unfairness.

I have tried to clarify for them and their subordinates the simple meaning of true leadership and encouraged them to carry that message down through their organizations. I have insisted that an authentic leadership mind is the key to an enhanced bottom line, and I have challenged them to translate immediately their increased understanding of the leadership mind to matters like increased productivity, more enthusiastic marketing, greater assumption of responsibility, intensified innovation, greater alertness to the customer and greater care for the customer, and more willingness to place the needs of the organization above their own. I believe that I have helped, at least I like to think so, to restore dignity to American business.

How? By private consultations, public lectures, and through help in designing company philosophies and credos and in carrying out that spirit through seminar series that penetrate deep into the organization. All that is done in the hope of permanently changing a culture which gives employees meaningful pride of membership.

In sum, what do I do? I try to *understand* and to *challenge* leaders. One way I have found I can do that is by writing, lecturing, training, and consulting on the personal rather than on the business side of leadership.

ACKNOWLEDGMENTS

Grateful acknowledgment is made to the following for permission to quote from copyrighted material:

Chapter 6, p. 30:

Roger Harrison, "Strategies for a New Age." *Human Resource Management.* Fall, 1983, p. 224.

Chapter 7, p. 36:

USA TODAY, Friday, October 31, 1986, p. 13A. Copyright ©, 1986, USA TODAY. Excerpted with permission.

Chapter 7, p. 36:

Viktor Frankl, *Man's Search for Meaning.* Boston: Beacon Press, pp. 210-211. Reprinted with permission of Beacon Press.

Chapter 7, p. 36:

Rollo May, *Psychology and the Human Dilemma.* New York: W.W. Norton & Co., p. 159. Reprinted with permission of W.W. Norton & Co.

Chapter 10, p. 63:

Roger von Oech, *A Whack on the side of the Head.* New York: Warner Books, 1983. Reprinted by permission of Warner Books/New York. Copyright © 1983 by Roger von Oech

Chapter 10, pp. 66-67:

"The Ultimate Gift from the Heart," *Newsweek,* January 20, 1986. Reprinted by permission from NEWSWEEK.

Chapter 16, p. 99:

Norman Cousins, *Human Options.* New York: W.W. Norton & Co., 1981, p. 131. Reprinted with permission of W.W. Norton & Co.

Chapter 19, pp. 157-158:

The passage about Elie Wiesel winning the Nobel Prize, from *Time,* October 27, 1986, p. 30. Copyright © 1986 Time Inc. All rights reserved. Reprinted by permission from TIME.

Chapter 20, p. 176:

Tom Robbins, *Even Cowgirls Get the Blues.* Cited in Daniel Yankelovitch, *New Rules.* New York: Random House, 1981.

Chapter 22, p. 233:

The reference to the work of Mihaly Csikszentmihalyi, in *Newsweek*, June 2, 1986, pp. 68-69. Reprinted by permission from NEWSWEEK.

Chapter 24, pp. 250-251:

Excerpt form "Managers and Leaders: Are They Different?", by Abraham Zalenik, *Harvard Business Review*, May/June, 1977. Reprinted by permission of the Harvard Business Review. Copyright © 1977 by the President and Fellows of Harvard College; all rights reserved.

Chapter 25, p. 269:

Excerpt from "A Gathering Glut. Auto Industry Faces Era of Plant Closings Due to Overcapacity," by Paul Ingrassi and Doron P. Levin, *The Wall Street Journal*, February 14, 1986. Reprinted by permission of THE WALL STREET JOURNAL, © Dow Jones & Company, Inc., 1986. All Rights Reserved.

Chapter 29, p. 350:

Excerpt from Notes and Comments," *The New Yorker*, January 13, 1986. Reprinted by permission; © 1986 THE NEW YORKER MAGAZINE, Inc.

THE HEART OF BUSINESS
workbook will be available in
1988. For more information,
write: Saybrook Publishing Co.
4223 Cole Ave, Suite 4
Dallas, TX 75205.